I0803037

Benjie's *Diary, 30 May '97, L'Atlas, rue de Buci:* "Walking toward our door from rue St.-Jacques, I look up. The early sun reflects off the modest steeple of St.-Séverin, illuminating the eight-hundred-year-old stone and spreading sharp-edged shadows among the buttresses, roof peaks and gargoyles. The gargoyles jut out over the street, blind and gape-mouthed, stained, wind-scored and eternal against a jagged lapis sky. *Seeing* this street is a humbling stroll through time and art. It's a miracle of history that has survived the depredations of countless generations of demolition-mankind. *Living* on this street is a stroke of remarkable fortune.

"I started out on Pearl Street in Tomah, Wisconsin, pop. 4,500. Now, my address is rue St.-Séverin, Paris. This might be the greatest impossibility since Tiny Tim had a Top Forty hit."

LAST KID BOOKS
by David Benjamin

The Life and Times of the Last Kid Picked

Three's a Crowd

A Sunday Kind of Love

Almost Killed by a Train of Thought: Collected Essays

Skulduggery in the Latin Quarter

Summer of '68

Black Dragon

They Shot Kennedy

Jailbait

Bastard's Bluff

Woman Trouble

Fat Vinny's Forbidden Love

Witness to the Crucifixion

Choose Moose

Dead Shot

Bistro Nights

The Melting Grandmother and Other Short Works

Voice of the Dog

Also by David Benjamin

SUMO: A Thinking Fan's Guide to Japan's National Sport

An Apartment IN PARIS

BY DAVID BENJAMIN

LAST KID BOOKS

Copyright © 2025 David Benjamin
Cover and Illustrations Copyright © 2025 Junko Yoshida

Excerpts from *Fragile Glory: A Portrait of France and the French* by Richard Bernstein, copyright © 1990 by Richard Bernstein. Used by permission of Alfred A. Knopf, imprint of Knopf Doubleday Publishing Group, a division of Penguin Random House LLC. All rights reserved.

Excerpts from *The Other Paris* by Luc Santé, copyright © 2015 by Luc Santé. Reprinted by permission of Farrar, Straus and Giroux. All rights reserved.

Last Kid Books
309 W. Washington Avenue
Madison, WI 53703

First Edition
March 2025

All rights reserved

No part of this book may be used or reproduced in any manner whatsoever without written permission from the author.

Printed in Wisconsin, United States of America

For more information or to order books:
visit www.lastkidbooks.com

Library of Congress Control Number: 2025906634

ISBN-13: 979-8-9917169-2-5

A NOTE ON THE TYPE
This book was set in Athelas, a serif typeface designed by Veronika Burian and Jose Scaglione and intended for use in body text.[1] Released by the company TypeTogether in 2008, Burian and Scaglione described Athelas as inspired by British fine book printing.

Printed and bound by Park Printing Solutions
Verona, Wisconsin

Designed by Kristin Mitchell, Little Creek Press
Mineral Point, Wisconsin

For Roberta Beardsley,
guardian angel

"Whoever does not visit Paris regularly will never be elegant."

— Honoré de Balzac

"Paris is sufficiently compact that you can cross it with ease, in a few hours, and it has no grid, forestalling monotony. It virtually demands that you walk its length and breadth; once you get started it's hard to stop. As you stride along you are not merely a pedestrian in a city—you are a reader negotiating a vast text spanning centuries and the traces of a billion hands, and like a narrative it pulls you along, continually luring you with the mystery of the next corner."

— Luc Santé

"Paris is always a good idea."

— Audrey Hepburn

HOTEL
Rue de Haut Pavé
et
May 23, 2014
Rue des Grands Degrés

Preface

Junko and I share a plethora of pet peeves. Prominent among them is the unfortunate happenstance of a favorite restaurant—especially in Paris—getting "written up." Soon thereafter, the joint starts drawing crowds densely composed of yuppie trend-followers and checklist tourists. This phenomenon—ruination by social media—can victimize whole cities. Paris and New York—the world's two most written-up cities (sorry, London!) are in constant peril of being overrun by Yelp-directed hoi polloi.

Paris somehow always manages to rise above, absorbing its annual influx of riffraff and then sloughing them off, like crab shells, in September.

A simple proof of how vastly chronicled Paris has always been, both by its denizens and visitors, is the bibliography at the back of this book, a list that barely suggests the thousands of pages and millions of words that have been spilled on the topic of Paris. This reminiscence is a drop in that ocean. To enrich my knowledge and enliven my narrative, I pored through all of these books and more. In doing so, I risked breaking one of the rules of economical prose.

Whenever a writing project requires homework, I've fought the temptation to show off by referencing every bit of information—even if superfluous or redundant—

accumulated in my notes and closeted in my brain. Anyone even skimming this memoir will notice that I've loaded it with quotes from other works by authors whom I read as I researched.

In doing this, I flouted my own rule. I justify this transgression partly because so many previous authors have written about Paris more eloquently, or profoundly, or more entertainingly than me. By quoting others, I reflect their glow.

But there's a better reason for speckling my chronicle with the observations of my literary forebears. For virtually every experience, every sight and surprise encountered in Paris, there exists—recorded somewhere—a previous observation, anecdote or shaggy-dog story. This is my alibi.

As I boned up diligently on Paris, reading material as far back as the sixteenth century, I perceived an unexpected trend. What I wanted to find—and quote—was commentary on Paris, not just as geography, but as an idea. I sought descriptive and insightful passages about the city, its byways and alleys, its people and mores, its moods and its spirit, its spectacle and grandeur. Of course, I found ample material in this vein, but I had to dig deeper than anticipated.

Many of the books I faithfully studied, from Jean Émile-Bayard, Janet Flanner and Kay Boyle between the two World Wars to Mary Blume at the turn of the current century, dwelt sparingly on "local color." Rather, many writers who came to Paris from elsewhere, who settled in, worked here and made names for themselves—Gertrude Stein, Robert McAlmon, Morley Callaghan, Irwin Shaw, etc.—offered in their memoirs only passing impressions of the city as a breathing character. Most typically, the foreign famous who hobnobbed among the Parisian luminati wrote less about the city and more about their hobnobbing, about the people they knew and the people they met—at which party, café or cabaret—in Paris.

A great deal written about Paris reveals little of the quotidian experience of life in the city. By comparison, my thirty-some Parisian years have been almost completely quotidian. Perhaps this is why my favorite "Parisian author" is Elliot Paul, who circulated among—and published—those famous Lost Generation giants but who preferred to write about the ordinary tradesmen, shopkeepers and seamstresses in his Left Bank neighborhood. The only "famous" character in my Paris story—and now largely, sadly forgotten—is Alain Bernardin, the founder and impresario of the Crazy Horse de Paris. Otherwise, everybody you'll meet in the following pages is unknown, although hardly ordinary.

This book, I would contend if challenged, is unusual—and worthwhile—because it's an everyday narrative about an exceptional and rather mysterious experience, the acquisition of an apartment in Paris. I've recorded the nuts and bolts, fears and frustration—and a hundred trips across the Seine to the Samaritaine department store—of that journey.

Real estate, of course, is a topic almost entirely devoid of entertainment value, even when the locale is the most coveted city on earth. I knew that before I started. I would not have written this story had I not decided to run amok with digressions, impressions, deviations, opinions and detours. As noted, I'm abetted in charting this meandering course by quoting authors who've gone before. Among my favorites in this respect is Alan Houghton Brodrick, whose extraordinary guidebook, *The People's France: Paris*, published before Arthur Frommer came out with *Europe on 5 Dollars a Day*, is the richest trove of piquant and erudite Parisiana in my library.

If our adventure in Parisian property has any value to the reader, it might be as a sort of primer, the first lessons of discovery in the world's most beautiful—and in the sweep of history—most important city.

Long ago, the heart of Paris was marked on the map as "Kilometer zero," the central crossroads in France from which all distances are measured. By establishing this milestone, Paris proclaimed itself a crossroads of the known world. Paris said to every other city: "If you don't start here, you don't know where you're going."

Once we had signed all the paperwork and made the down payment on our apartment in Paris, from that day forward, we knew—more than ever before—where we were going: Kilometer zero.

This is how we got there.

PITCHERS

1
Paris on My Mind

Every man has his own Paris. It is the first discovery one makes among cities—and the last. It is as personal as clothes, as food and drink, as books and pictures. There is no writer but has been influenced by his experience of it, no painter but has seen, after its own strange landscapes, all other compositions in sky and stone and water with critical, meditative eyes.—George Slocombe, *The Heart of France: Parisian, Provincial & Peasant*, 1934

Paris, once, is safe.

Paris, again, is playing with fire. After that—the third, fourth, fifth time back—you're a goner. It's a flea in your ear, an ache in your heart. Paris leaves an ember, smoldering, in your psyche.

Yet at the end no one ever left Paris willingly. The city became a state of mind which you carried with you for the rest of your life.—Shusha Guppy, *A Girl in Paris,* 1991

The emotional danger in coming back to Paris is that you're not awestruck any longer, not as exalted by its grandeur or humbled by its history—although it's easy to revive such feelings and succumb to them. Paris' sneakiest trick is its smallness. Despite being touted in postcards, guidebooks and travel brochures for its high spots—Sacré-Coeur, the Eiffel Tower, the Montparnasse monolith—Paris is a low city hugging the earth in old limestone canyons and long airy arteries radiating into clusters of narrow, cobbled streets where ancient beams and buxom caryatids support the doorways. Paris' seduction is its intimacy. Paris is like going back to your old neighborhood—if the old neighborhood were really as homey and welcoming as it seemed to be on the very best day of your most innocent childhood year. Paris is the best ice-cream cone you ever licked.

Paris nibbles at you. It warps your psyche. It colors your perception of everywhere else, and it alters your dreams. Paris sticks to you even when you make a conscious effort to push it to the fringes and appreciate somewhere else. This happened to us despite our previous intentions, in 1994. That year, Junko and I took our annual vacation to France by way of a long, cramped flight from San Francisco, with about a week scheduled for puttering around Paris.

Paris is devine. I mean Dorothy and I got to Paris yesterday, and it really is devine. Because the French are devine—Anita Loos, *Gentlemen Prefer Blondes,* 1925

Unlike previous Parisian pilgrimages, we were determined not to squander our every waking moment stuck in the city, eating and imbibing, painting watercolors, shooting photos and malingering in cafés. We committed to an "active" holiday, exploring hinterlands, seeing more of France than we could regard from the boulevard Montparnasse or the bridges of the Canal Saint-Martin. We would go on safari. We would explore *la France profonde!*

Ay, but here's the rub: Paris followed us. It clung all the way way south in our rental Renault. It haunted our room at the Hotel Ibis, seeping under our skin until it made us crazy. All this happened in a nice little city called Périgueux, which, in your Rand McNally, you will find in an area called the Périgord—a region of goose ranches, prehistoric diggings and undistinguished but amiable wines—halfway between Bordeaux and Lyon.

Périgueux ... makes a town of about 60,000 inhabitants, of limited interest to the visitor.—Rex Grizell, *Off the Beaten Track: Southern France*, 1994

In Périgueux, Junko and I had a fight. Not about Paris but about Paris.

Actually, this was The Fight—meaning that it was about money.

And Paris.

If you've been married—I mean, *really* married—met and ignited and collapsed into each other's naked arms, fondled each other's every protrusion and orifice, lived together tentatively, anguished over a lifetime of just one lover forever, wrote your own gooey vows, tied the knot blithely in front of an audience of people you rarely see anymore, pledged undying devotion, survived the cooling of the conflagration, found comfort in your mutual dailiness and found a certain fearful fascination in the Tilt-A-Whirl of marital moods—"What did I do wrong?" "What can I do?" "How can you say that?"—ever been distracted and unnervingly tempted by a strange, anonymous but alluring form as it bops on by—

you've gotten around to:

The Fight.

If you don't have The Fight, you don't have a marriage yet. You're rookies, steeped in delusion and blinded by denial. After you've done The Fight, you either have a marriage or you don't. The Fight is the continental divide.

Typically arising out of nowhere, it starts innocently in a setting unlikely to incite conflict—in leisure, in intimacy, in small talk.

But in Périgueux?

Well, yeah.

Benjie's Diary, 25 September '94, Périgueux: "Last night, the guidebook directed us to a bistro called L'Oison, where, at about 6 p.m., we tried to make a reservation. The proprietor responded bemusedly and said we could drop in any time. When we dropped, as promised, about 8:30, L'Oison was almost empty. We benefited from the end of the tourist season, about three weeks ago. Our hostess was a charming, genial lady who remembered us and our reservation attempt. She led us to a table by the window visible from the street. We would serve as bait for peckish passersby.

"Our waiter, Junko insisted, was the spitting image of Forrest Gump.

"I was feeling the first pangs of a virus, so my appetite was weak. I focused on fish. Junko ate regional specialties, *paté de campagne* and free-range *cochon*. A beautiful meal, even without an appetite. We had the perfect dessert—dried fruit (prunes, apricots, orange) soaked in some yummy, boozy fluid.

"After L'Oison, we walked the wet streets and found this town all the more appealing. Périgueux is a pile of rubbly streets and stone houses stacked around an overwrought cathedral on the banks of a river punctuated by elegant arched fieldstone bridges. Though it is probably unremarkable among a thousand similar French towns, no less picturesque and placid than all those similar French towns—which makes it ideal for strolling, sitting, drinking, eating, painting, writing—it's a thousand times more suitable for these pleasures than almost every city, town and hamlet in the Walmart-gutted U.S. of A. We could linger here indefinitely."

As I said, The Fight is always about money or manhood—by which, of course, I mean both. A woman may be frugal and prudent. She may be the wildest spendthrift since Imelda Marcos. But she will typically regard her stewardship of the marital treasury as her primary compensation for all the submissiveness and guile necessary to manage the gaseous thug to whom she had pled her impetuous troth. To keep the marriage intact, the woman administers the joint purse subtly, nursing the husband's illusion that he is the de facto Comptroller of the Hoard and the little woman merely a resident bookkeeper. When the façade crumbles, which it eventually does unless the wife is exceptionally clever and the husband singularly obtuse, The Fight ensues. In pursuit of some desired luxury, often revealed to be a device containing a motor, the male asserts his dominion over the family's fiscal fortunes. The woman, who knows both the bottom line and where the penny jar is buried, scoffs. Friction results. Combustion follows.

Benjie's Diary, 25 September '94, Périgueux: "One of the growing interests of this trip is the price of real estate around Périgueux. We've noticed ads for houses as low as 390,000 francs—less than $80,000. We could raise a 50 percent down payment on something like that. What a refuge it would be ...

"We're thinking, talking about it, tempted by the possibility."

By 1994, Junko and I had been making an annual hajj to Paris for six years. After several *vacances* in Paris, we had conjured a fantasy common among starstruck tourists: our own little garret overlooking the jagged rooftops and chimney pots of Paris. We had thought about buying from our French friends, Margaret and Jean, their vacant apartment—a sort of oversized broom closet where we had stayed on several visits—in the Sixteenth Arrondissement.

Gradually, through repeated exposure to Paris, after midnight walks along the *quais*—an autumn moon reflected in rain-slicked pavement that evoked the early noir of Louis Malle—our fantasy graduated to the solidity of a pipe dream. During Paris strolls, we began to pause at real estate storefronts to gaze at smeary Polaroids of *pieds-à-terre* while calculating franc/dollar equivalents. We carried on this pastime all over town—in the Marais, in the workaday Fifteenth, among the ethnic blocks in the Thirteenth. We even browsed, preposterously, on the Île Saint-Louis, which until the seventeenth century was a swampy pasture steeped in manure known as the Île Aux Vaches (Cow Island), but which today everyone tends to romanticize (and few can afford).

It was a lovely March evening, with just the faintest tang of spring in the air, and once I stumbled onto the Seine, at Pont de Sully, I was met with perfection. There facing me was the Ile St.-Louis, glowing softly and floating on the river like a vision, a medieval hamlet magically preserved in the midst of a modern city. I crossed the bridge and wandered up and down its shuttered streets half expecting to find chickens wandering in the road and peasants pushing carts loaded with plague victims, but what I found were tiny, swish restaurants and appealing apartments in old buildings.—Bill Bryson, *Neither Here Nor There: Travels in Europe,* "Paris," 1992

Steadily, our pipe dream took on a life of its own. It began to pick at the sutures and scabs that riddled the epidermis of our oft-surgered bank account. We had begun to ponder wild schemes of Parisian homesteading.

Our trip to the Périgord triggered a fresh onset of wishfulness. This half-discovered region of rural France infected us—well, me—with the prospect of a spectacular bargain. What about snatching up a cottage in the Périgord? Well, it isn't Paris, okay? But it is France, which is pretty much the same thing, right? Hey!—a whole house for the price of a cramped Paris flat with an eighteenth-century commode.

Inflamed by this deviant possibility, I led the charge across the bridge that lies fatefully between idle speculation and rash commitment. My mistake was that I got across and looked back, and oops! There was Junko, still on the other side—and the bridge was gone, washed away in a raging torrent of common sense. Above the metaphorical waters' roar, I could faintly hear Junko's voice shouting, "Benjie, what the *hell* are you doing over there?"

The Fight began.

Benjie's Diary, 27 September '94, Périgueux: "Boy, forget that! "We're not ready to buy no stinkin' farmhouse in no stinkin' France! First, we have to prove, once and for all, that we can save a few bucks on our own. This is the gist of last night's epic fight—which all started in an unnamed (but very good) restaurant somewhere in Périgueux's commercial center. It continued through the *centre ville* to our hotel (where mild violence ensued), then outdoors again, going 'round and 'round the cathedral 'til we were both exhausted by discussion of our financial prospects and occupational travails."

By the night of The Fight, I hadn't held down an actual job for four years, since I'd been fired—for the quaint offense of profanity—as editor of an erratic periodical enterprise called *Tokyo Journal*. I had since reconciled myself to being supported by my spouse and lucky in my dependence. I was a writer of mildly risky prose with a sponsor (Junko) who demanded that I keep writing despite a seamless continuum of publisher indifference occasionally spiced by an outright rejection. Nonetheless, I could hear now and then the muttering of an inner voice reminding me that the only legitimate husband is the hunter/gatherer in buckskin jockstrap winning the bread and bringing home the bacon. The only sort of man who lets a girl pay his bills, quoth the pesky voice, is either pimp or pansy.

Junko bore the brunt of my spasms of guilt. The night of The Fight was the mother of all macho regressions. I deteriorated into whining that, goddammit, the reason we can't do this, can't make our dream come true, can't have a vine-covered cottage in *la France profonde* is because I'm a good-for-nothin' unpublished unsuccessful probably-not-even-that-good parasite hack, that's what I am. We could build our castle in the air (I averred) if I were to swallow my pride and find a decent job, if I up and restored my self-respect with an alarm clock and a damn paycheck.

Get a haircut and get a real job,
Clean your act up and don't be a slob.
Get it together like your big brother Bob.
Why don't you get a haircut and get a real job?
—"Get a Haircut,"
George Thorogood and the Destroyers, 1993

Junko, common sense still flowing, said, "Benjie, Japan is crawling with respectable salarymen shackled to their alarm clocks and bringing home paychecks. I turned down every one who introduced himself or had my mother break the ice for him. I didn't marry you for normalcy, predictability or respectability. I knew what I was getting into and I knew I would be the one with the steady job. I want you to write. I don't care how long it takes for someone to get wise and publish your stories. We're doing fine without you on the payroll. Of course, I still think we should save more."

Benjie's Diary, 27 September '94, Périgueux: "Thanks to excessive fatigue, jet lag, eye strain and probably constipation, we both managed to unbreast virtually every anxiety that has visited our union over the past seven years. We purged ourselves. Still more residue left but not enough, really, to stuff a muffin.

"Today, we're muddling toward Lascaux."

Five years afterward, I remember the locale better than I remember most of what we said—well, hollered and whispered—throughout The Fight. We walked lap after lap of Périgueux's old city, its pavement humped, creased and treacherous with cobblestones, its passages as narrow as tenement hallways, damp and claustrophobic, its shadows Hitchcock silhouettes snaking along limestone walls and twisted beams. On one wall, I noticed a lonesome graffitus that read, simply, *"ANARCHIE."* Above it all, wherever we stood, the weird domes of the Cathedral of St.-Front leaned over and eavesdropped.

Périgueux has a very unusual cathedral. It is said to have been inspired by St. Mark's Cathedral in Venice, which itself was derived from the Church of the Apostles in Constantinople, built in the eleventh century, and since disappeared. The oriental domes and turrets of this cathedral of St. Front have become the symbol of Périgueux, as the Tower Bridge is a symbol of London, and are known all over France to people who have never been to the city. As it stands today, St. Front is almost entirely a nineteenth-century construction, and its cavernous interior is curiously lacking in atmosphere. For most visitors the most interesting thing about St. Front is the view of it from across the river.—Off the Beaten Track: Southern France, Rex Grizell, 1994

I think Junko was probably terrified that night. She had never been through this scene before. The Fight, if it goes wrong, can eviscerate a marriage. It strips away that veneer of pretense that two people can will away, with words of love, their differences and demons. I was scared, too, but less so than I had been in my two previous Fights. I knew how stubborn I was and Junko's equal obstinacy. But here we were in France, where we love to be, where we waste our savings, where we have conspired guiltlessly in dissipation despite my poverty and my emotional baggage and Junko's fiduciary prudence. By that night in Périgueux, we had already entangled ourselves so inextricably into a ridiculous cross-cultural union that there was no escape but foolishness. And foolishness, of course, had been the spark that got us started with each other and the glue that bonded us. That night, I sensed that Junko and I would bicker and rage 'til dawn and find ourselves gasping and enervated (with bruises on my biceps), staring across each other's coffee and restored by a recognition that all we'd been yelling about was Benjamin's unconvincing pose as a he-man and Junko's equally dubious persona as a penny-pinching Meiji Era housewife.

Benjie's Diary, 27 September '94, Périgueux: "We might have gone and seen Lascaux already, but they have lunch here from 12 to 2. This is France and lunch is sacred.

"We still have a strategy for owning lodgings in France (or Paris), but it awaits a larger nest egg."

Blue skies followed the quarrel. The countryside healed us. We roamed three bright, healthy days through the Périgord, from Périgueux to Saint-Cyprien and Beynac, through Pussay and Limeyrat, to La Roque-Gageac (where Junko painted and I wandered) and Domme, with an overnight in Les Eyzies (pronounced, delightfully, "Lazy Z") at a snooty ranchhouse called Le Centenaire.

Benjie's Diary, 28 September '94, Périgueux: "The Hôtel Le Centenaire is very elegant and comfortable—three stars. Dinner was huge—to the point of being oppressive—but we gnawed our way through all of it. We began with kir and little crunchy canapés, followed by three small dishes of mysterious French *kaiseki*. One: a little brown pyramid with piquant flavor; two, a yellow fluid speckled with parsley; three, a tiny terrine. Then, they hit us with *foie gras*—threes again: 1) *foie gras de confit du canard*; 2) *foie gras de canard roti*; 3) *foie gras de l'oie* (a big slab). This was a lot of *foie gras*, more than we'd ever eaten (about a year's worth in one swell foop). Our cholesterol level immediately leaped a hundred points (but it's the *good* cholesterol). On to the fish course, which was a nice caramelized sturgeon. No. Wait. Before that, I guess we had our third entrée, which for me was a mushroom terrine (hot) and for Junko a risotto with langoustine. Both were intensely rich, but after the *foie gras*, they seemed comparatively subdued. Then the sturgeon, then the meat. We had lamb, perfectly rare and lean. Not finished yet. By this time, we were nursing our wine. We'd never had to stretch one bottle through so many courses. We left some lamb on the plate because the *fromage* was still on the way. We each opted for a single cheese. I got Cantal, Junko something she didn't catch the name of, but it was yummy. Finally, dessert—an ice-cream confection piled on sandy sugar, surrounded by *fraises*. And coffee! Whew.

"The evening's entertainment came from Hiroshi and Sandra, our first Japanese tourist couple in the Périgord, who (for reasons unfathomable to human reason) decided to take an auto vacation to rural France, to the most expensive hotels and restaurants at every stop, only a month after the delivery of their infinitely fussy and dyspeptic daughter, Mari. Mari established that she would not be silent for as long as two seconds unless held, rocked, fondled, lullabied and coddled. This drama held our unwilling attention through all sixty-two courses of the repast of Hiroshi and Sandra, as well as ours. We developed an abiding hatred for little Mari and a mounting dismay with the presumption of two well-to-do yuppies who perceived no discourtesy in imposing their colicky excrescence on a restaurant full of people who were paying $300 to dine in quiet opulence. We speculated on Hiroshi and Sandra's motive for being here. We assumed they were stationed somewhere in France. Sandra was neck-deep in French duds, and she had embraced the native affectation of piercing her daughter's ears at birth, a sort of *circoncision des oreilles*. Hiroshi was less sartorially daring. He wore the typical Japanese male overseas uniform: formal golf clothes. We thought they might be embassy types but decided against that when we realized poor Hiroshi couldn't understand any cheese names except "paprika." Also, an embassy guy would dress better. We finally concluded he was a mere salaryman assigned to France, grossly overpaid, forced to take his vacation when the company ordered him to, compelled to haul his pissing papoose from *chateau* to *relais* to *hotel de ville* and eat *foie gras* while smelling on his shirt collar the delicate ambience of Mari-puke. Clearly, whatever Hiroshi's miseries, he had earned them. We, however, resented sharing them."

Smile on our tourists as you will, blush for them as you sometimes must, there is nevertheless something fine about them, something indomitable. On occasions one may think that many are so travel-blind that they ought not to tour Europe at all, for all the good they get from it. They might as well be counting steps in the courthouse at home as in Notre Dame. But that view is too narrow. At least, every one of them learns that the world is accessible, that foreigners are courteous and gentle people, and that there are national points of view other than their own. And that is something.—Robert Forrest Wilson, *Paris on Parade*, 1925

The lesson Junko and I took away from Le Centenaire is that, alas, we are—even at our pinnacle of pretense—mere one-star people (or maybe no stars at all). Dinner at the Lazy Z ranch house was our first venture into the galaxy of Michelin cuisine, and, well, we couldn't tell the difference. If, sometime before, we had blundered into a two-star dinner or a one-star brunch, we had done so without noticing the Michelin sticker on the window. But we would have said something—along the lines of "Holy shit!"—about the price. We've always been a little fussy about where we dine. So, we came away from Le Centenaire well-fed but no more impressed than we are when we patronize one of our star-deprived favorite bistros in Paris, with the bonus that we've never had Hiroshi, Sandra and their colicky issue to keep us company. We've come to accept about ourselves that our roots had sucked their sustenance from too much impure soil in our oblivious youth. Junko was an Ikegami proletarian who had eaten too much U.S. Army surplus bread and fried blubber for hot lunch in grade school. I was back-alley white trash from western Wisconsin, who ate roast squirrel and survived month to month on commodity distributions from Aid to Dependent Children. These childhood depredations had compromised our palates to near numbness. As we grew up, however, work and travel gradually refined our tastes and set us looking, wherever we go, for the happy medium of imaginative food that's nonetheless recognizable and not too costly, in an atmosphere welcoming and casual that is, in the French formulation, *genial.*

It is a sad but incontestable fact that people accustomed to plentiful but abominable food cannot acquire the taste for high-class fare readily.—Elliot Paul, *Understanding the French*, 1955

After finishing our leisurely tour of *paté* country, we had several days to indulge in our favorite place on earth. The drive north was uneventful. We rested overnight at Orléans, a city with a grand, pale cathedral topped by lacy towers but not much else to see in so short a visit. We found in Orléans a singularly depressing British pub and, improbably, an Australian restaurant which, to our dismay, served neither roast koala nor barbecued kangaroo. Neither of these oddities nor the cathedral were diversion enough to slow our rush back to trusty, crusty Paris.

While roaming the Périgord, Junko, my favorite watercolorist, had hit her artistic stride, and she was eager to continue painting. Barely had we returned our Renault that she was prodding me out of our hotel toward the mortal menagerie that mills on the place du Louvre in tourist season.

In 1202, in the west, where they still remembered the Norman Terror, Philip had built a keep nearly seventy feet high, with walls fourteen feet thick at the base. It was called the "Louvre," perhaps in memory of the Viking "Leovar" or camp. It was a strong-room for the royal archives and a royal prison as much as a tower of defence.—Robert Laffont, ed., *The Illustrated History of Paris and the Parisians*, 1958

The sun peeked out from the clouds that tend to move like freight trains across the Paris sky. Our Fight was forgotten. We sprawled on the paving stones at the place du Louvre. Junko painted the sightseers queuing and posing outside Mitterand's presumptuous pyramid. As with every change in the Paris profile, from the Eiffel Tower to the Centre Georges Pompidou, I.M. Pei's great glass triangle had triggered a municipal civil war that verged on bloodshed before dissipating into prideful coexistence with the startling, incongruous and thoroughly Parisian new attraction.

Indeed, the pyramid unleashed talk on a whole host of subjects, talk that had a particular Parisian flavor, precisely because of the belief among the Parisians that part of the city's essence and mission is to be without blemish ... And the entire debate about the Chinese-American's design, whether it was an elegant solution to a perplexing problem, as Pei maintained, or whether it was, as the critics charged, a desecration in the form of an Egyptian death image, had the special Parisian quality of intensity, cleverness and fervor, which could come only from a concern that something was deeply sacred—the very appearance of Paris itself—was at stake.—Richard Bernstein, *Fragile Glory: A Portrait of France and the French*, 1990

The Louvre plaza is the only spot in the city where tourists (to whom Junko and I frequently refer as "human clutter") seem to enhance the view. How naked the pyramid and its lagoons would look unpopulated by the throngs of wilted snapshooters. Like this familiar courtyard, this trip to Paris consisted mostly of familiar places, familiar doings. On a chilly Sunday afternoon, we ventured boldly into Fouquet's, the highfalutin' tourist trap on the Champs-Élysées, where Junko did a fine painting, watched over by the most beautiful woman (outside the Crazy Horse) whom we saw on this entire trip. She was darkly Levantine with slender legs and a possessive Anglo-Saxon boyfriend who had (we suspected) promised, by marrying her, to rescue her forever from the mullahs back home.

"We dine in Fouquet's very frequently, in fact almost always," James Joyce wrote to his son and daughter-in-law on 1 July 1934. "It has become a chic prize-ring. The other night an advanced lady slapped a perfect gentleman's face on account of another perfect lady's being with him."—Noel Riley Fitch, *Literary Cafés of Paris,* 1989

Also familiar was L'Ecluse, one of our favorite wine bars. It was, in the 1950s, a cabaret where Eric Hazan remembers hearing "for the first time Georges Brassens [1], and later Barbara." [2] Having read Hazan's mention of her in *A Walk Through Paris,* I had to look up Barbara, a *chanteuse* with a haunting voice tinged with wise pathos whose big "hit" was "L'Aigle Noir" ("The Black Eagle"):

Un beau jour
Ou peut être une nuit
Près d'un lac

Je m'étais endormie
Quand soudain semblant crever le ciel
Et venant de nulle part
Surgit un aigle noir ...

Just across the Seine was the secluded place Dauphine, a veritable oasis in the hurly-burly of the city's center. Remarkably, it is still recognizable from a description by Elliot Paul almost a century ago.

The place Dauphine is a quiet little square on the Ile de la Cité, with a small park in the center and a few obscure hotels and old residences ranged closely on all sides. Not fifty yards away is the busy Pont Neuf, where market trucks and wagons rumble all night long to help in the colossal task of feeding Paris, but the sounds that reach the place *are softened and subdued. On the eastern side, the jail, the Palais de Justice, and the Saint Chapelle introduce an atmosphere of spiritual and temporal authority which does not overshadow the square. There are dim doorways, shuttered windows, time-stained walls and in the center a few chestnut trees beneath which are short cement walks and a half-dozen benches. Two street lamps, spaced well apart and cloaked with foliage, furnish just the right amount of light.*—Elliot Paul, *Hugger-Mugger in the Louvre*, 1940

Benjie's Diary, 28 September '94, Paris: "We shlepped to the place Dauphine and made our long-delayed reservation at the bistro Paul. Then we slowly made our way back to the hotel, dropping in on a favorite Left Bank hangout, the bistro Mazarine, which is the poor stepsister of the ever-trendy and youth-infested La Palette. We ordered cheese, wine and bread and stifled our appetites because the hydra at the door of Paul, who had the look of a defrocked Dominican nun, ordered us not to show our ugly faces 'til 9:45.

"Yes, S'ster."

Years before this visit, I'd been pink-slipped by a magazine called *Tokyo Journal*. After my dismissal, which I welcomed, my candle continued to flicker and gutter on the Tokyo English-language literary scene. This continued even after Junko and I fled Japan in 1993 and settled experimentally in Silicon Valley. From California, I wrote a column called "Lost in Babylon" that ran weekly in the *Mainichi Daily News*. A journey to Paris always helped to nicely fill my editorial hole.

From Benjie's column, Lost in Babylon, Mainichi Daily News, Tokyo, 19 October '94:

PARIS—My favorite city. In fifteen years of returning here, I haven't changed much. My French is still excruciating, and I still tend to get lost among all those skinny Left Bank streets, which all seem to end up at the Institut de France ...

But as little as I've changed, Paris has altered dramatically—perhaps not for the better. Nowadays, the only certain victims of The Attitude are those foreigners capable of no French whatsoever ... Today, in once-cruel Paris, you can get prompt service and even a measure of grudging courtesy if your language skills are merely pidgin and your pronunciation hopelessly Texan.

On this year's pilgrimage, it was only by accident that Hotlips and I stumbled on the last redoubt of The Attitude ... in place Dauphine, a secluded village tucked into the heart of Paris, a shady plot where tourists rarely tread and ripe buckeyes bomb the unwary. Among the last defenders of Parisian *hauteur* are the Sisters Sans Merci, three black-clad defrocked nuns who preside over an intriguingly creaky bistro called Paul.

There is no Monsieur Paul in evidence, nor has there been for years. I suspect that, one night, like some troublesome victim in a Roald Dahl story, he was served up to the customers with a sprinkling of capers and a side of *pommes frites*, because his presence annoyed Sister Mary Rhinoceros, Mother Superior of the Sisters Sans Merci (the face of Wallace Beery, the dental work of Bela Lugosi, the body of Ray Nitschke, the discreet charm of Quasimodo). I'm not sure which convent she was thrown out of, or when that happened, but I can only assume (rather charitably) that her offenses had to do with eviscerating live cats and setting fire to novices—or vice versa (or worse). Sister Mary Rhino spotted me as an enemy of France the moment I made our dinner reservation and hesitated when she snarled the phrase *"dix heures moins le quart,"* which, alas, I first took to mean "ten bricks shy of a load." But I recovered. But! No ...

Too late. She knew what we were—and what we were *not*. When we returned that night for dinner (promptly at ten bricks shy of a load), Sister Mary Rhino marched us to the foreign ghetto—several tables with no view of either place Dauphine or the Seine, but close to a kitchen door which the Sisters kept in constant motion—and sound. Throughout our meal, it regaled us with its refrain: "WHOCK WHOCK whock whock whocketa whocketa WHOCK WHOCK ..." never resting, always restored to voice in the nick of time by one of the flying nuns.

Our waitress was Sister Max von Sydow (see *Three Days of the Condor*) ... who greeted us by shouting, "No!" when we asked for the chicken. "NO CHICKEN LEFT!" Okay, mea culpa, Sister, it's cool. How about the burf? Sister Max summoned her fellow waitress, Sister Klaus Barbie. They loomed above us for what seemed a lifetime, Sister Klaus kneading the grip of her riding crop before she finally, almost imperceptibly, nodded.

We sighed with relief. The burf was allowed, along with the famous snails—which seemed like any ol' snails, but Sister Max served them with a flourish, arranged on a tin plate and dropped from a height of 24 inches.

Incoming!

Clang!

"Ah, merci!"

But she was gone. WHOCK whock whocketa ...

We looked around. The scenic tables went to certified Parisians, most of them spending less than we, skimping stylishly on the "plate da jure." Sister Mary Rhinoceros passed among them, fawning and purring in magnificent Parisian French, frequently striking the pose that won her fleeting fame as the 1944 poster child of the Vichy government. Our ghetto neighbors, all of us clustered near the deadly jaws of the Whocker, were two Scandinavian ladies, a German couple who got no slack from the Sisters despite babbling textbook French, and a family of French gypsies who spoke dialect.

Sister Mary Rhino inspected us regularly, glaring at our plates, piling crockery and linen on tables around us, reminding us that we were eating in the storeroom and indicating that closing time was nigh and she needed her beauty sleep (my estimate was 250 years). Purely to aggravate the Sisters Sans Merci, we lingered. They had us penciled in for a twenty-minute "four-mule," and we dragged it out to damn near an hour and a half. There was one more crisis, when we wanted *framboises* for dessert and Sister Max von Sydow bellowed, "No!"

Only *"un"* serving of *framboises* remained, she cackled triumphantly, to which I trumped, "Say bone! We only wanted *un*! Bring it on, moncherrry!"

After all, Hotlips and I had a surprisingly swell time at Paul—probably thanks to the nostalgia triggered by an unexpected resurrection of The Attitude. There is nothing like a duel of wills, nothing like the specter of nationalist contempt and possible violence—nothing quite like being a brazen Jet on Shark turf—to lend spice and adventure to a mere plate of "ay-mince-ay da burf" and a "dummy-botay" of "vannored in air." Eventually, reluctantly, we drained our espresso to the dregs and stood to leave. We would have strutted proudly past Sister Mary Rhino, but she was teething her fangs on a table leg, too busy to note our passage. So we strolled among the box seats to the back door. The Sisters Sans Merci, of course, offered no thanks for our patronage. The only counterpoint, as we hummed the tune to "Over There," was the murmur of our Alliance Française French and the trademark melody of Paul sans Paul, still ringing in our ears as we crossed the Seine to a kinder, gentler, but sissier Paris.

WHOCK whock whocketa WHOCK.

Before we headed back to California, we also returned to the Crazy Horse de Paris, where we had first gone five years before—to behold the tall, unnerving, ironic naked dancers.

Before I knew Junko, I'd been married to a woman who spoke French and loved Paris but blanched Catholicly when I wondered aloud what the Crazy Horse was all about. She deemed this subterranean cabaret a near occasion of sin and banned me from ever darkening its scarlet doorstep. "Okay, sweetie," I said, "no big deal." But my curiosity—piqued by the allure of the forbidden—festered for a decade until the era of Junko who, like me, harbors a certain mischievous appreciation for flashing curves and nude flamboyance.

What we expected on our first Crazy Horse foray was a stylish tit show. We came away chastened. Style had so transcended tits that barely a jiggle stuck in our memory. There was something unique here, and wonderful. A year later, a second trip to the Crazy affirmed our hypothesis that here was a burlesque show like no other, ever.

The next year, I resolved not to settle for just another peek at the babes. Hoping to sell a feature to a stateside magazine, I wangled an interview with the man behind the Crazy Horse, Alain Bernardin. Our hostess for the meeting was Polly Harper from Chicago, who had danced in the Crazy chorus as Polly Underground. She ushered us into his office 'round midnight, after the late show. Well into his seventies, Bernardin was a dervish of perpetual motion. His welcome was gracious but distracted. He would sit with Junko and me for a moment talking compulsively, then stand, rattle off an order to Polly and burst from the room, disappearing into the Crazy Horse's warren-like premises on the boulevard George IV. The room was red, and Bernardin was suddenly gone. All we learned, in the first five minutes, was that after Bernardin had acquired the lease on the building from a kindly old lady. He had tried to start a nightclub with a Wild West motif (hence the title). That was 1949, and the saloon idea bombed. Undaunted, Bernardin contemplated other American themes. His inspiration was his discovery, in the centerfold of a girlie magazine, the greatest ecdysiast of all time. "She was sumptuous and *venusienne*," he wrote in a memoir. "Tall, blonde, platinum, exotic and unlike the common run of *femmes fatales* and amateur celebrities. The face of this sculpture of Aphrodite fascinated me. Under this photo, the caption said that this was Lili St. Cyr [3], the queen of American burlesque."

I began experimenting with stripping. I met a girl. She said, "I'm a dancer." She was eighteen, long blonde hair. She had been working in a Brazilian group. She had a great deal of energy. She wanted to turn the audience on. It was her hobby—which was just what I was looking for. She danced for me as Rita Renoir ... Now? She's 65.—Alain Bernadin

Bernardin admits that his first shows were amateur hours. But then, with Rita Renoir, four other dancers and a handful of comedy acts, he began a forty-year experiment in the refinement of what he called a "parody" of the American striptease. The show's satiric vein comes through the stage names Bernardin—and only Bernardin—conferred on Crazy girls. Melody Bubbles, Lady Chinchilla, Bertha Von Paraboum, Sofia Palladium, Bettina Uranium, Prima Symphony, Magda Magnum, Candy Capitol, Capsula Popo, Vicky Toboggan, Bibi Acoustic, Usha Starlight, Trucula Bonbon, Vanilla Banana, Tiny Semaphore, Bulba Butterfly, Betty Buttocks.

Meanwhile, long before stripping in the U.S. devolved into pole-dancing, dry-humping and hardcore raunch, Bernardin diverged into an uncharted realm of imagination. At the Crazy Horse, Bernardin turned his naked women into a breathing screen. Light glided and burst, darkened and flashed across fluid curves and restless flesh.

I'm an artist. Well, I don't know if I'm a good artist ... but I want everything to look like a painting, the light, the makeup, the costume, the little g-string, everything. Altogether it must look like a painting, in motion.—Alain Bernardin

Writer journalist Bertil Scali recalled that Bernardin's emergence in 1951 occurred in "a magical Paris after the war, when anything was possible—that époque of insouciance and a shortage of great men, and of dancers who once more mingled with patrons in smoky little cellars." In the best of Bernardin's times, which stretched through the seventies, everyone who was anyone had to be seen in the Crazy's intimate blazing-red saloon.

Salvador Dali and Caésar [4] came and found inspiration. Fernand Raynaud [5] and Raymond Devos [6] came and played. Charles Aznavour came and sang. And above all, Rita Renoir, Tricia Boogaloo or Nouka Bazooka came to dance.

—Bertil Scali, *VSD* magazine, 1994

By the nineties, however, the Crazy was a little passé. Bernardin sensed the slippage and groped for ways to reverse it. He was all the more frustrated because he was a control freak for whom no minutia was irrelevant. He allowed no subordinate the tiniest decision and protected his girls like a jealous dad. He reputedly spent a week in London combing the city to find just the right shoes for his hat-check girls.

The most important thing in theater, in ballet, in opera, is maintenance. You must want a standard, as you have to make it better every day. Better than yesterday. Not as good as tomorrow.—Alain Bernardin

He likes to construct and destroy, and change it. I don't know how many times he changed the dressing rooms. One day, you'd come here and you wouldn't know where your dressing room was.—Ivan Kraus, "The Blackwits"

The visual spectacle that Bernardin created, in forty years of tireless tinkering, invention, revision and relentless rehearsal, was often brilliant and consistently startling. His dancers were the best-paid and best-drilled in Paris. But beneath the impressionism of light and motion, beneath the crimson allure of the Crazy girls, Bernardin's ironic misanthropy lurked. This was the undercurrent that kept Junko and me coming back. Bernardin had taken to heart the second syllable of "striptease." He had noticed that his audiences, flocking into the Crazy from all over the world, settled into their plush red seats with the expectation that they would be entertained with the lowest denominator of amusement, sleaze and jugs and shaved pussy. They believed the Crazy was a den of iniquity, and iniquity was what they were paying for—exorbitantly. Bernardin steadily lost all tolerance for this base motivation. He ended up liking his customers less and less.

By the nineties, there was a Betty Boop duality to Bernardin's Crazy Horse show. The 1930s Betty Boop cartoons, many censored by the Hays Office [7], always worked on two levels—one to appeal to children and literal-thinking adults, the other for an entirely separate audience attuned to *double entendre* and elliptical smut. For every beautiful patch of skin Bernardin unveiled, there were acres only suggested, or inferred so deftly that few in the audience sensed the maestro's deceptions. Besides, everyone was so busy trying desperately, hopelessly, to peek between the girls' thighs.

We try to make a little magic ... I try to get people to fantasize from what they see—to see what they don't see. To think that she did this, but no, she didn't do this. Did she? ... Without that effect, it's nothing.—Alain Bernardin

As he grew increasingly detached from the audience, Bernardin nurtured a chorus line of women—even buck naked—whose style was intimidating. Akky Masterpiece, arching her back, discarding her g-string and freezing the front row with a dazzling grin, was the quintessence of the Crazy. Bernardin's women were tall, lean, proud and—in Bernardin's word—"aggressive." No pose they struck onstage was submissive. Hands on hips and nude to the ankles, they gazed down at their spectators, shouting, strutting, laughing. They were shameless, scary, unapproachable. Touch one and she would sear your fingers.

Like all great men, he demanded everything from his performers. "One enters the Crazy Horse as one enters a convent," he told his dancers, "half in love, half terrified."—Bertil Scali, *VSD* magazine, 1994

Junko and I had begun our "interview" with Alain Bernardin around midnight. We were there 'til nearly dawn as our host sat, stood, paced, talked, emoted, burst from the room and vanished for a half-hour at a time. Even absent, he kept us busy and fascinated by sending others to us—soloists Akky Masterpiece and Friday Trampoline, and two extraordinary puppeteers, Ivan Kraus and Nadezda Munzarova, "The Blackwits," who were fixtures of the Crazy Horse's non-naked program.

As I explored the "idea" of the Crazy Horse, it grew clear that my challenge was to express the difference between this show and the rigidly ritualized GYN exam that nowadays passes for striptease in America. I was convinced that Bernardin had sculpted a Galatea while the rest of the world—using the same tools—had punched a peephole in the ladies' room. I've since often struggled to express how thoroughly singular the real

Crazy Horse is from its analogues, imitators and namesakes in a thousand strip malls and red-light zones from Las Vegas to Manila.

[Alain Bernadin] succeeded in making a very erotic show without being vulgar. You can never see inside the girls' legs. It's very classy. When you take a look at Crazy girls, they're not like the type you see in Pigalle—not hard. He'll never take a girl who has a naturally sexy face. He prefers very innocent-looking girls. Pretty faces but interesting pretty faces. Very fresh girls. Sportive girls. That makes the difference.—Akky Masterpiece (Akké Alma)

Benjie's Diary, 18 November '98, Le Saulnier: "I was thinking last night of how to explain the Crazy Horse to Fuller. He treats it as a Combat Zone strip club—pole-humping and dollar bills in g-strings. Best I can do to dispel that expectation (if I try at all) is to emphasize that Bernardin's ideal woman was a sort of Amazon—or a Venus in living marble. She's the sort of woman who is stunningly, immediately desirable but—at first impression—perfectly unattainable. She's out of any guy's league. She is too beautiful, erect, proud, athletic and forceful to approach. This is with her clothes on. Bernardin placed these Venuses and Amazons in the most vulnerable possible position—naked in front of hundreds of people. But the aspect he sought in his women, which he instilled and encouraged, was their power to become even scarier, even more untouchable, in the nude. When they were motionless, they became artworks, Venus, *La Joconde, La Maja Desnuda,* the odalisque. *You don't touch the art.*

"And when they moved, they kicked, leaped, strutted, threw their heads back, swirled their hair and laughed. To consider touching one was to consider caressing a live electric wire. You faced the prospect of a spike heel in the teeth, or having your glasses snatched off your face and flung from the stage like a stolen stocking cap. Worse, you expected to be disdained.

"These women are too good for you—any of you." This was Bernardin's insight and his intent. This attitude radiated from girls like Akky—in her brazenness, in her *hauteur,* her posture, her eyes looking at you, into you, through you, both sympathetically and mockingly.

"She knew why she was onstage—because she is magnificent. And why you are in the audience. Because you're not."

The Crazy Horse, it's not like anything else. I've never done anything on stage where there's less clothing, and I don't want to take my clothes off in another show—because it wouldn't be like this.—Friday Trampoline (Caroline Mills)

When I saw my costume, it was so small. I said where's the rest of it. Is this my hat?—Akky

Junko and I eventually found a friend in Akky, despite her teasing me as a *"prude Américain"* and egging me into blustering protest. Akky laughed at me, and Junko joined in. This exchange happened during a rehearsal at the Crazy Horse, as we watched Bernardin alternately raging, cooing and nitpicking among his *danceuses déshabilles*. That day, Akky offered a remarkable insight. "Bernardin says a woman should not sag. She shouldn't droop," said Akky. "He insists that we're proud. Bend back and hold your tits high. It's so much more beautiful. Isn't it?"

She showed us. Suddenly, in the taut curve from neck to knees that Akky had formed with her body, there was something of Brancusi and a memory of Kiki [8]. She radiated an erotic force that had not been present a moment before.

In the ultimate tribute, his masters, like Marcel Duchamp or Max Ernst, came by the Crazy sometimes to talk with him. A genius of sophisticated eroticism, he revolutionized the spectacle du nu. *"Bernardin is truly the reinventor of the way a man looks at a woman," said César.*—Bertil Scali, *VSD* magazine, 1994

The dark side of Bernardin's art was his withdrawal from his public and from the Paris society that had once made his club a mecca for the artistic and entertainment elite.

Sometimes, I'll see him sitting in the front row, watching the performance, perfectly attentive ... What he's doing here he's doing for himself, and he just lets in three hundred people to watch his show with him.—Ivan Kraus, "The Blackwits"

In the fall of '94, a month before Junko and I were booked for another trip to France, Bernardin went into his office. The last show of the night was playing before less than a full house. For more than a year, Bernardin had been struggling with the Crazy's faltering finances and distancing himself from people closest to him, who had been more a family than a workforce. Lately, his performers were demanding higher pay and more star billing. Akky, almost a daughter to Bernardin, was litigating her salary and threatening to leave. Creditors were leaning hard, and his children were pressuring him to loosen his grip on every tiny management detail.

A little after midnight, Alain Bernardin killed himself with a bullet to the brain. He was found slumped on his desk. He was seventy-eight and in perfect health.

We saw Polly at the Crazy Horse a month later. She said that everything was going fine, but it wasn't. Bernardin's children had taken over, the club's hospitality had lost its ardor, and the Crazy girls? Well, they were making small mistakes onstage. In the finale, "You Turn Me On," they just weren't brassy enough.

Benjie's Diary, 3 October '94, Paris: "After the show, we met Akky at the exit. She is beautiful with her clothes on. We found out that her law studies are going well, that she's planning to leave the Crazy Horse in a month, that she has a new boyfriend, that she has a chance to work in Vegas choreographing her own act (maybe). [9] We stood together on Ave. George V and had a mutual admiration society and made absolute promises to rendezvous in America. I hope we succeed.

"She told us that Bernardin had steadily cut himself off in the last several years. He'd had battles with suppliers, costumers and vendors, but he had also alienated journalists who didn't have my patience or my offbeat needs. I might have been the last journalist to conduct a really extensive interview, and that was three years ago. He had even alienated his girls by refusing to negotiate higher salaries. We all suspected that the cost of his isolation was that he no longer felt close enough to his protégés, to the brainchild that made his life worth living, in a society for which he harbored an abiding contempt.

"He could not simply relax and pass the baton. He had to go out with a bang, one last 'Screw you all!' ... He died of pride."

In 1968, in Prague, when the Russians were shooting people in the streets and throwing artists in prison, we were a group of six or seven puppeteers. We found an article in a Prague newspaper about the Crazy Horse. Desperate to escape, we sent a card to Mr. Bernardin, saying, "Please help six or seven crazy Czechs get out of Prague alive." A few days later, we received a state contract, signed by Bernardin, to appear at the Crazy Horse in Paris. Of course, there was no job for us, but the contract was our ticket to freedom ... I sometimes wonder what would have happened if my letter had disappeared before Mr. Bernardin had read it. My whole life would have been changed.

Bernardin said, "That would never happen. I do everything myself." The Crazy Horse is a one-man show. Bernardin is just one Bernardin. There is no other like him.—Ivan Kraus, "The Blackwits"

Perhaps the bad vibes surrounding the Crazy Horse left us a little discouraged. Maybe, back in Périgueux, The Fight had tired us more than we realized. So, just before departing Paris in that autumn of '94, Junko and I decided that we would start taking our vacations elsewhere. Paris, we agreed, had turned a trifle stale. We were moving, we thought, to grooves too familiar.

Benjie's Diary, 2 October '94, Paris: "Still enjoying ourselves, but not feeling the adventure as intensely. We're going to modify our Paris schedule, from yearly to every three years. After three years, Paris will be full of change and sorely missed."

Junko and I had made dumbass resolutions in the past, but this proposed three-year Paris agenda took the cake. Eight months later, we were already heading back, eager for the sort of incomparable surprises that seem a part of the everyday Parisian experience. We were ready to start our search for an apartment in Paris.

Just then a young woman's voice, penetrating and perfectly pitched, free of all accompaniment, rang out in the streets below. We went to the open window and watched her, barefoot, shiny hair streaming down her back, as she belted out one show tune after another in English. Her voice was strong and clear and not to be confused with anyone else's. Two diners sitting under an awning on the curb didn't appear to appreciate her, perhaps because they'd just been dazzled by three tap dancers dressed up as ducks, a tough act to follow.—Edmund White, *Our Paris: Sketches from Memory*, 1994

Benjie's Diary, 3 October '94, Paris: "Coming back to the hotel Saturday night, Junko and I passed, on the *quai*, a naked man on a bicycle. Smiling, waving. He was thoroughly enjoyed by all his spectators."

Panthéon
Sept. 19, 199

2
Boo Air

Franz, old man, Paris is one of the cities I would like to share with you sometime. Of all the cities it has the most beautiful varied light. The domes of Sacré-Coeur look like pearl onions floating in the mist.—James Wright, a letter to Franz Wright, 1979

Some people are born Parisian, some people achieve Paris, but most—when you get down to true confessions—have Paris packaged by a travel agent, along with Naples, Madrid and the Côte d'Azur, and thrust upon them. If this experience allows for even a brief stolen moment of unharried absorption (a lingering *verre de* Beaujolais at Le Départ Saint-Michel, a stroll through the Tuileries after a summer shower, a Dixieland band on rue de Buci), those who've seen Paris can't keep it discreetly to themselves. They will vent. If you've been a sightseer in Paris, a business tripper, a transit passenger, a student, a romantic reading Janet Flanner's gossipy dispatches to *The New Yorker,* it comes over you ineluctably and starts to nag at your subconscious—the need to share Paris with someone special or beloved, with someone you expect to appreciate it or maybe just someone who has no choice but to go where you tell him, or her, to go. This is what happened to my Uncle Harry in 1918, whose Parisian propellant was Black Jack Pershing, followed by a timely armistice that got Harry to Pigalle before the trenches, the Bosch or the flu could cut him down.

Harry spent the rest of his life sharing Paris over his kitchen table in Tomah, Wisconsin.

I also got drafted to Paris, in 1980, pre-Junko, by a Previous Wife (PW) whose thirst to share Paris was unquenchable. Guided by this French-fluent woman who was familiar with the territory, my Parisian novitiate was a cakewalk. We suffered no slights, not a single humiliation at the mercy of a surly waiter, nor even an elbow in the ribs from a crone in a queue. Our only crisis was a one-day Métro strike when all taxis were *occupé* and even the hotels were full, and we had to walk hurriedly (she was almost sprinting, and I had to keep up) at midnight—through northern Paris' throngs of Arab and Algerian purse snatchers (none of whom we actually saw; their concealment was superb and their forbearance, as they ignored us entirely, quite hospitable)—to our tourist *pension* near the Périphérique. On that vacation, PW and I ran the full tourist gamut—Eiffel Tower, Notre Dame, La Coupole, the night-blazing *bateaux mouches*—so that, years hence with Junko (who had, in college, hit Paris and done the checklist exhaustively in the company of an effervescent fusspot named Chikako), we were free to focus on graveyards and oddities and watercolors and to wonder why the towers of St.-Sulpice don't match.

Nonetheless, on my first visit, the ease of Paris, thanks to PW, was exceptional. Paris has never been notably cordial and welcoming to the Nike-shod throngs who invade every summer. If tourism were physics, Paris would be relativity. Moreover, my first foray occurred long before the bicentennial, which, in tribute to profit, domesticated many unruly natives. Before the bicentennial, Paris could be, for the transient of delicate sensibility, torturous.

When King Edward and Queen Alexandra attended the gala performance at the [Comédie] Français *in May 1903, out of respect for what were considered the prejudices of the British, the famous actress known as* La Belle Otero [10] *was asked to exchange her stall for a box. The King had a very cold reception when he arrived in Paris. One of the members of the suite said, "The French don't seem to like us very much, Sir." To which the King sagely replied, "Why should they?"*

—Alan Houghton Brodrick, ed., *The People's France: Paris*, 1950

I remember noticing a newlywed couple on the same flight with PW and me, from Boston to Paris. The pair were bubbly and cuddly, bright-eyed with anticipation of a honeymoon in the world capital of romance. Snuggling in their seats, sharing a small red phrasebook, they interspersed kisses with hesitant stabs at French dishes and first-aid questions.

"Oo-way la vay-say?" she asked adorably.

"Ma famay malade. Javoo dray oon ombulants!" he replied, tenderly.

After the flight, they disappeared. At last sighting, they were holding hands at Charles de Gaulle. We didn't see them again 'til our return ten days later, at Logan Airport. They were hard to miss.

The bride was charging into traffic outside the international terminal, shrieking back at her luggage-laden spouse, who was carrying three bags and viciously kicking a fourth through the exit doors.

"I'm NEVER," screamed the bride, "NEVER going back to that FUCKING country as long as I live!"

She halted in front of an oncoming bus and pointed

j'accusingly at her husband. "You were no help at all, you son of a BITCH!"

The bridegroom stumbled over his kicking bag and staggered into the roadway, barely dodging death on the grille of a taxi. The bride seemed untroubled by her true love's brush with mortality. "FUCK Paris!" she shrilled conclusively as she simultaneously flipped the finger at a bus driver.

Then, again, she vanished from our lives, trailing son of a bitch and baggage.

I hope you have a section in this book about the people who should never come to Paris.—Roberta Beardsley

Benjie's Diary, 7 May '98, place Maubert: "We ... headed over to rue Bonaparte for a cheap meal at the Restaurant des Beaux Arts ... we had a genial, ironic young waiter and an unobtrusive American couple beside us. The Americans ended up confused about paying the bill because they didn't take coffee after dessert. While they were waiting for *l'addition*, the waiter was waiting for them to order coffee.

"They were followed [at the adjacent table] by the Vacationing Young Couple from Hell. The male half, dour and monosyllabic, posed no problem to the management. The female—let's call her Carol—was one great, peeled, throbbing, ambulatory neurosis. She kept talking incessantly, entirely about herself, about the impression she thought she made on other people and about the male half's perception of her (which, we concluded rather easily, boiled down largely to fatigue). But she bridged over to paranoia with the arrival of our waiter.

"Carol's French vocabulary extended little beyond two words: *"merci"* and *"beaucoup."* This was insufficient to the challenge of ordering—in a French restaurant—food that contains no milk. As we got to know her, we gathered that Carol was lactose-intolerant … Judging from her conversations, she had seen or experienced nothing of Paris, and she gave little indication (beyond her explosive anti-milk harangue at our kindly waiter) that she even knew she was in France. Junko and I later agreed in whispers (lest Carol overhear) that she should stay safe and sound back home in The Town Without Milk. There, she can talk about herself among accustomed and patient listeners, with the added bonus of not annoying the strangers at the next table.

"Anyway, from some product package she must have seen, Carol conjured two additions to her *répertoire du français*, which she flung deafeningly at our mild and bemused *serveur*.

"'Sands-lay!'" she snarled.

"Absent an immediate reply, she continued: 'Is this sands-lay? No milk! Do you UNDERSTAND? SANDS-LAY!'

"'Oui,' said our waiter. '*Sans lait. Mai …*'

"She roared on through the menu, impatient of the waiter's efforts to guide her to something—anything—without milk in it. He was handicapped by the hitch that most of the sauces concocted at the Beaux Arts tend to be cream-dependent. To assist in her show-and-tell rant against dairy, Carol pointed—well, jabbed her index finger threateningly—at our table, indicating that wine was okay. She wanted WINE! But that stuff—the shit on my plate—NO! No milk! Sands-lay! Understand?

"He understood.

"She found another French word: 'FISH!'

"Well, 'fish' isn't French, okay? But she pronounced the 'i' like a long 'e.' 'Feesh!' Nice try.

"'Can I have a feesh, sands-lay? No MILK!'

"She said this four times, louder with each iteration. The waiter surrendered and promised he would convince the chef to heat a slab of fish 'nature,' nothing on it at all—the quintessentially Parisian dinner. The waiter backed away hurriedly, almost falling on top of me in his haste, as Carol renewed her battle cry.

"'Sands-lay ... No milk ... Plain feesh! ... SANDS-LAY!'

"Then she lapsed into her angst-laden stage whisper, seemingly laboring to convince her male half to stick by her, through thick and skim, despite his likely yearning to flee into the Paris night—and the relative quiet of car horns and police sirens.

"I pictured him plotting an alternate plan, to strangle her in bed. But there I was again, walking in another man's moccasins."

Paris is, in my opinion, the most complete city in the world ... it is, at one and the same time, the political, literary, scientific, financial, commercial, pleasure and fashion capital of a great nation and the whole history it represents ... Bores do not find in Paris the same indulgence extended to them as in some other towns in Europe ... In Paris, it is advisable to hide one's painfully acquired knowledge under a certain grace of manner ... This sort of prudence is so common in Paris that foreigners often think it is a city of pure luxury and easy-going morals, for pleasure is well in evidence. People come to Paris to escape from their everyday life, to enjoy themselves. Thus visitors can easily acquire quite false ideas about the most mysterious nation in the world—one which is, moreover, the most open. —Paul Valéry

After my first Parisian idyll, it took me seven years to get back. I was solo, working on a book about inventions for Arthur D. Little, Inc., interviewing the two remarkable Communist adventurers who co-founded Club Meditérranée, Gerard Blitz and Gilbert Trigano. While in Paris, I cultivated acquaintance with Margaret Orsal, the head secretary of ADL's Paris office, a woman who would take one look at you and decide forever—passionately—if she hated or loved you. If you were Dutch or Belgian, you were already predisposed toward Margaret's lifelong cold shoulder. But she tended to favor Americans. Add to this advantage my tendency, when I travel, to seem incompetent, tongue-tied and vulnerable. These flaws triggered Margaret's mothering instinct. She and her gracious, gangling husband, Jean, adopted me, brought me home from my fleabag hotel and fed me. I wrote Junko all about Jean and Margaret in my daily letter to Tokyo.

A letter, Benjie to Junko, 25 March '87: "We had drinks back here at La Régence-Étoile, and they promised me a weekend in Jean's homeland, Chantilly. Now, I have to see if I can manage it. Margaret is a treat. A little wine and she laughs like a teenager. I was tired after a long day of interviews and a fruitless search for the men's underwear department at Galeries Lafayette. So I was less enthusiastic about Margaret's invitation to supper. But I made it back to ADL-Paris, found her … and then tagged behind Margaret to her apartment. She gave me a Pernod and we chatted. Then Jean arrived. A warm, expansive man who's been unemployed for three years but sustained by France. His French accent is lilting and dense, but he works so caringly to speak English that I'm touched … After a lot of discussion whether to go out or have an omelette in the house, we took the advice of Margaret's boss, Michel, and headed to Le Congrès Maillot. Not far from Étoile. Lively, smelly, ornate, multi-leveled, red carpets everywhere … Jean had the special of the day, *bar* (sea bass), I had *lotte* (monkfish) and Margaret had the Crustacean Delight, a whole mess of raw and cold stuff like oysters and *ebi* and *moules*. And a crab in the middle! A fun meal, with strawberries at the end. The first *fraises* of the season."

Two years later, Jean was employed again, keeping books for the American Hospital in Neuilly. Jean and Margaret had moved to Paris' very-near suburbs, in Courbevoie. Their Paris dwelling, on rue Dufrenoy in the fashionable Sixteenth, was vacant. So, on our next vacation to Paris and subsequent returns, Junko and I occupied rue Dufrenoy. This arrangement changed in 1993, however, when Margaret had to rent the place to an OECD [11] functionary to help defray taxes and cover the mortgage in Courbevoie. Perhaps having to switch to hotel-dwelling after mooching off Margaret and Jean compelled Junko and me to ponder more seriously the purchase of our own *pied-à-terre* in Paris.

Meanwhile, we were graduating from apprentice tourist to journeyman status—not much of an advance, but enough that we could presume to look down our nose at the rookies, the chipmunks and the thundering Germans.

Benje's Diary, 11 September '90, Paris: "Funny weather all day. The sun wandered in and out—mostly out. After the usual breakfast (f56), the waiter recognized us and praised Junko's drawing of the boulevard Jules Sandeau—we headed for the Île de la Cité. Junko drew the Pont Neuf, then we crossed over to the boul-Mich and ended up having lunch at a nice spot on the rue de la Harpe. Then to St.-Julien-le-Pauvre—another drawing while I went to Shakespeare & Co. Found three rare paperbacks (f50). Afterward, Junko and I finally had Berthillon ice cream (f16). A walk past Notre Dame, a visit to the Memorial to the Holocaust Départées. Then a pause at a café on Île St.-Louis. Another book, Ray Mungo's *Total Loss Farm*, with poems by Verandah Porche, sister of Spot [12] (f25) actually less than that because the bookstore guy (Abbey Books) [13] was out of change. Finally, Les Deux Magots. Snotty waiter. Wine (f64) steep. We're going to a Bach/Vivaldi concert tonight at St.-Germain-des Prés. Late supper. This place is still fun."

Of all the bridges which were ever built, the whole world who have pass'd over the Pont Neuf must own, that it is the noblest, the finest, the grandest, the lightest, the longest, the broadest that ever conjoin'd land and land together upon the face of the terraqueous globe.—Laurence Sterne (quoting a Parisian), *A Sentimental Journey*, 1768

At the tip of the Ile, in the place where the morgue once was, the Crypt of the Departées, with its portcullis on black blades, its two hundred thousand symbols representing the two hundred thousand missing, its earth from the camps and ashes from the crematoria, and its unknown corpse.—André Malraux, *Anti-Memoirs, 1967*

There was a ceaseless coming and going at the great fair which since 1486 had flourished under the protection of the Abbey of Saint-Germain-des-Prés. It was a place of brawling and fighting no less than of amusement and trade; there were to be found such rare and fashionable novelties as tea, chocolate and tobacco. All the tradesmen of Paris were represented at the fair of Saint-Germain, but especially French pastry-cooks, Italian sellers of soft drinks, and managers of dance-halls.—Robert Laffont, ed., *The Illustrated History of Paris and the Parisians*, 1958

Even by 1990, our Paris paths were fairly predictable. After café crème and croissants with the morning's *International Herald Tribune* and its two-day-old baseball scores, we took the Métro to a familiar corner, then strolled off randomly, sometimes on beaten paths, sometimes into the French unknown. We moved slowly, feeling for the city's rhythm, pausing at windows and turning corners expecting the unexpected. We let Paris decide our course and impose its detours. We never traveled far without stopping for Junko to work on a watercolor, for me to prowl an intersection sneaking photos of people or snapping postcard clichés, or receding into a café to read Mungo and Porche.

Paris, for anyone inclined to chill out and tune in, invites loitering.

Paris invented the flaneur *and continues to press all leisurely and attentive walkers into exercising that pursuit, which is an active and engaged form of interaction with the city, one that sharpens concentration and enlarges imaginative empathy and overrides mere tourism.*—Luc Santé, *The Other Paris*, 2015

The heart of Paris is like nothing so much as the vast interior of a house. Buildings become furniture, courtyards become carpets and arrases, the streets are like galleries, the boulevards greenhouses. It is a house, one or two centuries old, rich bourgeois, distinguished. The only way of going out, shutting the door behind you, is to leave the city's center.—John Berger, "Imagine Paris," *Harper's Magazine*, 1987.

During the average two weeks in Paris, Junko would do twenty paintings. I would burn fifteen rolls of film and we might hit one museum. We still have dozens of museums on our backlist, but they're not going anywhere. Our favorite museum until we discovered the Musée Nissim de Camondo and Gustave Moreau's weirdly wonderful mansion/museum near Pigalle—was the Marmottan with its enveloping, circular salon of Monet waterlilies. Our favorite eatery for years was L'Échaudé St.-Germain, largely because its table-hopping mom-and-pop proprietors made Paris' best dessert, a hot apple tart with *crème anglaise*. This confection, if served to Louis XVI as his last meal, would have sent him to the guillotine with a spring in his step, a song in his heart and a big, wet, sloppy kiss for Monsieur de Paris. [14] Our favorite walk was usually after midnight, on the unglamorous rue de l'Université from the Quartier Latin all the way to the Eiffel Tower, whose lights usually flickered off (closing time was 1 a.m.) just as we arrived there. Then, we crossed the Seine to Trocadéro and along avenue Georges Mandel toward rue Dufrenoy. Our favorite pastime, besides painting and reading, was probably watching the tourist parade, especially the pairs of young Japanese women, whom we came to call "chipmunks" because of their nervous alertness and tendency to shiver all over, squeak and scurry off, inevitably toward a shop bearing the logo of a famous designer.

There is an infallible test for detecting a tourist in any metropolis in the world—simply look for a man standing in front of a cutlery or luggage shop with his mouth ajar, gazing vacantly in at the manicure sets, razor strops and collar-boxes and jingling the change in his pockets.—S.J. Perelman. *The Most of S.J. Perelman,* 1942

The tourist of Perelman's day coveted luggage and cutlery. Nowadays, more likely, he jingles his change over a brasserie's bill of fare, mentally calculating the price—at the current exchange rate—of *coquille St.-Jacques* or a *cotelette d'agneau*. For us, the lure of Paris gradually evolved into a room—or garret, or *atelier*—with a view and a functioning toilet. Even while sponging our accommodations off Margaret and Jean, we had begun loitering at the window displays of realty offices. Living in Tokyo, we knew how to measure apartment floor space in meters rather than square feet, which made our window-shopping less mathematical. Our Tokyo flat, just big enough for two people who didn't mind the occasional doorway collision, was forty-three square meters. We specified our imaginary Paris place at fifty square, and we started pricing apartments—just for fun—whenever we passed a display of three-by-five Polaroids that depicted rustic parlors with fireplaces, exposed beams and a glimpse of a claustrophobic kitchen.

In those days, a dollar was four francs. Fifty square meters on avenue Victor Hugo or in the Seventh was selling for close to a million francs, or $250,000. Steep. But in the Thirteenth, in the Fifteenth or the not yet gentrifying Marais, prices were lower. They were almost ... imaginable. Still, the notion of buying an apartment in Paris?

C'mon, man!

Preposterous, impractical ... to quote Vizzini: "*Inconceivable!*"

[In 1814] The [occupying] Cossacks themselves disdained the luxuries of Paris, but drank deep of its earthier pleasures. The term bistro—the Russian word for "quickly"—is said to have come into usage at this point to describe the kind of no-nonsense restaurant favored by Cossacks.—Andrew Hussey, *Paris: The Secret History*, 2006

Meanwhile, we ate, we drank. We came to understand that in Paris, the best use of a dollar, a yen, or a franc was to end one's day with the sort of repast unthinkable back home, or unlikely in almost any other city. One of our regular bistros was Chez René, a trencherman's paradise on the boulevard St.-Germain. For several years running, we had very strange luck with the people who occupied neighboring tables—hollow-cheeked, arachnid herbivores from the Heartland.

Those, on the contrary, to whom Nature has refused the aptitude for the pleasures of taste, have the face, the nose and the eyes long, whatever may be their height—they have in their appearance something "lengthened"—these are the people who invented trousers.—Jean Anthelme Brillat-Savarin [15]

Benjie's Diary, 8 September '93, Paris: "We dodged raindrops 'til our reservation at Chez René came due, and we were welcomed at the door by the enthusiastic barkeep.

"'Monsieur Benjamin!'

"We were placed between a French couple gorging on sausages and, on the other side, two Americans on tour—a kind of reverse Spratt family. Mr. Spratt could eat no lean, his wife could barely look at fat without curling a lip. They are an incongruous couple at Chez René, a country-style restaurant that serves meat in large portions in thick, dark, long-simmered sauces. The *coq au vin* is great, *boeuf bourguignon* the house specialty. *Saucissons* hang from the rafters. Wine flows liberally, with a bias toward Beaujolais. Into this scene comes Ma Spratt, tee-total vegetarian. She drinks naught but water and orders a hearty repast of green beans. That's all. *Haricots verts*.

"As the waiter delivers her dish of beans, he says, *'Trés chaud! Trés chaud!'*

"A difficult phrase at which Ma Spratt says to Pa Spratt, ignoring the waiter, 'I wish he would stop talking to me in a language I don't understand!'

"As far as I can discover, the Spratts are from Florida, or perhaps some godforsaken border state like Kansas. I gather that Ma Spratt belongs to an arts and crafts group back in Starkville, among whom accumulations of small, unsightly, mass-produced figurines is the equivalent of trophy-hunting for white rhinos. Else there's no point in ever setting foot outside the city limit.

"Pa Spratt, in marked contrast to his emaciated wife, orders food appropriate to the setting, accompanied by Scotch and water. I picture the amusement of the waiter as Pa Spratt shouts, much too loud, *'Un autre Scotch!'* providing entertainment to the merry bartender and the French patrons.

"As Pa Spratt settles down to a plateful of lamb chops—nicely rare with a pile of dauphine potatoes—Ma Spratt hails his repast by reminding him, probably for the 5,000th time in their incongruous marriage, that 'Your mother always encouraged you to overeat.'

"I suddenly picture that mother, God rest her soul, a jolly fat woman who had the strength—if only she had acted on her intuition—to strangle this bitch before she'd set her hooks into her passive putz of a little boy.

"However, later we note that Pa Spratt has devised ways to taunt his tormenter. With the ruins of his meal laid below him, he says, 'Well, I sure didn't leave much meat on those bones.' Yeah, his mother taught him to overeat whenever he got the chance, and he does it with panache.

"However, as Pa Spratt begins to eat, he notices that his bread is unaccompanied. We begin the best international exchange of the evening.

"Pa Spratt: 'Hm, there's no butter for my bread.'

"Seeing the specter of death by arteriosclerosis perched on Pa Spratt's shoulder, Ma Spratt scowls darkly. She allows as how Pa could go without butter for once in his bloated life. Pa declines her advice.

"Ma Spratt: 'Well, margarine is all right. But they don't have *that* here.'

"Meanwhile, Pa Spratt manages to snag a waiter.

“Pa Spratt: ‘Butter! Can I have butter? For my bread?’

“Waiter: *‘Qu’est-ce que c’est* Ba da?’

“Pa Spratt: (A light bulb appears above his head) ‘Boo air!’

“The waiter is quizzical.

“Pa Spratt: (Louder) ‘Boo air!’

“Waiter: ‘Boo? Air?’

“Pa Spratt: (Louder and slower) ‘BOO! AIR!’

“Here the waiter, mystified, wilts visibly and cocks his head, looking deep into Pa Spratt’s eyes for some clue to the meaning of this strange device, ‘boo air.’

“Pa Spratt: (Beginning to pantomime spreading motions in which his left hand plays the role of a slice of bread) ‘Boo air. Butter! Ya got butter?’

“Waiter: (A fellow countryman of Marcel Marceau, interpreting Pa Spratt’s gesture, his face suddenly alight) ‘Ah! *Buerre!*’

“Pa Spratt: ‘Christ! That’s what I said. Yeah. Butter! Boo air. You got it? Gimme butter.’

“Waiter: *‘Ah, oui, monsieur. Buerre. Un moment.’*

“Junko and I could only deduce that Pa Spratt had discovered his rare word of French—‘boo air’—by reading it off a butter pat at his hotel, at breakfast.

“The Ma and Pa Spratt Show had its moments, but Junko and I were wearying of the strain. The Spratts are a sort who can start fraying your nerves during a shared elevator ride from the lobby to the mezzanine. We couldn’t wait for them to leave, so we changed our commentary from Japanese (at which I’m limited) to English (at which Junko is fluent) and kvetched in undertones. Eventually, Pa Spratt compelled the waiter, rudely, to summon a taxi. The waiter returned shortly and announced, with undisguised relief, *‘Le taxi arrive.’*

“Hooray. They were gone.

“Did I mention the decaf? Well, Junko made the prediction, after five minutes next to Ma Spratt, that her café would be decaffeinated. An apt perception. The amazing coincidence is that two years before at Chez René, almost in the same spot, Junko and I had endured beside an American couple—younger, newlywed—equally uptight. The bride had also ordered nothing but rabbit food, and had demanded decaf. Two years ago, Chez René was less prepared for ascetic weirdness. Then, the joint had no decaf.

"Last night, *pas de problème*. We even heard a French couple—our sausage hounds—ordering decaf. And now there's a French magazine, advertised on Métro billboards, called *Top Santé*—top health—with copy that reads, 'Protect Your Liver!' The morbid American fear of dinner-table death is like a contagion. While AIDS travels east to west, hypochondria creeps west to east, pinching and sickening every culture in its path."

In the heroic age before the First World War, there were men and women who ate, in addition to a whacking lunch and a glorious dinner, a voluminous souper *after the theater or the other amusements of the evening. I have known some of the survivors, octogenarians of unblemished appetite and unfailing good humor—spry, wry and free of the ulcers that come from worrying about a balanced diet—but they have had no emulators in France since the doctors there discovered the existence of the human liver. From that time on, French life has been built to an increasing extent around that organ, and a niggling caution has replaced the old recklessness.*—A.J. Liebling, *Between Meals: An Appetite for Paris*, 1959

Despite repeated subjunctive immersions at the Alliance Française, Junko and I still don't know much more French than Pa Spratt. Nonetheless, we've always made a point to use every word we've learned—even if it's wrong or outright ridiculous. Our oft-pathetic effort to speak French is a fundamental Paris-café icebreaker, although it requires a ritual of repetition that many tourists can't seem to fathom. The rule is that you never say anything just once.

I've often pronounced some unmistakable French word like *"de l'eau"* (da low) flawlessly, only to have the waiter knit a peevish brow and say, *"Pardon?"*

This is where a lot of neophytes panic. A well-meaning non-French person has spit out two French syllables in perfectly rounded tones, direct from the phrasebook pronunciation guide, but the only reply, from a certified Frenchman, is that patented Parisian stare of sardonic incomprehension. Thus chastened, the tourist mutters, "Um, water?"

The waiter, triumphant, switches to English. "Water! Of course, *m'sieur.* Why didn't you say so?"

But not me. Or Junko. Not anymore. Because we know that Parisian waiters *never* understand French spoken by a foreigner the first time, even though they actually *do* understand. You have to persevere. The game—linguistic chicken—is to make the foreigner repeat his French, if he dares.

So I persevere, with the same diction, *"De l'eau, s'il vous plait."* The waiter nods placidly and asks what sort of *eau* we prefer. This is a more complicated exchange, but it proceeds fluidly, despite my rotten French, because the game is over—for now. Dessert will initiate a whole new battle of wills.

I was always curious about why Parisians are so prickly. By and by, I concluded—lacking a better explanation—that this is the "New York syndrome." Parisians, I posit, are the New Yorkers of Europe. They're mean and rude because *hauteur* is their birthright, insolence their rite of passage. My analysis was altered in reading Elliot Paul, my favorite among all modern chroniclers of Paris. There is, in fact, a history of Parisian rudeness.

Concerning the tourists, the Middle-of-the-Road coalition and the Communists are sharply divided. The government leaders want Americans to come and spend dollars. The Reds slander Americans, collectively and individually, in their newspapers every day, and by exerting pressure on the members of public employees' unions within their sphere of influence, try everything possible to make a tourist's life insupportable. Communist writers refer to Americans as a drunken "master race," the members of which want to reduce French citizens to a colonial status. No minor news item that reaches the offices of L'Humanité *or* Ce Soir, *the Communist organs, is too trivial to be falsified in order to make Americans appear barbarous, degenerate, greedy or vile.*

Of course, the relatively friendly French newspapers seldom get anything about America or Americans straight, and unintentionally, sometimes cause as much damage as the sworn enemies of the United States. Of whatever shade of public opinion, Paris newspapers have an utter disregard of people's names and plain facts.—Elliot Paul, *Springtime in Paris*, 1949

Nowadays, Parisians are politer. As a rule, there are few hostesses as horrid as Sister Mary Rhinoceros at Chez Paul, and there are few actively misanthropic waiters. The typical Paris *serveur* is a cool professional, a careerist. Very likely, he started as a teenager as a kitchen hand and will retire in his sixties with a substantial state pension. Watch him move between tables and chairs, never bumping a patron, never disturbing a *tête-à-tête*. He doesn't walk, exactly. He shimmers, like Jeeves [16].

There is none of the little-girl charm or the boy-next-door friendliness of American restaurants. In Paris, the waiter does not introduce himself by name. He does not smile a great deal or spend a lot of time in ceremonious politesse. You sit at a café correctly, which means you manifest a certain composure; you don't gawk at the passing world, and you know what you want to be served. And then you are served correctly, with a quick, nimble formality and an economy of motion, by a practitioner of the métier, *who knows how—oh, so subtly, with a hint of condescension in his* oui, monsieur, *or a hard stare that lasts just a moment too long, or perhaps a sudden departure just before your business has been transacted—to put you in your place if you seem to be inadequate to the ritual.*—Richard Bernstein, *Fragile Glory: A Portrait of France and the French,* 1990

Once, I was actually moved to compliment a Parisian waiter for his gracious restraint—he chose not to strangle two of his customers—at a café on the rue de Rivoli. At this joint, called Le Carrousel, tourists in vast numbers collapse for rest in the midst of exchanging traveler's checks so they can buy t-shirts, coasters and plastic eiffels. Many of these tourists are *oban*, a Japanese term favored by Junko. *Oban* neatly summarizes that army—or *"obatarion"*—of post-menopausal matrons whose petty grievances eternally, illogically outweigh their obvious affluence, their impenetrable complacency and their surfeit of creature comforts. For an *oban,* no inconvenience is so small that a federal case can't be made of it. Japan, of course, is the mecca of the militant *oban*. But she is a universal phenomenon and, alas, she can always afford to travel, if only to confirm the couthlessness of every society but hers, back home. Ma Spratt, for example, was an *oban*.

Benjie's Diary, 2 June '97, rue de Rivoli: "Ah, here's my *salade Parisienne*.

"Two American tourists, women—*oban*—behind me.

"'Hello!'

"'*Oui, madame.*'

"'I want an omelette.'

"The waiter repeats her demand, pronouncing the word properly.

"'No! Omelette! I! Want! An! Omelette!'

"The waiter is a saint. He's in his fifties, been through this dialog before.

"'*Oui, madame. Une omelette.* And to drink?'

"'An omelette! I want an omelette!'

"'Yes, madame. A nom-lut. And to drink?'

"'I don't want it raw. Not raw!'

"'*Pardon?*'

"'Raw! You make them raw here!'

"'*Madame? Roi?*'

"'No! Not raw!'

"'*Not roi?*'

"'Cook it! Well done! Not raw!'

"'*Ah, oui, madame.* Well *done*. And to drink?'

"'Sprite! You got Sprite?'

"Why do all sixty-year-old American women who come to Paris order Sprite? Is this some sort of movement I've overlooked?"

The German buses are parked in perfect rows, like tanks lined up for inspection. The drivers polish them with towels while the German tourists lope off after their führer*—meaning "leader," whether of tours or bigger enterprises—to buy another five dozen postcards. When such a group passes noisily by, silence seems to fall. Maybe I only imagine it, but my impression is that the French avoid noticing them in the same deliberate way one ignores something unfortunate on the sidewalk.*—C.W. Gusewelle, *A Paris Notebook*, 1985

Rue des Barres, Paris
June 6, 2015

In Paris, it's true, the only women who wear minks are Italian tourists and local prostitutes, but the Italians usually carry a cellular phone as well, so there's generally no confusion (Ciao, Mamma, siamo a Parigi!).—Edmund White, *Our Paris: Sketches from Memory,* 1994

Over the long haul, it seems to us that tourists are peerless in their rudeness, but also harmless, because they are reacting out of linguistic weakness and cultural fear. Open rudeness from a Parisian, on the other hand, can scar its victim for life—partly because it's a surprise out of nowhere with no evident incitement, partly because it's so stylishly understated. Usually, when you get cut dead by a Parisian, it arrives as little more than a wordless, dismissive sneer. To convey disdain, silence trumps vocifery.

Notwithstanding the occasional humiliation, Junko and I felt Paris growing on us. Certain sights had become so familiar that we began to need them. Certain tastes and smells and sensations were a necessary form of intoxication. Certain activities were only possible in Paris, and certain delusions about ourselves, as artists, or as bon vivants, or as citizens of the world could only be entertained—without giggling at our pretense—in the rarefied realm anent the Seine.

Every man of talent, every artist, every man worthy of the name, every cock with brilliant plumage, spreads his wings and flies to Paris.—Balzac

As an artist, a man has no name in Europe save in Paris.—Friedrich Nietzsche, *Ecce Homo,* 1908

Benjie's Diary, 31 August '93, Le Carrousel: "Junko's across the street, starting on her second image of the day—which includes the building I'm at and the gilded statue of Jean d'Arc. I'm drinking some French beer called Mützig Old Lager. It tastes like the French version of Bud. Adding to the ambience is the fragrance of the nearest sewer, But all is not crummy. I can see Junko at work."

Rimbaud was less than impressed by Paris and growled in his letters home that he had found the city to be no glittering capital but rather "Parmerde," a disease-ridden place that smelt of shit both day and night.—Andrew Hussey, *Paris: The Secret History*, 2006

Junko's an instinctive artist with a kind of idiot affinity for lending vitality and color to city scenes. Her talent is less evident in rural landscapes and is sorely lacking in portraiture and figure studies. But put her down in Paris—against a pissy-smelling wall, with a Staedtler waterproof pen and a palette of aquarelle tablets, and she has powers that defy explanation. Notre Dame or the Port St.-Denis, or a crowded café in Les Halles springs into dancing lines, vivid hue and buoyant personality. All year, Junko rarely draws and never paints. She's too busy. In Paris, Junko's painting is the guide and meter of our daily movements. We go where Junko feels like painting. We linger as long as the painting takes. We're merry or moody depending on Junko's satisfaction with her latest effort. Mostly, they're good. They tend to improve with each passing day as Junko finds her groove. Hence, leaving Paris is a painful regression into an existence without bright new pictures or, at least, with only those we can see on TV.

Paris is most beautiful when one is about to leave it.—Robert Brasillach

For me, Paris is a sort of Neverland where I never feel vaguely apologetic about my craft. It's a vacation from American culture, where anti-intellectualism is a deep strain from which even I suffer. Americans regard with an attitude of dismay the idea of an entire lifetime spent just writing stuff down. At a party, the first question anyone asks me is what do I do, to which I reply, "Writer," to which they ask—evidently hoping for some sort of commercial application—what do I write, followed by my reply: "Well, books."

"What *sort* of books?" they persist.

I grind my teeth.

In Paris, by contrast, I reply, *"Ecrivain,"* and the reaction is unpredictable, variable, almost always respectful. This vocational inquiry is never, in Paris, an interrogation. Often, it is enough to say that I write. No further probing follows. There's something implicit in being a writer, for me as it was for my expatriate forebears and demigods, Fitzgerald, Dos Passos, Orwell and Morley Callaghan. Writers have always fled to Paris, often—like James Jones—foolishly. Paris improves no one's writing nor, usually, his or her income from writing. Many productive writers come to Paris and stop writing. Sinclair Lewis couldn't write here at all. Writers starve in Paris as self-piteously as they starve in Greenwich Village or Milwaukee. But in Paris, there is a validity, intangible and rarely found elsewhere. In Paris, the writer feels that his or her work is a worthy calling—and not an embarrassment to Mom.

What accounted for this charm of Paris? It was not a rejection of the United States. Living abroad—in Paris, on the Riviera, in London, Rome, or the Hague—has never made me feel alien to America. I am American to the core, no fonder of these prestigious places than of others, less celebrated, where I lived rewardingly—Boston, New York, Rockport, Massachusetts, Chelsea, Vermont, or even the city where I was brought up, Fall River, Massachusetts, which for outsiders is distinguished only for the Lizzie Borden murders. Why then should the thought of being marooned in America have made me, in my dreams at least, so miserable? I was in Paris, where I wanted to be, and the thought of being anyplace else was intolerable.

Paris was a city in which the expression of all ideas was permissible, at least in the part of its society that I entered. There was no dominant body of public opinion so sure of its own standards that it dared tell everybody else what to think. This nearly complete tolerance and freedom often led to extravagance, but extravagance was more interesting than well-worn ruts. Everything of intellectual importance was happening in Paris, and I was privileged to be occupying a ringside seat at its immense cultural crisis. Paris was open to all ideas, to all opinions, to every mode of thinking. That is why we were happy there. And that is why being exiled from its freedom was translated by me into a series of nightmares.— Waverley Root, *The Paris Edition: The Autobiography of Waverley Root, 1927–1934*, 1987

Besides the spiritual sustenance Junko and I, as artistic wannabes, derived from Paris-the-grand-illusion, there was a mighty physical force that stopped us at each real estate window. We had begun our Paris infatuation as hotel-bound tourists. Then we had switched to "our own place"—although it belonged to Jean and Margaret. After a few years, we had to return once more to hotels, cozy places called the Hotel de Nevers and Hotel de Nice, but hotels nevertheless. We had to buzz ourselves in, disturb the concierge if we came in late, fend off the housekeeper if we overslept, decide the night before whether we felt like breakfast in bed or *un petit-déjeuner* in the sun. Each visit to Paris required a new, strange room, sometimes noisy—the Hotel de Nice overlooked a late-night hangout for motorcycle enthusiasts—sometimes stuffy, sometimes grubby, always too small, unhomelike and unfamiliar. The neighbors changed daily, and the phone was a pain in the ass. During our rue Dufrenoy period, we had graduated to a second-class cabin. Now, we were back in steerage. We'd been spoiled. Now, cut down a peg, we were testy, and chronically tired.

There's a vital difference between being a tourist and being in your own town. That difference is a bed, nothing more, nothing less.

A tourist has nothing, because even the bed, loo, water tap, is rented by the minute. Laying your head down is at somebody else's behest. But if it's your own pad, you can tell everybody else to clear off and shut the door on the blighters. The difference is tourist tiredness, that state of utter weariness where you get taken for every penny, when you buy stupid things, when con merchants come out to play on the bones of the gullible. Exhaustion's a grim mutagen. Even the smartest tourist eventually begins trading dollars for dimes, hard currency for zlotniks.

—Jonathan Gash, *The Great California Game,* 1991

When we returned to Japan, or America, we would confess to friends our preposterous yearning for a place of our own in Paris, and the response was often the equivalent of "What sort of books do you write?"

People would knit a brow and ask, "Why Paris?"

Some of these friends had actually been to Paris but had left uncharmed. Perhaps they had suffered the trauma of an arrogant waiter or lost a wallet to a pickpocket, eaten a bad oyster or couldn't find pizza sold by the slice, or had shivered through a cold ride on a *bateau mouche*. Maybe their tour guide had just kept pushing them from site to site to t-shirt store and back onto the bus without a moment to pause and turn slowly on a private axis ... and *see* Paris.

Margaret, all her life a Parisian, once stood on her nephew Fabrice's apartment terrace, not far from the Élysée Palace, with a fourth-floor view across the Seine to Les Invalides and farther off, to the lights of the Eiffel Tower against the twilight.

"It's like opening a jewel box," said Margaret, the enchanted native.

I do not deny its beauty, but it's a waste of electricity.—Greta Garbo, *Ninotchka,* 1939

Eventually, what Junko and I told people as we tried to justify this lunatic compulsion to own lodgings in that stuck-up city on the Seine was this: although we have less than the normal middle-class interest in owning real estate, we would like a fixed address. And if we must own land, then why not own it in a place that expresses not where we are but where—ideally—we would prefer to be more than anywhere else on earth?

Above all, Paris was a good address. It was the one grand display window for intellectual talent, and if you were at all interested in the way the intellectual cloth of the time was being cut you had to be there, even if you couldn't do more than press your nose against the window.—Morley Callaghan, *That Summer in Paris*, 1963

Besides, if we had our own place, we could hide—when we needed relief—from all those Yank tourists whose self-assurance never seems to match their attention span.

Benjie's Diary, 28 September '94, Lascaux, the Périgord: "A gray dawn burst into sunshine. We had an informative visit to Lascaux II, the perfectly copied facsimile of the Lascaux caves, which were closed in 1962 because of violent oxidation from human breath. The only drawback, although amusing, was the crowd with whom we were forced to view the cave. At one point, our guide, a clipped and fastidious young woman with a British lilt, explained that the artists of Lascaux had lit their work with spoon-shaped lamps made of sandstone, filled with deer fat, with juniper twigs serving as wicks. The juniper twigs burn white smoke, which prevents carbon buildup on the walls. The guide flashed her torch onto a display of lamps in the room where we all stood elbow-to-elbow listening, a room in which the only sound was her voice (except for the whining of a one-year-old brought into a dark, damp, crowded cave to gaze at giant images of monsters on warped and sweaty walls amid evocative, frightening shadows—brilliant parents!). Within two minutes of the guide's disquisition on lamps, a voice from the throng: "Excuse me, but it would seem that the people who painted these pictures would need some light. How did they light the cave, and why wouldn't some sort of torch leave carbon deposits on the cave walls? Huh? Tell me that, smarty-pants." The guide rolled her eyes, took a deep breath, shone her light again on the lamp display and repeated her previous speech. Junko and I said a silent prayer for the girl's sanity."

Tourists will always be a morbid fascination for me, partly because the Americans tend to embarrass me, but partly because, secretly, I feel their pain. I am, at bottom, irredeemably one of them. Occasionally—and against Junko's objections—I shock myself by offering befuddled sightseers a shred of solace they don't deserve.

Benjie's Diary, 25 May '97, near the Champs-Élysées: "I was at Métro FDR, waiting for my train. (You can't imagine my satisfaction knowing that there will always be a Paris subway station named after Franklin Delano Roosevelt and never a Paris subway station named after Richard Nixon.) Across the tracks, the four most obvious American tourists in Paris. All in their sixties. Two women, two men. None exactly lively, but at ten in the morning, the men both looked totally played out, by life if not by Paris. One shuffled to a bench and sagged into it. The other, tall, rawboned and potbellied, was so indifferent to appearances by now that he'd given up holding his mouth shut. He just shifted his feet in aimless circles, gaped and gawped. Both guys were wearing baseball caps with golf logos. The two women, all slacked, permed, raincoated and chickenlike, fussed and nattered happily over a map of Paris—one of those useless maps with the Galeries Lafayette ads and the infinitesimal Métro diagram. None of the foursome had the foggiest. The women were trying. The men were resigned—like Charlie on the MTA—to ride forever 'neath the streets of Paris.

"The old guy sitting down seized a bold initiative. He spotted a passing Parisian *yoot*. He caught the *yoot's* attention. He said, loudly enough to hear halfway down the tracks, 'Is this the right way to the Loov?'

"The *yoot*, true to his Parisian code, went imbecile. 'Loov? What's a Loov? If there was a Loov, do I look like I know where it is?'

"We were, of course, on the Métro line that goes straight to the Louvre. Except that my four bumbling countrymen were on the wrong side of the tracks. They were aimed for La Défense. The *yoot* was vamping for time, backing away, determined not to reveal every Parisian's most darkly held secret: the location of the Loov.

"'To hell with this,' I said to myself.

"'Hey!' I shouted. 'It's over here.'

"The old guy looked at me.

"'Just go up the steps and cross over,' I said.

"The four old folks consulted one another, peered at me suspiciously, re-checked with the *yoot*—who denied all knowledge of the steps, the Loov or the other side of the tracks. He slipped away.

"The tourists decided to believe me. They worked up an ounce of adrenalin and moseyed toward the staircase at the end of the platform. The old guy who had saved them all from a day wandering the sterile barrens of La Défense caught my eye and waved a thank-you. I waved back.

"I never saw them again.

"They're probably still at FDR, crossing the tracks, pausing now and then to shove a nitroglycerin tablet under the tongue of old Slackjaw.

"P.S.: There was a strike of museum attendants that day. The Loov, if they ever got there, was closed."

Published in six languages and color-coded to help tourists find their way through confusing spaces, it provides the precise location of six masterworks that many first-time visitors feel it is crucial to see—among them, the Mona Lisa, the Venus de Milo and the Winged Victory. No museum is happy to encourage tourists to proceed through the building at a gallop primarily or exclusively in order to stand before a half-dozen celebrated pieces. But something had to be done for the peace of mind of those staff members who preside over the information desk: they were bored beyond endurance by the number of tourists wanting directions to those works.—Helen Dudar, "The Hungry Museum"

The Louvre is the book in which we learn to read.—Paul Cézanne

We always try to end a visit to Paris with a good memory. For a long time, the best guarantee was dessert at L'Échaudé St.-Germain. One reason we enjoyed this restaurant, which is unlisted by Michelin and unnoticed by most guidebooks, was that its clientele was a pleasant balance of habitants and aliens. It sat far enough off its namesake main drag (boulevard St.-Germain) to draw a mostly Parisian patronage. But because it resided in one of the city's most heavily trod tourist quarters, it enticed a trickle of fascinating foreigners.

Benjie's Diary, 4 October '94, St.-Germain: "After the Rhumerie, L'Échaudé St.-Germain, where our immediate table-neighbors were Moose and Betty Sue. American newlyweds fresh from the playing fields of Ohio State. Her eyes were blank, hiding mandibles of emasculation, her mouth taut and mirthless. A scary ex-cheerleader with a plan. Moose was large and naive, but he had a hollow leg—a useful appendage with a wife like Betty Sue. Also nearby, three Australians, one a European boulevardier and (apparently) travel agent, who had undertaken the Journey of a Thousand Clichés, hitting every famous sight and hackneyed stopover from Northants to Palermo. He laboriously led his Aussie hayseeds through the entire leaden itinerary, leaving no wet rock unturned. And across from us, an argumentative bilingual French couple, who started by negotiating the *formule* with the waitress, spilled wine spectacularly in mid-meal and finished by sharing the famous apple tart. Besides them, we were the only apple-tarters in this corner of the bistro. Pretty odd. L'Échaudé St.-Germain is a splendid place for dinner, but to go there and not finish with the *tarte fine aux chaudes pommes* is like going to the Périgord and passing on the *foie gras*.

"Then, as Junko began to fall asleep at the table—a regular feature of an evening on the town, especially if there's a bottle of Sancerre—we hurried our coffee, paid our tab, slipped past the desserting Aussies (*crème brûlée* and chocolate ice cream) and walked to Ler Putty Pont for a last hot drink. A stroll to the hotel in the Paris night, puffy clouds against a black sky between wonderful dirty buildings, monsters spitting water on the rue de Grenelle."

The corner was like a great bowl of light, little figures moving into it and fading out, and beyond was all of Paris. Paris was around us and how could it be alien in our minds and hearts even if no Frenchman ever spoke to us? What it offered to us was what it had offered to men from other countries for hundreds of years. It was a lighted place where the imagination was free. Men have to make room for such places in their thoughts even if they never visit them.—Morley Callaghan, *That Summer in Paris,* 1963

Margaret had described Paris as a jewel box, Junko's analogy is more of a jack-in-the-box, with a surprise around any corner we might turn. For instance, there was an incident on the boulevard St.-Germain, as we were passing the storied place Maubert.

Place Maubert, from the late nineteenth century until the 1960s the domaine of the clochard, *was the center of the trade on secondhand tobacco, of which there were two grades: coarse, gleaned from cigar ends and pipe scrapings, and fine, twice as expensive, collected from cigarette butts.*

On Maubert there were sock darners, birdseed vendors, public writers, confectors of sugar pipes and little windmills with feathers as blades, gluers of paper bags and cones for grocers, and people who made the rounds trying to sell dubious objects they'd stolen or recovered from the trash.—Luc Santé, *The Other Paris*, 2015

Junko stopped and looked up rue des Carmes, adjacent to Maubert. Uphill, emerging regally from behind a barricade of buildings suddenly, was the Panthéon, repository of the bones of the Republic's heroes. The view was from the rear, with no façade, just a long Parisian street, then a wall, and then the great mottled dome whose massiveness made the columns on which it rested look spindly. Junko froze to the spot, awed and charmed. She didn't leave the view for more than an hour, until the painting she'd begun spontaneously was finished. The Panthéon's pop-up trick is one of the surprises, one jack coming out of the box, that made Junko—made both of us—return again and again until, insidiously, we needed to become, at least in our delusions, Parisian.

To be Parisian is to have an identity that transcends social class, economic distinction; it is to belong to a world apart, to an intellectual and moral category not of class, race or gender but of a qualitative difference from the rest, an essential worldliness, a heightened expectation—as F. Scott Fitzgerald put it in a different context—of the possibilities of life.—Richard Bernstein, *Fragile Glory: A Portrait of France and the French,* 1990

Years later, Junko discovered to her infinite delight

that Eugène Atget, the turn-of-the-twentieth-century photographer who had painstakingly transferred onto glass negatives virtually every street and alley of Paris, had seen and shot—at the precise angle chosen by Junko—the same unromantic view of the Panthéon. No façade or feature on the rue des Carmes, or in the aspect of the Panthéon, had altered in a hundred years. The only addition was a few street signs. These Junko faithfully included, after which she was scolded by Fabrice, Margaret's artful nephew, for excessive realism.

Fabrice, of course, like so many of our favorite Parisians, is an irretrievable romantic. But me? I like the signs.

We do not say anything special to each other, only that Paris is beautiful. But in that word beautiful there are centuries of lives, of wars, of work, of faith, of deaths. Paris is indeed beautiful, the last of the great cities of the world which has kept its soul, which works like a well-oiled machine. Paris is beautiful. It aches to say so. One's arms are never big enough to hug such an immensity.
—Etel Adnan, *Paris, When It's Naked,* 1993

Rue de Buci 8/12/18

3
Paris or Bust

There is, however, a real satisfaction in living in Paris from the great number of sensible, knowing and polite company with which the city abounds above all other places in the universe. I once thought of settling there for life.—David Hume [17]

For a few months after our trip to the Périgord in 1994, Junko and I toyed with the fancy of mortgaging a thatched cottage in Ireland on the theory that Galway is close to Paris (somewhat in the way a hedgehog is related to a peccary). This Irish pipe dream did not grip us long or firmly. It let go entirely one California night in front of the television.

"It's Paris," Junko suddenly expostulated, "or nothing."

I was watching a Special K commercial, the one in which the woman in the short black skin-tight dress admires herself in the mirror.

After a moment, Junko said, "It's Paris or nothing."

"Say what?" I replied crisply. The Special K woman had swiveled to regard her derrière. Pleased with the view, she purred.

"Paris," said Junko one more time, "or nothing."

“What? What about Paris?” The woman in the commercial had changed into sweatclothes and was noshing on breakfast food. Interestingly, the actress—Paige Turco—in this Special K ad later turned up (also in sweatclothes) as a semi-regular character in *NYPD Blue* as Greg Medavoy’s lesbian jogging partner and sperm recipient.

I glanced at Junko.

“Look,” she said, “why do we keep going to France every year?”

Paige Turco, once more in her clingy *petite robe noire*, had cocked a hip at the mirror, said “thank you” to the Kellogg’s people and had cut away to the next sales pitch featuring a group of bungee-crazed slackers slurping Mountain Dew soda pop.

I looked up.

“Well,” I ventured, “Paris.”

“There you go,” Junko snapped back. “Why did you go ape over the idea of buying a house in the Périgord?”

She was dredging up The Fight.

“Well, I just figured—”

“Why?”

“Well, Périgord is nice.”

“Why?”

“Okay, it’s cheaper there, okay? For the amount of money we’d have to raise for a down payment in Paris, we could buy a whole—”

“Aha!”

“Aha?”

“There it is.”

“There what is?”

“Paris!”

“Yeah, Paris,” I said, waxing a bit testy. “But the idea was to get a toehold *someplace* in France, closer to Paris than we are—”

"Bullshit, Benjie."

"Okay, you're right. It's not Paris. But—"

She kept cutting me off.

"If we had a place in Périgord," Junko reasoned, "or somewhere else, every time we flew to France, we'd land in Paris and then we'd have this all-day trip to get to this other place rather than—"

I cut her off.

"So, what's your point?"

"We wouldn't be in Paris."

She had a point.

"What we want," said Junko, "is a place in Paris. Or nothing at all."

"Paris or bust."

"Yes."

"You're right," I conceded with all due magnanimity.

"I know I'm right. I've been right all along."

"So when?"

"When what?"

"Paris."

"Now."

"How?"

"No idea."

"Right."

The commercials ended. *ER* returned. We sank back into the televised agony whose name cannot be uttered, between the emotionally impotent Dr. Green and the procreatively obsessed Dr. Lewis.

Meanwhile, during ads, Junko and I affirmed our commitment to Paris. Thanks to the distracting anguish of Drs. Green and Lewis, this decision didn't exactly sink in. Nor had we asked, at that point, the recurring question.

Why Paris?

France is a country where the money falls apart, and you can't tear the toilet paper.—Billy Wilder

Later that night, after another Thursday of must-see TV had segued limply into bloody-pavement film on the local news, Junko and I had time in bed to coldly assess the unreasonable urge to nest in Lutetia. Indeed, why Paris? This became our main theme (along with what the hell is Dr. Green's problem, anyhow?).

Paris is clearly a destination that elicits powerful feelings. Love. Hate. Fury. Bliss. An old friend, Charles, born and raised in Hungary, had formed his opinion of Paris from a 24-hour layover, during which he rode the elevator to the obligatory top of the Eiffel Tower in a drizzly fog while he was afflicted with diarrhea, a condition that he insisted on describing in clinical detail. This ordeal triggered Charles' encounter with a timeless Parisian horror: the public toilets. Charles hated Paris and vowed to never again set foot there. On the whole, he would rather be in a Transylvanian swamp.

It is on the Troisième Étage that we discover the most ridiculous feature concerning the loos of the Eiffel Tower. However fantastic a feat of engineering it may have been to construct a loo 898 ft. above ground level, and even though the first person to use it may have been our own King Edward VII at its inauguration in 1889, it seems absolutely mad and ridiculous that this loo, which could have the finest view of any loo in Europe, has frosted glass in its square porthole of a window; and therefore no view at all.—Jonathan Routh, *Jonathan Routh's Guide Porcelaine to the Loos of Paris,* 1996

Marty Gold, one of Junko's journalist colleagues, is another Paris basher. Interviewees dread Marty's inquisitions because he can ask the same question for hours without variation or fatigue. Marty once assailed me through an entire evening with a relentless, unwavering "Why Paris?" third-degree. He was persistently incredulous at my every attempt to explain, because he couldn't imagine English-speaking people voluntarily returning over and over to a city where reliable reports had proven that the natives speak French publicly and evidently intend to persist in speaking French.

Father was, moreover, helpless in Paris without Mother because he did not have French and thought she was fluent in it. It was an illusion she maintained as long as they traveled together.

"If you talk English to them, they double the price," he used to say.—A.J. Liebling, *Between Meals: An Appetite for Paris*, 1959

Besides the language, there were good reasons to question the wisdom of setting up a regular circuit of Parisian visits, not the least of which was the inconvenience of transit.

Benjie's Diary, 30 August '93, Paris: "We got here the hard way, with a crisis even before we left the house ... We looked in the legendary black thing [18] and voila, Junko's passport was missing. This didn't make sense. We always keep our passports in the black thing. Whenever we go overseas, we take along the black thing, with passports tucked inside. The black thing and passports are inseparable. 'Black thing' is our synonym for passports.

"But!

"Yes, Junko had recently gone to the Japanese consulate

in San Francisco to get her passport renewed. The new passport somehow never made its way into the black thing. It was nowhere in any of the black thing's myriad slots and compartments. It was lost. Gone. We were four hours from our flight, and Junko had not the wherewithal to enter France. We started rummaging, panic filling our throats. While I went to the car to fecklessly rifle the glove box, Junko climbed into the bedroom closet. While I was in the garage, emptying a map envelope, I heard a cry.

"'Huh?'

"'Benjamin!'

"'Huh?'

"I stepped out of the garage. Looked up. Junko hanging over the edge of the balcony, waving a little blue book—new color and size for Japanese passports.

"'I found it.'

"I had left it in the black portfolio (which I almost never use) that I was carrying when we went to S.F. for the passport. I'd forgotten. Somehow, Hotlips had remembered the portfolio and went for it like a dog after a weiner. Astounding.

"But we were not yet out of our hole. Nor are we today. Crisis #2 struck after we'd stood in line at the jury-rigged World Airways counter (yes, Virginia, there is a World Airways, apparently running cattle-car charters in and out of Paris, hauling Frenchpersons like bike baskets jammed with vertical baguettes). We faced two (apparently) French World Airways clerks who told us, in an excess of passionate solicitude, that—whoa!—Junko had neglected to bring along her green card, without which, alas, (Scene ... Junko: 'Benjie, should I bring along my alien registration card?' Benj: 'Hm, well, you don't want to risk losing it in some far-off foreign outpost. Better we should leave it safe and sound in the bosom of home and hearth.' Junko: 'Okay, honeybunch. It's so nice having a wise and decisive male authority figure in the household to guide my way through the vicissitudes of expatriatehood.'

Benj: 'It's nothing, Hotlips.') she would never be allowed to set foot in America again, save my paying an enormous fine, which would also be assessed against World Airways, thus plummeting the airline back into receivership and breaking the hearts of a million peripatetic but thrifty Frenchpeople. However, the two resourceful and slightly devious ladies, perceiving our onset of panic and denial, immediately started plotting a solution.

"Which emerged like this: They would gladly send us to Paris. No skin off their noses if we never made it back. Not much skin off ours, either, if you ponder the dilemma of being trapped in Paris, unable to ever return to Silicon Gulch.

"So, we were given seats 4E and 4D on World Cattleways Flight 410, which placed us next to M. Pied, whom we referred to surreptitiously as 'Ashi-san' [Mr. Feet], who greeted us by skooching down his seat, settling all his weight on his sacral spine, digging his knees into the seatback in front of him and planting his feet on my seatback pouch.

"Large, bare feet.

"He managed to maintain this position for ten hours. From this position, he slept, grumbled, rooted and flailed his elbows effectively. He established an enviable standard for silent annoyance on an airplane. This performance was enhanced by the width of the seats, roughly equal to the length of a Japanese watermelon.

"The flight was fully booked. Weary Frenchfolks, returning from a month in America, as far as the eye could see. The attendants—except for one tall Frenchman probably drummed out of service at Les Deux Magots (for smiling at an American?)—were surly and incomprehensible. One kept zipping past with a cart, saying, *'J'oi, choi mmphglxlzj?'*

"We responded by saying, 'Um ... huh?' But by then he was twelve rows away and moving like a zephyr.

"On the other hand, after detaching from Ashi-san, we had an effortless arrival. Our bags emerged early. We had no customs formalities because our plane was a chartered boxcar loaded with 90 percent sun-browned *vacanciers* draped in L.A. Lakers merchandise. In a trice, we found a bus to Opéra, and I remembered the exact Métro station, impressing Junko. Rue du Bac, where we are staying at the Hotel de Nevers, posed a small problem. Initially, we turned right when we should have gone left. But I halted midway, left Junko, reconnoitered, returned and steered us back until we found our skinny hotel, squeezed between two large entries. We haven't been here long enough to even note what occupies those entries. Time, in the immortal words of Dave Lammers, will tell.

"Our evening was a delight. Although we were prostrate with fatigue when we climbed the four flights of winding stairs to our tiny room (the mice are hunchbacked), we were revived by the allure of the Paris streets below."

Dripping roofs, sweating walls, slippery pavement,
Cracked asphalt, streams filling the gutter.
That's my road—with heaven at the end.—Paul Verlaine

The rue du Bac was, originally, a track cut down to the river-side in the fifteen hundreds to facilitate the carriage of stone, wood and other building materials to the construction of the Tuileries Palace for Catherine de'Medici. As where the track debouched there was no bridge but a ferry, the way took the name of rue du Bac, which it has kept.—Alan Houghton Brodrick, ed., *The People's France: Paris,* 1950

The "why Paris?" issue will always dog us, but it plumbed whole new depths with the proposition of buying a "home" there. Marty Gold and the other devil's advocates had soured on Paris merely through the experience of *visiting* the city, once—briefly. As Junko and I considered the proposition, we vacillated between our love affair with Paris and the sometimes exhausting challenge of daily coping, speaking French, rustling up our daily bread, dodging the dog shit on the sidewalks, changing Métro lines at Châtelet.

It is a concert hall whose acoustics are incredible but whose audience is hard to hold. It is also a bazaar, a den of thieves, an unofficial social agency, a flower shop, a public urinal, a bedding place for the homeless, an asylum for the harmlessly deranged, a fashion show, a political stage, a stink, a rush of wind.

Last, and almost incidentally, it is a means of transport, a system of hidden arteries through which the city's lifeblood flows. It is the Paris métro.—C.W. Gusewelle, *A Paris Notebook,* 1985

Sometimes the smells, the footsoreness, the persistent sense of being an outsider—having to gird one's loins for the simplest task, from ordering a cup of coffee to buying postage stamps—felt far more tangible than our ethereal infatuation with the myth-wrapped City of Light.

Benjie's Diary, 30 August '93, Paris: "We made it to the rue de la Huchette, and Junko sat down there on a street corner that smelled of piss. Junko did a really good drawing of rue Xavier Privas, with new effects from her new pens."

Zola himself walked with pencil and notebook in his hand, taking notes and making sketches. Balzac ran right across Paris, between his printers, his coffee dealer, his visits to houses to find a dwelling for "the foreigner," Madama Hanska.—Eric Hazan, *A Walk Through Paris*, 2016

Benjie's Diary, 30 August '93, Paris: "Now we're at a favorite dive—Le Mazarin—having a cup of espresso and settling into an onset of jet-lag ennui. At least I am. I'm getting this post-traumatic feeling that it would be too difficult for us to move to Paris because there are all these people speaking in perfectly grammatical French, eliding consonants like plane trees shedding leaves in the autumn, and me—who can't remember the French words for "French words."

The fundamental education of French children is not a local haphazard affair. It is directed and controlled from Paris, with a minimum of ecclesiastical interference or obstruction. Nearly everybody, except Apaches [19] or the moderately low-priced prostitutes, speaks very good French, and if a slight accent of Marseilles, Strasbourg or Quimper is discernible, the provincial flavor does not distort the language. Even the Parisian thugs and loose women can speak clear, correct French if they are in the mood for elegance or politeness.—Elliot Paul, *Understanding the French*, 1955

Remember, a few scant months before Junko's real estate ultimatum (during the Special K commercial), we had departed Paris resolved to return less, to wean ourselves from the breast of Brigitte Bardot. We'd had, we averred, our fill of Lutetia. We would spread our wanderlust in a wider circle. This was, of course, a dumbass decision. It could not hold. It flouted reality. It defied desire. It flew in the face of common sense. Barely had we hit the runway in San Francisco than Paris began blowing in our ears, like Fifi in a Beaubourg doorway.

Junko had at least one European business trip scheduled in 1995, to Montreux, and we were already plotting how to deviate that junket through Paris. We couldn't stay away. The occasional discomforts, anxieties and affronts that Paris inflicts are the *poivre* in the sauce. Paris is the rare city that uplifts the lives it entangles.

Every spring I fall in love with the same woman, and it happens the same way every time. After work at the typewriter, I take a walk in the sun, and there she is, as striking as ever, and there I am, struck dumb as Dante seeing Beatrice.

So Thackeray's hero fell in love at the Louvre with a woman standing there, silent and majestic, her hair light and her eyes gray, looking thirty-two but born 2000 years ago. Her name was Venus de Milo.

For me, it is Paris.—Joseph Barry, *The People of Paris,* 1966

Why Paris?

Our most selfish reason for wanting quarters of our own in Paris was to husband tangible evidence that we are different from—no, better than—the hordes of Kodak-snapping dilettantes who throng the rues and boulevards as soon as school lets out in Illinois. It isn't true that elitists emerge naturally, genetically, from the upper crust. The hardcore snobs are people like us who've achieved moral and cultural superiority by picking it up in the streets from rich friends, snooty guidebooks and artsy-fartsy postcards. Junko and I had begun our Parisian studies by examining, and then proceeding to avoid almost every notable tourist attraction in the city. In subsequent excursions, we identified our favorite tea salon, restaurant, wine bar, bookstore, jogging path, public garden, secret garden, midnight stroll, even our favorite bridge. We could give directions (in pidgin French, if necessary) to almost any site within a kilometer of the place de la Bastille. We were seasoned Lutetiaphiles, and still ... glimpsing us on the street,

Junko in her straw hat and me in my Red Sox t-shirt, who could tell we knew Paris better than your average cluster of lobster-palace rubbernecks from Lubbock?

Any Parisian can circle on a map of the city three or four districts where if you go there gawking and careless, you are all but certain to be relieved of some of your goods. Americans, with their inviting hip wallets and loose-flapping coats, eyes raptly on shop windows or historic sights, leave a blood trail that a Gypsy can smell for blocks.—C.W. Gusewelle, *A Paris Notebook*, 1985

Benjie's Diary, 10 November '98, Café Beaubourg: "I scurried home past Notre Dame ... the square where there is a constant performance of the Quasimodo Follies.

"You have tourists milling in couples, threes and fours, intermingling with tour groups all staring raptly at a guide usually mounted on a bench or auto barrier, bloviating on the cathedral's history, the story of the Hôtel Dieu, the legend of Esmerelda, etc. Among these marks circulate gypsies working scams, shlepping infants (who serve as handy distractions), rifling pockets, snatching cameras. There are always street performers, who are typically a letdown (unless the guy who blows fire shows up). The rollerblade acrobats can be, however, as diverting as the portrait 'artists' are incompetent.

"Of course, there are mimes. And no one to shoot them.

"Amidst all this, the sightseers strive to take photos of Notre Dame. For the last four years, this has been complicated by scaffolds. They've obscured one tower, then the other as crews painstakingly strip the grime and pollution off the limestone.

"Still, the visitors must have the photo. Proof that 'we were here.' They pose clutchingly, and the scaffolds are captured forever, blurry and unsightly, in the shoebox where the family stuffs its photographs.

"Lately, this farce is aggravated. The renovators have shrouded the famous façade—all those saints and apostles and kings and demons extending around the great doors—in plastic.

"You have a wall of industrial-strength Saran Wrap, then up pop two towers.

"And still they take their pictures.

"And they will go back to Arizona. They will say: 'This is us at Noater Daim. You know? The church? The hunchback and all? Course, it doesn't always have all that plastic there. But underneath, they have statues. Hundreds of 'em. They won't let you inside the plastic. But they're there. Hundreds of statues, the guide said. Anyway, that's us. At Noater Daim.'"

Notre Dame was as busy a place as Old St. Paul's, as we can see from a precious miniature by Jean Fouquet representing St. Vrain, Bishop of Cavaillon, casting out devils in the north aisle. The cathedral was full of priests, canons, bigots, beggars, beadles, loafers, choir-boys and incense. On every hand were rich silks, gilding, paintings, brocades, golden shrines, carpets, pictures, statues and images. For the Fête-Dieu *or Corpus Christi, the church would be transformed into a garden of flowers, and on Whit-Sunday, doves with lighted wicks of tow fluttered about until the birds—their feathers all burnt—smashed to the floor.*

—Alan Houghton Brodrick, ed., *The People's France: Paris,* 1950

It is there, the Cathedral. Somewhere in astral space travel the echoes of men who toiled, the thoughts of the architect planners, the devout who prayed, the élite who approved. After eight centuries, the foundations are solid, the stones, arches, windows, doors, transepts, nave and buttresses, aloft the gargoyles, add up to Notre Dame, Our Lady of Paris. She catches the glow and the dimness, the aloofness and interdependence, the rise and fall, and visually exemplifies what spirituality She failed to protect—a rich man's church in a poor man's community.—Elliot Paul, *Springtime in Paris*, 1949

Why Paris?

People are often surprised at the amount of traveling Junko and I do. No more than we are. Secretly, we're ambivalent about travel. We like to go, but like those golden agers on the bus tour, we deplore adventure. We want to know what's in store, in detail. Wherever we venture, we dip a cautious toe and peer with trepidation around the potted palm. We prefer the benign surprises that loom upward suddenly against a cornflower-blue firmament or shimmer against a starlit night. The surprises that smell bad, taste funny or brandish automatic weapons tend to put us off our feed. In Paris, we know where the bad smells come from, and we've come around to the notion that they're not so bad, after all. We've likewise gotten used to (or begun to savor) the funny flavors. The guys with the guns are under strict instructions from the Prefecture of Police to leave alone the foreigners with money. Paris is adventure with little peril. It is a safari of small, pleasant, inexhaustible shocks. It is splendor in a frame of ominous Atlantic clouds with an occasional whiff of ammonia (as though Nelson Algren was brought in as the realism consultant).

Perhaps more important, we have learned in Paris to make ourselves vulnerable to the spontaneous grace note. If you go out in Paris not looking for something remarkable, not expecting more than a *verre* of Muscadet in a patch of sun, the city will provide. The city will burst forth in beauty, or drama, or unsolicited good fellowship. The secret is to have no defenses.

Benjie's Diary, 31 August '93, rue de Rohan: "I can see Junko at work ... After she painted Ste.-Clotilde, we went back to our hotel because of the capricious Parisian weather. Clouds rolled in and cold breezes wafted. God, what a treat after equable, sunny, constant, tedious California. (This is great. Junko sits there on the fence at the end of the Louvre, drawing, looking up, and crowds keep stopping to peek over her shoulder. She's a celebrity wherever she sits down.)"

I passed on to the Isle de la Cité, the Palace of Justice on my right and in a moment, on my left, rising above the open place before it, appeared the rich facade and the strong truncated towers of Notre Dame. In the silence and the dusk before dawn nothing was visible of the modern city, only the ancient towers of the Palace of Justice and of Notre Dame, and it was possible for a moment to believe that you had arrived in the Middle Ages.—Waverley Root, *The Paris Edition: The Autobiography of Waverley Root 1927–1934*, 1987

Benjie's Diary, 26 December '97, 16, rue St.-Séverin: "'You can observe a lot just by watching.' I think Junko and I both subscribe to the Yogi Berra school of travel, which is a little offbeat but not weird. People who don't travel much, or who always go to different places briefly, find themselves in a constant state of semi-panic, with a list of 'sights' as long as an orangutan's arm. So, 'seeing' the 'sights' boils down to a series of glances, glimpses and peeks. They never watch and they come away bereft of observations.

"We kept coming back to Paris because we knew we would look, watch, observe and stare fixedly, sometimes for hours at one spot, or a few thousand spots, and we would never run out of 'sights.' Paris is an embarrassment of sights, most of which permutate, expand and get better the longer you watch.

"One of my Paris habits is to stand on an ordinary corner,

usually after coming up from the Métro, not moving, just scanning until I see some detail, a café front, a café patron, a quirky sign, a flowered balcony, a row of windows and shutters brushed by the sun and punctuated by ironwork, geraniums and reflections of the passing clouds—or all of these at once. I take photos of the most arresting vignettes before moving on.

"Paris in summer is a dappled limestonescape seen between wreaths of trembling leaves. In winter, the curtains fall to the ground, and the buildings are exposed, soaring along the Seine and breaking out in statues. Paris expands in winter, goes soft in spring, bloats with tourists and contracts in reaction against them in the hot months and then goes elegantly to seed in autumn. All these changes in the city's thousand niches—making their transitions out of step and at their own leisure—deserve watching.

"Notre Dame changes by the moment, a hundred times a day. Glance and you see little more than chipped rock. Watch and you see her breathe, shudder, float, pout, preen, swell and sigh.

"Even our own little church of St.-Séverin, with its low-rent gargoyles and its entrance in the back, is a startlingly different neighbor when its steeple changes backdrops from gray sky to blue."

The lights! How they made the old streets cozy! And the river, how refreshing and unhealthy! And the moon! Smells of heat, of pavements, of new leaves! Wherever France had been, she was then at the place St.-Michel. Wherever France was going, so were those Parisians present. Beside the Seine in silver black. In the aspic of the moon.—Elliot Paul, *Springtime in Paris*, 1949

Benjie's Diary, 25 May '97, rue St.-Julien le Pauvre: "While Junko was painting the church of St-Séverin today, from rue

This is good!
Two smokers on a café
on the boat!

Galande, I got to be downright cozy with the waiter at La Friterie [20], Henri.

"Junko followed St.-Séverin by doing the church of St.-Julien-le-Pauvre while sitting at La Friterie. Henri posed for the painting. Junko added him to the composition. He signed his portrait. Everybody loves Junko."

For a painter, the mecca of the world for study, for inspiration and for living is here on this star called Paris. Just look at it. No wonder so many artists have come here and called it home. Brother, if you can't paint in Paris, you'd better give up and marry the boss's daughter.—Alan Jay Lerner, *An American in Paris*, 1951

Benjie's Diary, 4 September '93, rue de Buci: "From the concert, it was our resolution to have dinner at La Coupole. But we were running early. It was only 8:15 (closing time for most restaurants in Tokyo), so we decided to walk down the boul-Mich to boulevard Montparnasse. It was a cool, leisurely stroll that led to annoyance ... The main problem was the fashionable crowd at La Coupole [21]. As soon as we stepped through the door, we were snagged by a pretty hostess in a quasi-tuxedo (called, for some reason, a *smoking* in French), who determined swiftly that we were two for dinner, at which she steered us toward the 'bar,' more of a blond-wood holding pen, and gave our names to 'Jean-François.' Jean-François was a harried, supercilious drill sergeant in expensive duds with Brylcreem in his hair. He sorted us out from the rabble long enough to collect our name, then consigned us to the rear of the corral, pinned between the backs of the patrons at the bar and the asses of the people jockeying for position to be recognized a second time by Jean-François. Clearly, during rush hour at La Coupole, once is not enough. Were we eager to elbow ourselves in circles among testy, better-dressed

Frenchpeople for an hour, our only reward the privilege, granted by Jean-François, of sitting by the toilet door and eating bathtub curry at thirty-five bucks a plate? Or would we rather blow this clambake?

"We blew. Junko, impressively, made the decision. She had long anticipated an intimate *soirée* at La Coupole, as a kind of obligation to Paris and silent eulogy to Jean-Paul Sartre and Simone de Beauvoir.

"But our annoyance was not over. We fled boulevard Montparnasse, to the Métro to St.-Germain-des-Prés, and steered toward rue Jacob, one of Junko's favorite rues. We had a choice between two bistros, Le Boeuf a Table and Chéz Papa, at the latter of which we'd once had a convivial lunch with an effervescent hostess and two amiable French kibitzers observing Junko as she painted an aquarelle.

"We chose wrong: Chéz Papa. The bubbly lunch hostess had been replaced by Mlle. Icepussy, likely valedictorian of her graduating class at L'Académie Française des Bitches. In a half-empty restaurant at 10 p.m., she pulled the shocked, appalled *'Oh? Pas de réservation!! Quelle dommage'* routine and—like B'rer Fox—consigned us to the unprestigious table we wanted anyway, near the door. Thereafter, although she engineered a campaign to ignore us for twenty minutes, she kept bumping into one of us as we did a tag-team maneuver to the *toilettes* and back. With each encounter, Mlle. Icepussy peered at us as though we were smeared with human blood and clutching meat cleavers. Eventually, however, Chéz Papa reverted to form and turned out to be fun. Our waiter was a small, jovial guy who scurried around solicitously and almost gave us our dessert before our entrée (apparently because he read our order upside-down). The food was only *ordinaire* (for France), a nice *rhumsteack* and better *pavé de saumon*, but the accordion was great. This was supplied by a wandering minstrel with the face of a Hollywood character actor (I thought of Dub Taylor and Brian Dennehy). He flitted in front of Chéz Papa, twiddling merrily at French medleys, then plunged in among the diners to collect tribute for his chaotic music. He did this so engagingly that everyone ponied up a few francs. He even negotiated with the man next to us to trade 50f in change for a single 50f note—at which juncture Mlle. Icepussy descended and tried to oust the musician from the premises. Here was the evening's highlight. The accordionist responded with reluctance and high dudgeon. He had her outclassed. He could make jokes and hurl insults with his voice and add harmony with his squeezebox. The harder she fought him, the nimbler he dodged, and the more we clientele smiled and cheered. Mlle. Icepussy melted with fury, and the minstrel retreated at his own pace—unbeaten, untied, unscored upon ... After that, Mlle. Icepussy sweetened a little. When we'd arrived, she treated us like peasants from Ohio. But, as we lingered and—apparently—fed ourselves with the dignity befitting a Parisian bistro, she allowed a *soupçon* of respect ... grudgingly."

As did everyone else, I got drunk at La Coupole when I landed for the first time in Paris. From the terrace, I saw all my heroes passing—I was young ... With Anaïs Nin, [Henry] Miller and [Alfred] Perlès [22] we were the three musketeers of La Coupole. We played chess there. One might say that Perlès almost slept there ... as for Anaïs, she quarreled at the bar with her lovers and her publishers. She really liked men, but on all fours, if possible psychiatrists and if possible weeping. —Lawrence Durrell

Why Paris?

Our mounting desire, in the early months of '95, to plunge our funds and our future into Paris property was a complicated mixture of accumulated experiences, indelible impressions, unfinished paintings, literary itch and unexpected vistas.

We gradually realized that we had just begun to collect the dividend of our investment in Paris in currency other than money. Paris takes feelings and compounds interest in them, expanding one fleeting sensation into a wealth of memory, temptation and passion. If you're a trifle romantic in Minnesota, you're Yves Montand in Paris. If you're occasionally erotic in Boston, you're shamelessly Colette in Paris. If you're manly in Memphis, you're Hemingway in Paris, strapping on your boxing gloves and chucking Morley Callaghan in the chest. If you're mildly tragic in Texas, you're Édith Piaf in Paris, weeping into your décolletage.

For Junko and me, Paris had become a particular feeling, an intensity we felt nowhere else. Nor did we wish to feel that way anywhere else. Paris was the only place we wanted to feel this way, feel this much, feel each other.

Junko feels more an artist in Paris than anywhere else because the city is a work of art that preens before her palette. I feel more a novelist there, where storytellers and philosophers still claim more respect than barons and propellerheads.

To feel these self-indulgences, we didn't just want to return to Paris regularly, which was possible and pragmatic. We wanted to be sure of Paris, to always have it, better than Bergman and Bogart (who always had it but never made it back). We wanted to have to return to Paris, even against our will or better judgment. We wanted a corner of it to ourselves, the certainty of adventure always in prospect, an emotional refuge that inevitably—after jet lag had worn off and our rusty French had creaked again into motion—exalted us.

I look into these courtyards. Narrow sidestreet doors, hung with signs that read, "Cour Privée," block a passerby's access. But I look. The courtyard's size is a surprise, three and four stories up, and as many as six doors opening into living quarters. The yards themselves are cobbled stone. The smell of drains, of heat on the broad humped stones and grayed walls, of moss and lichen, of clay flowerpots that have just been watered. White lace curtains over the windows. Like Eugene, I feel that Paris life looks wonderful. I want in.—Judith Moore, *A Postcard from Paris*, 1984

Or ...

Maybe we were just being petty. Maybe we just wanted proof that we're smarter—or cooler—than the average bear. What finer evidence of one's superiority than to be Parisian? Maybe, for example, I just wanted the symbolic distinction of being a writer in Paris, to be treated with a little more deference when I bought a book at Shakespeare & Co., Sylvia Beach's historic Left Bank bookshop (long since transplanted by George Whitman from Sylvia's storefront on rue de l'Odéon to the quai opposite Notre Dame).

Long before our eyes had ever seen Sylvia Beach's entire printed text in Paris and before our hands had ever lifted the full weight of its 730 pages, Joyce's Ulysses *had become part of the library of our minds. As we learned by listening and by watching Sylvia in her bookshop, to accomplish her publishing feat, she became Joyce's secretary, editor, impresario and banker, and had to hire outsiders to run her shop. She organized international and local subscription lists for the book to help finance its printing. After typesetting had begun at Dijon, in a kind of postscript ecstasy of creation, Joyce scribbled some ninety thousand words more on the costly, repeatedly reset proofs, making a four-hundred-thousand word volume, of which Sylvia managed to have two copies printed for his fortieth birthday on February 22, 1922—one for him, one for her.*—Janet Flanner, *Paris Was Yesterday, 1925–1939*, 1972

Benjie's Diary, 2 September '93, Notre Dame: "Our trip took a turn for the better this morning on our way out when Minon, our concierge, handed us a fax from Ron Wilson assuring us that he had found Junko's green card and had already FedExed it! We headed forth with a spring in our step. While Junko was at rue des Ursins painting, I crossed the island to Shakespeare & Co. to browse the cheap shelves out front. I don't like going inside anymore because the place has become steeped in literary pretense and posturing. Such as today. A middle-aged woman with a New York accent and trailing husband. She was dressed in Long Island casual and was doggedly buttonholing the old fart, George Whitman, who long ago supplanted Sylvia Beach as the patron-in-residence. She was explaining that 'I've sent out sixty copies and gotten twenty-five acceptances.'

"George seemed unmoved. Asked if she'd been published.

"'Not yet, personally, but my partner has. Edith Lipschitz La Fleur. She's my partner. *A Rage of Chenille.* Perhaps you have it here. Do you have it here?'

"The old fart was squirming in his seat. The husband of the budding authoress/nag was pitching in, praising the work of E.L. La Fleur. 'It's really very good.'

"Apparently, the objective of this woman's mission to Paris was to wrest from the old fart an invite to some private reading room upstairs redolent of binding glue and rat feces. The old fart, eager to get this harpy off his case, got up, creaking from his comfortable chair. He led the harridan and her sycophant into the mildewed recesses. These days, S & Co. is constantly under siege from these importunate aspirants to literature ... The place is haunted by the grim gravity of twentieth-century prose—Hemingway, Miller, Woolf, Gertrude Stein, Kerouac ... Not a chuckle among 'em.

"However, I found in the unheralded refuse outside the stoop an unread (by me) Ed McBain, a Richard Condon and an out-of-print P.G. Wodehouse—*The Girl on the Boat*. All for 60f, and not a word, cordial or otherwise, from George.

Why you want to write is more than I can understand. Writers are the most dreadful bounders. I've seen them in cafés in Paris, down-at-heels, inky fellows with scrubby beards.—P.G. Wodehouse, *French Leave,* 1956

We would sit there all evening with just one cup of coffee each, and no one protested. How such cafés made any money I cannot think! Seeing papers and manuscripts spread over the little round tables, and hearing snippets of text as he went past, the waiter assumed we were writers and left us alone.—Shusha Guppy, *A Girl in Paris*, 1991

Meanwhile, back in California, the local news anchor began hyping his "top story tonight," the birth of a kangaroo at the San Francisco Zoo. Junko and I turned off the newborn joey, nestled into the dark and—safely 8,950 kilometers from the spell of Paris—reviewed our motivations. Yes, we wanted to be the Paris writer and Paris artist starving and lovemaking in our Paris garret. But we were probably too old and affluent to pull off this fantasy. We had long since concluded that owning a "home," the hackneyed American dream, consisted largely of being somewhere on earth, usually by birth or sheer chance, and fashioning a sense of belonging in this random locale by buying a quarter-acre of it and painting the mailbox blue. Instead of this benign bourgeois obligation, our objective was to buy, if and when we could afford it, a quarter-acre (or a few square meters) of a destination entirely of our choosing. If we must own a home, we reminded ourselves that we would own it not where—for the moment and out of necessity—we *are* but where we *want to be*.

Paris was where we wanted to be.

Paris or bust.

Thing was ... we had not the dimmest idea of who sold Paris property, or how to reach them, or what to say (in French) if we ever did.

"So," said Junko finally, "call Seville."

"Seville?"

"Yes."

"Why do *I* always have to call?"

Yes, I reflected afterward on the terrace of the Deux Magots while polishing off a final cognac, my Paris sojourn had been one narrow squeak after another, but I had survived, and who knows? Perhaps like a fine Damascene blade, my nature had been tempered, made nobler by the fires of adversity. Up the boulevard St.-Germain from the place de l'Odéon there came a bedraggled American girl streaked with mascara, her eyes beady with vengeance.—S.J. Perelman, "Paris on Five Dolors a Day," *Eastward Ha!*, 1977

Benjie's Diary, 11 September '93, Aeroport Charles de Gaulle: "Going home, our airport ordeal was no ordeal at all. Knowing that we're on World Airways—the Armpit of the Skies—we checked out of the Hotel de Nevers very early and reduced our travel fuss by taking a cab to a big quonset hut at Aeroport Charles de Gaulle called Terminal T9. Torquemada would have loved it. Then we sort of maneuvered and surveilled, keeping tabs on the activities of the World Airways staff 'til we saw them start removing queuing-up hardware from the crematorium. And we pushed our little cart to the scene of the impending war. We squoze in right behind a young woman from America who'd been hauling her parents around Europe for three and a half weeks. Now she was awaiting her mom's

EKG results to find out if the old gal was certified healthy enough to fly home.

"My thoughts wandered to Charlie on the MTA.

"In the end, we were among the first in line at check-in. The American girl had slipped behind us because her luggage was more complicated than ours. The only hitch was this rich guy from L.A. who started pushing his cart past ours just as the windows were opening.

"RICH GUY: *(In a simpering, effeminate hairdresser voice, subtly falsetto)* Ahem.

"ME: Just a minute.

"RICH GUY: *(Trying to move his cart around us and the American girl, who was still ahead of everyone else in line and struggling to batten down the stuff on her cart so she could make it move)* He said we should move forward.

"ME: *(Waiting for the beleaguered American girl)* Just a minute.

"RICH GUY: Excuse me.

"ME: *(Stopping him)* We're waiting for the people in front of us.

"RICH GUY: (Still jockeying) The man back there said we should move forward.

"ME: Right. We're all going to move forward, just as soon as these people are ready. They were here *first*.

"RICH GUY: *(Sniffing aristocratically)* Well! Thank you.

"ME: *(Inaudible)* Yeah, well, fuck you, Reginald.

"We both wondered what Reginald and his Gwen Wedgwood wife were doing on this Flying Toilet cattle car anyway. Their cart was heaped with Louis Vuitton luggage and bottles of Meursault. They could have sold one bag or two bottles and upgraded to Coach class on a respectable airline, like Aeroflot or Air New Jersey. They obviously did not relish hobnobbing with riffraff like me. I posed the constant danger that I might get too close and soil Reginald's Members Only flight jacket. Still, for all their distaste, we watched them later as they went elbow-swinging into the boarding queue. And they were stymied once more because the World Airways minions were boarding us strictly by row number. So, there stood Reggie and Gwendolyn, right up front, tripping people with their Meursault, watching as row upon row of the unwashed marched past them onto the bus.

"Eventually, we all made it onto the Pigpile of the Wild Blue Yonder. We stop in L.A.

"We'll never get home."

I'd love to be a tabletop in Paris, where food is art and life combined in one, where people gather and talk for hours. I want lovers to meet over me. I'd want to be covered in drops of candle wax and breadcrumbs and rings from the bottom of wine glasses. I would never be lonely, and I would always serve a good purpose.— Maureen Johnson

CAFE DE LA GARE
CAFE de
LA GARE
DANSE

4

The American Woman

They tell me in Paris, if you don't buy your gown from Roberta, you're not dressed at all.—Randolph Scott in *Roberta,* 1935

It seemed sensible in this era of multiple listing services to begin our quest for Paris property by calling a company—any company—that sells property. We knew one.

We called Jackie Copple at Seville Realty in Menlo Park, California. Jackie was the real estate lady who found us an apartment when Junko and I moved from Tokyo. Getting into Paris realty by way of hometown Jackie Copple was weird, but it worked, sort of. After suppressing her alarm at the sheer folly of our proposition, Jackie steered us into a one-month courtship with a London outfit called Havard International and its courtly proprietor, Peter Havard Johnson. I began sending him a series of lengthy, nakedly self-revelatory, halfwit faxes.

Fax, to Peter Johnson, Havard International, London, 23 April '95: "In essence, we're seeking a place as close to 50 square meters as possible for about 1,000,000 francs. However, we have, in our perusal of a year-old copy of *De Particulier à Particulier*, stumbled upon apartments as high as 1,300,000 francs, which we would find difficult to resist—and we naturally assume that the negotiated price might be somewhat less than the listed price. On the other hand, we understand there is a European tradition of 'key money,' which could result in a self-canceling balance of apparent price vs. real price. Anyway, we assume your agent in Paris will help."

Most of my fax blitzkrieg relied on a childlike faith, entirely cockeyed, that Havard was a real estate office, much like Seville, crawling with perky, mercenary divorcées like Jackie, eager to help us buy an apartment and collect their percentage.

Fax, to Peter Johnson, Havard International, London, 23 Apr. '95: "5ème: We love the Fifth [23], in fact the whole Left Bank, although again, we're aware that most places might be a little above our preferred price. We'd be happy in almost any location in the whole area. A typical desirable listing [from *De Particulier à Particulier,* the magazine of direct owner-to-buyer home sales]: ***Prés Mouffetard, 2 pieces, au 6ème, 45 m2, cuisine, salle de bains, rangements, bien distribué. Clair, calme. Exposé sud-est, parfait état. Parquet, moulures, balconnets. Cave. Immeuble ancien. 1,000,000 F.***"

It is not true, as some would have you believe, that apartments in Paris are both impossible to find and savagely expensive. Not both. But always they are one or the other.—C.W. Gusewelle, *A Paris Notebook,* 1985

While Junko and I were cheerily memorizing esoteric realty terms like *parquet, moulures* and *balconets*, Peter Johnson persevered in getting across to us that Havard does not normally *sell* real estate in Paris. Havard, he explained tactfully, deals mostly in expense-account rentals to corporate executives who need to live in exclusive neighborhoods with prestigious addresses in fashionable *arrondissements*, like the Sixteenth. We were not Sixteenth-worthy. However ...

Peter knew this woman.

She was American.

She'd been holed up in Paris since Mitterand [24] was a comrade.

She could help us, maybe.

And get us off Peter Johnson's fax machine.

If she felt like it.

Fax, to Peter Johnson, Havard International, London, 14 May '95: "We need to know if we will be put directly in contact with your agent (the American woman) in Paris, rather than working through London. Secondly, how soon will we be able to communicate with the American Woman? As you probably recall, we plan to be in Paris from 14 June through 18 June. However, we will be leaving for Europe before that, on Wednesday, 7 June. Hence, time is short for us to share information with the American Woman."

Peter Johnson said, g'head. Call the American woman. I did.

She wasn't home. I left a message.

Fax, to Peter Johnson, Havard International, London, 14 May '95: "Will we be able to receive from the American Woman listings in advance? We would be grateful to receive 'sample listings' of apartments, even though these specific places might not be available when we reach Paris—because it's helpful to ascertain what sort of listings are available to Havard Int'l and how these possibilities match our needs. Even more desirable, of course, would be 'live' prospects, apartments still likely to be available when we visit Paris."

The first maps of Paris represented the city as a circular or oval space; indeed, it was commonly described as being round like an egg. They also looked at the city sideways on, presenting north on the right and south on the left (hence the present-day divisions between Right and Left Bank).—Andrew Hussey, *Paris: The Secret History,* 2006

Another phone call to the American woman failed. But I also had her fax number. Nothing like a letter of supplication—er, introduction.

Fax, to Roberta Beardsley, 21 May '95: "Mr. Johnson probably told you how eager we are to buy our apartment in Paris. This is true, but we have recently reviewed our unseemly frenzy and realized it's not a sound negotiating position. Nor is it wise to impose a host of unrealistic expectations on an agent, like you, whom we've never met and who has never had the opportunity to ask us a single question. Therefore, we have agreed between ourselves that we will NOT expect to find our dream *pied-à-terre* while we are in Paris in June for only five days."

Paris is a good place to live but a bad place to die.
It is where the beggars warm their asses making fires
from the bones of the dead.
—François Rabelais, *Pantagruel*, 1532

Time passed. Again, I called the American woman.

She answered.

"Yeah? Whaddya want, Mac?"

No, that's not what she said. What I'm conveying here is the spirit of what she said.

She had my fax. She'd gotten our messages. She knew we were going to keep calling. Evidently, she had not been looking forward to our relationship.

We learned later that Roberta Beardsley is one of the social linchpins of the expatriate milieu in Paris. She had so many friends, acquaintances, associates and protégés clamoring for her attention that she could kill one every day for a year and still have more characters in her circle than Cornelius Ryan piled up, like cordwood, in *The Longest Day*. She didn't need Junko and Benjie to help her while away the empty hours of her bleak Paris exile.

Nor did she need, she explained in the midst of a party that was raging over her shoulder, a couple of slickers from way out West using a trumped-up real estate dodge to finagle a tour of the locked courtyards and secret gardens of Paris. She'd fallen for a similar scam once and nobody was gonna make a sucker of Roberta twice.

Paris is a secret city, and you may guess that it is so if you look at a groundplan; there are streets enclosing great masses of buildings—but what do the walls hide? There is so much room within.—Alan Houghton Brodrick, ed., *The People's France: Paris*, 1950

The American woman was posing a point I had not pondered. There had always been sealed courtyards and forbidden arbors in Paris, hidden behind great doors.

The peace of great doors be for you.
Wait at the knobs, at the panel oblongs.
Wait for the great hinges.
—Carl Sandburg, *Smoke and Steel,* 1920

In bygone times, many of those doors were open, or unlocked, or flimsily secured. The doughty tourist could sidle through the untended breach and feast his or her senses on a parked bicycle, a row of *poubelles*, several sun-starved shrubs, a suspicious cat and six stacked stories of black-eyed windows. Nowadays, most of the doors of Paris, great and otherwise, are twice locked, first with bolts, next with electronic entry codes. Like anyone else, Junko and I, in our wanderings, had occasionally rattled a lock, just to see what might be behind. But we had never—honest!—thought of enlisting an unwitting denizen in a scheme to break and enter the length and breadth of Paris.

You pressed a button, and the small door in the middle of the gate clicked open to let you enter into the cobble-stoned courtyard. A staircase at the far end, its stone steps hollowed in the middle by centuries of use, led to her home on the fifth floor.—Shusha Guppy, *A Girl in Paris*, 1991

Suddenly, this American woman was accusing us of subterfuge. If what she suggested were true, we had hatched a cunning plot. By posing as condo shoppers, using a vulnerable and ingenuous real estate factor as our dupe, there would be virtually no walled redoubt we could not penetrate, snapping snaps, taking notes, rifling armoires and handling every pill bottle in a thousand medicine chests. We might be cat burglars casing a caper or terrorists planning an abomination or, worse, we could be a couple of yuppie voyeurs wasting La Beardsley's time.

I hadn't expected our Parisian real estate lady to be suspicious of us. Suspicion is a trait not common among real estate ladies for whom the sale is Xanadu. I tried to assure Mme. Beardsley that we had already spent years considering our French folly. We had already shuffled mile upon mile of Paris streets, gazing raptly at real estate displays, studying their muddy Polaroids and feverishly calculating franc/dollar/yen equivalencies. We were serious, I said. Dead serious. We had even visited Simone Signoret's grave, right beside Yves Montand (and far, far away, thank God, from Jim Morrison) at the awesome Cimetière du Père-Lachaise. We were ready. We had tried to get Paris out of our blood. We had traveled elsewhere, I insisted, to the Périgord, for example, to Tahiti even! And Las Vegas. But Paris kept summoning us back, like Anthony's mother [25] screaming through the streets of the North End that the spaghetti was getting cold, calling us home.

Anthony!

Really, lady. We're hooked on Paris. Cross my heart ...

ANTHONY!

Everything I saw—the chestnut trees, scattering their leaves along the walks, the wide bridges clustered with bookstalls at either end, the medieval town of Ile de la Cité over which Notre-Dame raised its ponderous, Gothic stones—evoked that strange pang which even first-time visitors to Paris recognize, with some astonishment, as nostalgia. *A buried memory seems to stab at your consciousness in Paris, and you follow in the steps of an elusive phantom of* déja vu, *but never quite catch up. So deeply embedded in the world's dream of freedom, youth, art and pleasure has this city become, that the feeling that the stranger in Paris feels is a feeling of* return. *Perhaps one misses friends so keenly there because all of one's senses are pitched to such a keen note of receptivity, and one vibrates with an awareness that one longs to share.*—John Clellon Holmes, *A Wake in the Streets of Paris*, 1987

Mme. Beardsley was obviously preoccupied. As we argued cordially over the phone, the ruckus in her kitchen, stirring intimations of the pie-fight scene in *The Great Race,* roared on. Over the clamor, I managed at least to convince the American woman to undertake some preliminary research on our behalf. I told her our dates in Paris, in June. These four days were sandwiched between two of Junko's business excursions to Montreux and Eindhoven. We'd call her from Montreux, I said, okay?

"Yeah, yeah, if you wanna."

Not what she said. Just how she sounded.

I hung up.

"Shit."

"What's wrong?"

"She thinks we're amateurs."

"Aren't we?"

"Well, yeah."

"Maybe if you sent her another letter."

"Flowers," I said. "We should've put *flowers* on Simone Signoret's grave!"

Paris is famous for her croissants, her art treasures and her general cachet, but perhaps she is less well known for her necrography. Yet nothing illustrates the slender line between life and death so well as the cemeteries of Paris. Stone figures seem to start up from their beds as if hearing a noise, or dance as if they had been turned to marble without warning. To visit these burial grounds is to be struck with wonder.—Judi Culbertson and Tom Randall, *Permanent Parisians: An Illustrated Guide to the Cemeteries*, 1986

Fax, to Roberta Beardsley, 6 June '95: "In responding to your concerns, it's important first that I thank you for all your warnings about the difficulties and expense involved in the sheer madness of buying a Paris apartment. We began this little quest somewhat aware of the tribulations that await us. You have enhanced that awareness. However, you haven't discouraged us.

"For this reason:

"Junko and I aren't really interested in owning a 'home of our own' simply for its own sake. We're interested in Paris. The only place we yearn to possess acreage is in Paris. Anywhere else on earth, we're perfectly happy to rent, mooch or camp out. Paris is where we want to stick out a root and hold on. This is not a particularly wise or abstemious desire, but we've got it, we like it and we're disinclined to be talked out of it.

"This means we're prepared to endure a plague of adversities and indignities to reach our dream."

Well, last night I dreamed I heard you callin' my name.
Your voice was music to my ears.
Well, I woke up this mornin' in a hotel room,
Drownin' in my tears.

Roberta, where are you?
Can't you hear me call?
I'm a thousand miles away from home
With my back against the wall.
—Phil Wiggins and John Cephas

We heard no more from the American woman before our departure for Switzerland, where we were attending the International Television Symposium. The journey was typically arduous, including two flights from San Francisco—in the smallest seats currently available on a public conveyance not under investigation by Amnesty International—to Frankfurt to Geneva, a train from Geneva to Montreux, and then ...

There was this cute little narrow-gauge mountain train that carried us to the hotel reserved for the press in a hamlet called Caux.

Benjie's Diary, 10 June '95, Montreux: "The natives of Montreux are distinctly uncivil, moreso than the average around Paris. They're not rude, just reluctant. For instance, the train—actually, a funicular—to Caux. I was carrying two large bags, standing in line to mount the narrow steps and squeeze the bags through a narrow door. Old lady beside me looked disapprovingly at the bags as I maneuvered toward the bottleneck. In French, in a voice of distant reproof—as though addressing the luggage rather than me—the old lady: 'Shocking! Have you never heard of baggage carts?' Me, the clever American, finally spot, to my right, attached to the front of the train, the baggage cart. So I dispatch Junko to find seats, and I shlep to the cart, saying as I pass the old lady, '*Merci beaucoup!*' She doesn't exactly nod acknowledgment. More like an involuntary shudder. In a moment, I'm on the train experiencing a rare moment of Swiss hospitality (an oxymoron). The conductor, exuberantly, helpfully, tells Junko and me that our Eurail passes are so much dogshit on the Caux funicular, and it'll cost us about twenty dollars to ride one mile up the mountain. 'Ho ho ho!' Meanwhile, Junko has managed to seat us knee-to-knee with the old lady, who glowers at our 23.60-franc ticket stubs and keeps mumbling, *'Trop cher, trop cher ...'* Not to the conductor either. God save us from the kindness of strangers."

The press hotel in Caux turned out to be one of the memorable ironies of our many travels. Mountain House was a decrepit palace operated by a mob of arthritic peaceniks called Moral Rearmament [20]. Its handful of staffers reminded us of Mormons, only poor and ambivalently secular. Although reserved for the international press, Mountain House was the only hotel in the greater Montreux metroplex with no telephones. One phone line, guarded by a matron in sensible shoes, connected the registration desk to the world. She alone, in all of Caux, was allowed to touch the dial. The rest was silence, and stately decay.

Benjie's Diary, 10 June '95, Montreux: "The hotel is one of the great derelicts of Europe. Perched halfway up the mountain overlooking a lake, it has been bankrupt and used only for conferences since the 1930s. It's built, literally, to accommodate maharajahs. The grand ballroom is vast, with bay windows that encompass the Alps and Lac Léman. For its age and state of disuse, it's in great shape. As a hotel, it's yellowed and musty and down at the heels. It's an architectural Norma Desmond."

Without a phone, except at the press center in Montreux,

we didn't call Mme. Beardsley right away. Toward the end of the conference, we left a message on her machine. Otherwise, Junko was preoccupied with covering seminars and fighting the inevitable struggle with phone links, dataports and telecom servers. I stayed busy trying to explore Montreux, finding precious little worthy of exploration. I shambled along La Léman, drank costly coffee by the shore (careful not to antagonize the waiters) and took a few desultory photos. I made a side trip one rainy day to Interlaken, consisting entirely of a train ride and a lonely lunch of Swiss cuisine. Desperate for diversion, I finally dusted off my press credentials and covered a panel discussion for Junko.

From Benjie's column, Lost in Babylon, Mainichi Daily News, Tokyo, 5 July '95:

I happened, unexpectedly, upon a vivid vision of Tomorrowland last month while following Hotlips to a confab called the International Television Symposium & Exhibition in Montreux, Switzerland.

(Montreux, by the way, a village on Lake Geneva as dull as it is expensive, is known affectionately among the landlocked Swiss as the "Vaud Riviera," "Vaud" being French for "Not The.")

To kill some time, I attended a session entitled "Info Highway Gridlock: Clash Between Market Reality and Public Policy," whose apparent focus was to determine the broad human impact of such revolutionary social changes as the convergence of telephone, television and wireless communication technologies under the control of a handful of colossally rich men (plus a few favored government officials in a few colossally rich nations).

Coincidentally, the panel's experts consisted almost exclusively of people who are colossally rich themselves or had been surgically attached—mouth to teat—to someone who is. The co-chair was a WASPette think-tanker named Lady (as in "Hey, Lady, you gonna eat all that?") Dougan. Her co-chair was George Vradenburg, a Hollywood mogul who recently worked as head mouthpiece and shoeshine boy for Rupert Murdoch, a guy known affectionately among his toadies as the Mussolini of Multimedia.

The scene I witnessed in Montreux, even before anyone spoke, was a microcosm of the century to come. First of all, since my session was not about technology nuts, bolts and commerce, but about the human implications of technology, most convention-goers avoided it for fear of contamination by affective sympathies. Hence, most of my fellow witnesses were empty chairs. The big party was next-door, where wall-to-wall capitalists listened to techno-tycoons handicap the future of terrestrial broadcasting. This is how things are going to be in the twenty-first century—cloistered nerds and boardroom strategists plotting the fate of humanity in a locked room, while "society" listens through the walls to an occasional muffled burst of laughter and applause.

Of course, my panel adhered to the symposium norm. It consisted of nerds and main-chancers who joined to depict a deliciously warped view of a society where they rarely set foot. Lady Dougan, for instance, noted smugly that the all-seeing tyranny of "Big Brother" has never materialized—despite the prediction of wet blanket George Orwell in *1984*. So now, concluded Lady Dougan, it's too late. The imagined Apocalypse has not happened as imagined. Ergo, there can be no Apocalypse. The danger has passed. Don't worry. Be wealthy.

(Just think! Orwell could have probably short-circuited the rise of Adolf Hitler by writing a Holocaust novel called *1926*.)

The population of sessions, mine and the loud one next-door, consisted entirely of white people. This is an issue far more significant than anything any of the panelists said. The twenty-first is shaping up as the White Century.

The devil, you say? Look at the rising political leverage of women and minorities everywhere, and you say, "Hah! You're wrong, coaxial-cablebreath!" But I say look again. The focus of all the world's chronic have-nots is a tangle of intractable social problems and eternal dilemmas, all of which require the begging of money from powerful white males. While women and minorities wring their hands over infant mortality, AIDS, drug addiction, gun control, starvation, homelessness, joblessness and institutional bigotry, the HHIC (head honkies in charge) are huddling together to set the hundred-year agenda for their enrichment and greater empowerment. They are negotiating the codes and standards, algorithms and firewalls that will determine every idea, every word, every utterance and every note distributed everywhere by telephone, television, satellite and computer. They're spinning the worldwide web. They're prescribing the news and divvying the spoils.

The sole dissenter on my Info Superhighway panel was a Russian UNESCO official, Henrikas Yushkiavitshus. Right now, he said, 84 percent of the world's economy enriches the upper 20 percent of people in the wealthiest nations. The bottom fifth of humanity squeaks by on 1.4 percent of world GNP. Not all of this bottom fifth lives in Africa and Asia. Some of the hungry, pestilential and info-deprived live in Chicago, Los Angeles, New York, West Virginia, Mississippi. Almost everyone among these economic dregs is not the least bit white.

One of the amusing paradoxes of this discussion was provided by Chairman Vradenburg, who defended as "anti-elitist" the consistently tawdry and exploitive content of Rupert Murdoch's media empire, from supermarket tabloids to jiggle shows and race-baiting on the Fox Network. Vradenburg, who champions the unregulated concentration of communications power in the hands of Orwellian piggies like Murdoch and TCI cable czar John Malone, simultaneously derides the tendency of 'cultural elites' to criticize the shlock and crap that constitutes most of popular broadcast entertainment. "Murdoch," said Vradenburg of his old boss, "competes with content. He offers content that people want."

In other words, folks, you think life is crap? You're right! Have some more crap.

Vradenburg's vision is the populism of the coming White Century. A few oligarchs take command of the tollgates on the info superhighway. They feed electronic bread and circus—movies-on-demand, cartoon marathons, infomercials, video games, video shopping, video workouts, video polls, video tits, video ass—to a mass of humanity who have ceded control of their destiny because they lack the technical knowhow to run a computer, because they don't have a computer, because they don't even recognize the word "qwertyuiop," because they have no electricity in their village, or because they went to public schools in Niggerland. Fortunately, Murdoch and Vradenburg, and Hollywood and AT&T, will provide them the content they want: electronic sedation.

Crap.

The final note on the plutocrats' version of the info superhighway's "social" significance appeared a day later. The daily newspaper of the International TV Symposium published a 33-inch feature about the "Info Highway Gridlock" discussion. According to the approved transcript, Henrikas Yushkiavitshus was not listed, wasn't mentioned, wasn't there, didn't utter one gloomy word.

On the official tape (accessible, of course, on the Internet), the Bolshevik was erased.

Freed one day, Junko and I spent an afternoon in Lausanne and visited one of the world's most extraordinary museums, the Musée de l'Art Brut, consisting largely of art created by inmates of asylums. It was blessed sanity after the symposium.

We fed ourselves adequately, which is par for the course in Switzerland, where the cuisine rarely exceeds the hospitality.

Benjie's Diary, 10 June '95, Montreux: "The meal, to a captive (the last train had come and gone) clientele at the Caux Station, was expensive but better than adequate. Mountain House, of course, has no restaurant nor even a vending machine with Zagnut bars and Oreos. No room service. They cleaned two of my shirts, though!

"Anyway, one of the highlights of our meal at the station restaurant was that everyone who ordered the *plat du jour*—but we went a la carte—got a tasty-looking bowl of cheese spread to go with their bread. Enviously, we dubbed it *'le whiz du fromage.'* We wished we'd gotten some. Junko thought the term, *'le whiz du fromage'* was a hoot. She almost fell over laughing. But she was really tired."

The best of America drifts to Paris. The American in Paris is the best American. It is more fun for an intelligent person to live in an intelligent country. France has the only two things toward which we drift as we grow older—intelligence and good manners.—F. Scott Fitzgerald

Finally freed from Switzerland, were were bound for Paris, where we billeted in the Marais at the Hotel des Chevaliers. We called Roberta Beardsley and made a date for the next morning. She was crisp and eager. She told us we had a busy day—no, a busy week—in store. This didn't energize us. We were weary from five days among the chilly Swiss and TV delusions.

Our rendezvous with her was scheduled slightly after dawn. We hadn't had time for breakfast, or even coffee. Our first apartment was on rue Jean-François Gerbillon, somewhere in the Sixth Arrondissement. We were supposed to meet on the street. We had never seen Roberta before. How would we recognize her? No problem. She would recognize us.

We recognized each other. We were the towheaded American and the cuddly Japanese woman. She was ... unmistakable.

"That's *gotta* be her," I said to Junko.

Legend has it that two visiting English ladies in the 1920s took a taxi to Montparnasse to find the famous night life. As their taxi stopped in front of the Dingo, Florence Martin, an American girl from the Folies Bergère and a regular at all the Montparnasse bars, emerged from the Dingo shouting a string of obscenities. The ladies looked at each other, and one said, "This *must be the place!"*—Noel Riley Fitch, *Literary Cafés of Paris*, 1989

From along the quai, rising over Circe's right shoulder, striding into the broad walkway in front of the Départ, a caped woman, hair flaming red and her face an instantly endearing portrait of sweetness and confusion beneath an excess of florid cosmetics, halted. She looked both ways, then peered into the café, her eyes visibly focusing and finally fixing themselves on Chester Quinn. A moment passed while recognition gradually dawned on her disarmingly ingenuous visage.

The woman, as crowds elbowed past her, straightened to her full height of —perhaps five feet, two inches and spread her arms upward and outward like Jeanne d'Arc surrendering her body to the flames, her soul to God, and her undying spirit to La Belle France.

"Chester!" she cried.

"Here we go," said Quinn.—David Benjamin, *Skulduggery in the Latin Quarter*, 2019

Spotting Roberta Beardsley, I thought of those rare lady professors who roam the campuses of small liberal arts colleges, swirling with scarves and capes and trailing a sneakered entourage of earnest Joyce fanatics or the brooding acolytes of Hesse or Burroughs or Sylvia Plath. Coincidentally, for that entire week, Roberta carried everywhere a dog-eared copy of a novel by one of those contemporary stylists of sentence-cult prose—Gaddis or Auster or Ondaatje or somesuch—whose tomes the educated classes guiltily purchase by the thousands but rarely read and never enjoy. Roberta admitted she'd been flogging the damn book for a month but couldn't find the thread.

Of course, we liked Roberta immediately. She was slim and kinetic, but substantial. She eschewed formalities, treated us as though she'd known us all her life, exploded with words, none of them closely or carefully linked together, and hustled us into a nearby building to look at the apartment under consideration.

Benjie's Diary, 20 June '95, Eindhoven: "Roberta works for Havard International, but not in any strict sense. She's more of a stringer. This explains her reluctance to commit to us when we were talking on the phone and faxing between California and Paris. However, she had turned eager while we weren't looking. My last fax had convinced her that we are real prospects and not just a couple of peeping Toms conniving to infiltrate the mews and *cours* of Gay Paree. So, while we were funiculing in Switzerland, Roberta, a non-stop talker in two languages (both of which came out mainly as English), had set up three-plus frantic days of apartment-hopping. We ended up *seeing* fifteen places, with Roberta checking out two others without us ... Since Roberta had offered the rule of thumb that you look at twenty-five possibilities, then take No. 26, we got pretty close to quota in three days. We got to walk up to a lot of fifth floors *sans ascenseur*. We got into a lot of mildewed corridors and weed-grown courtyards. We saw some of the worst carpets in the civilized world. We discovered that closets are considered an affectation in France. We studied French plumbing, including the curious device called a *broyeur*. This is, in essence, an in-sink-erator for sewage. And if you drop a tampon into it, whole neighborhoods are inundated in shit."

In retrospect, our first Paris apartment inspection was probably traumatic. For the money we expected to spend, about a million francs—which came to around $200,000—we anticipated apartments that were, well, livable. The joint on rue Jean-François Gerbillon resembled student housing in Morningside Heights the week after evacuation.

Benjie's Diary, 20 June '95, Eindhoven: "A plain, squarish, vacant apartment, fourth floor with an elevator, near St.-Placide. It's hard to remember because it was a week ago, and we didn't take it very seriously. The kitchen was bare, run-down but fairly spacious. The toilet, *salle de bains* were hopeless."

The ideal lodging was the rare and elusive chambre de bonne, *or maid's room—that garret beneath the roof that epitomised* la vie de bohême *and afforded maximum freedom. The service staircase that gave access to it might be steep and bare, but at least it was hidden from the habitually ill-tempered and censorious concierge.*—Shusha Guppy, *A Girl in Paris*, 1991

According to the cliché, Paris is a work of art. Its streets are corridors of history built by emperors and megalomaniacs, its squares asymmetric jewels of sculpted stone and phallic flamboyance, its gardens emerald oases, its skyline a jagged polygraph of domes, spires and terra-cotta chimneys sprawling on a cloud-ragged canvas of capricious sunlight. The cliché, actually, is accurate, but every canvas has a backside—frayed edges and corroded staples, naked slats of wood framing nothing but smears and smudges, flyspecks and a lifetime of dust.

The man who either disdains or fears to walk up a dark entry may be an excellent good man, and fit for a hundred things, but he will not do to make a good sentimental traveller.—Laurence Sterne, *A Sentimental Journey*, 1768

The backside of the Paris canvas is where we tramped behind Roberta for four wearying days in June. Behind each locked doorway were the signs of a swamp turned into a city more than two thousand years ago, detritus that possibly dated all the way back to Camulogène [27] and the Roman occupation. We crossed damp courtyards littered with cigarette butts discarded by doughboys after the Big One. We navigated hallways sifting with plaster and pungently cloudy with mold spores, where François Villon might have pissed during his school days. Most staircases we scaled were steep and claustrophobic, with peeling paint and treacherous banisters that creaked with pain and wobbled in their sockets, a few of them winding around retrofitted elevator shafts too narrow to fit a casket, vertically. We were reminded vividly that in an old city, the parts that don't show don't get a regular coat of paint or new screws in the hinges. The backside of Paris squeaks, reeks and crumbles, but, I guess, gracefully. Junko and I soon learned to judge our expectations of a prospective apartment by the state of the corridors, the health of the (usually dead) plants in the *cour* and the aroma of the stairwell. We got around to dismissing offhand any building in which the sweaty sheen of wet rot seeped from the hallway walls. If a building was merely dilapidated but swept, dry and solid to knock, our spirits rose.

After seeing three or four candidate flats, we began to divide Paris apartments into three categories. You had your Naked Derelicts, your Furnished Travesties and your Counterfeit Renovations. Alas, each of these rubrics ruled out the joint's purchasability.

A Naked Derelict was simply a suite of two or three square rooms, stripped to bare (twelve-foot) walls and splintered wainscot. It was usually equipped with a toilet that would tempt an agoraphobic princess to opt for crapping in a public alley. Typically, this sort of place had no bathing facilities, a kitchen not much roomier than a Buick glove compartment and a century's worth of assiduously ground-in grime.

A Furnished Travesty was a dwelling still occupied by

an owner. It often featured a trapezoidal floor plan, no right angles, Dostoyevskian lighting and one, inevitably superfluous, architectural non sequitur that would have to be destroyed to save the apartment.

Your Counterfeit Renovation was a slovenly effort to conceal the place's previous status as a Naked Derelict. Over a period that Junko, Roberta and I estimated to have been no longer than forty-eight hours, a crew of Three Stooges wannabes had swept through a once-decrepit shell with plaster trowels, paint rollers and sheetrock. By the time we arrived, the spanking-new bone-white latex paint had already begun to bubble up in spots where rainwater still flowed unimpeded through the walls, the freshly glued kitchen tiles had already begun to lose their grip—tinkling and clinking pianically as we gingerly trod the floor—and the carpet had parted company with the baseboard and begun to curl toward the middle of the room like Hokusai's famous wave.

In every case, we weren't more than two minutes into the latest Counterfeit Renovation before Roberta and the real estate agent of the moment launched into a maddeningly redundant ritual of mutual tsk-tsking, which led inexorably to the concession that this dump, like all the others before it, lacked the sort of lavatory normally recognized as a human necessity in the civilized, weekly-bathing, hair-shampooing, toilet-sitting world. This would commence an extensive discussion of where the pipes had been cemented somewhere deep in the building's walls and floors and how much demolition might be required to reach, rip out and relocate them. Next, either Roberta or the shark du jour would point to a wall whose cracked and melancholy aspect suggested that it was not Atlas holding up the whole building, and they would agree that it could be knocked down to accommodate some American (or Japanese) architectural frivolity—like a closet. Or a shower. Roberta and the agent would while away a blithe and incomprehensible quarter-hour discussing (which

Roberta eventually translated) pipe diameters, vast ochre stains on a hardwood floor, new walls and doorways, the pong emanating from an antique brass grating, and various fixtures and furnishings that we would have to buy at Parisian prices before seven or eight steroid-swollen Olympic powerlifters would have to be hired to winch whatever-it-is up six stories from the street, swing it through a window, thence to be wedged into a living-room niche that some long-past French carpenter-cum-extortionist had hewn from the apartment's original Daliesque floor plan.

Often, Roberta's dialog with the agent devolved into commiseration over the perversity of an interior decorator in charge of the renovation, who had slapped up some brand-new, paint-stinking, thoroughly impractical and occasionally bizarre configuration. Typically, fixing this abomination, its pillars and archways, its upcroppings and outjuttings, would involve the knocking down of walls and the plunder of the wiring within.

One Counterfeit Renovation featured a circular kitchen, its diameter just wide enough to hold a sink and refrigerator, or a sink and a range, or a range and refrigerator, but *not* a sink and a range *and* a refrigerator. Which of these three appliances would we like to keep in the living room?

Another Counterfeit Renovation had a closet-size toilet situated in the kitchen, between sink and range, with a door that swung out and banged against the range. This was an arrangement so singular that we all just stood mute for several minutes marveling at the dazzling stupidity of whoever etched the blueprint.

Two of our more curious Furnished Travesties were apartments of slightly less than fifty square meters. In each, one-fourth of the precious floor space was a hallway, without doors, covering and squeezing the entire length of the apartment, like a railroad track running through a ballpark.

None of the anomalies, oddities and monstrosities fazed

Roberta in the slightest. She had already seen every mutation Paris had to offer. The antidote to our fast-lowering expectations was to keep us on the move. If there was always something new to gape at, we couldn't pull up, sit down and surrender to despair. All the while she hustled us from shipwreck to shipwreck, Roberta was the ideal Paris companion. She wasted no time pointing out tourist attractions that, she assumed, we had already ogled. We scurried beneath the steeples of Notre Dame without genuflecting. We fled past the Panthéon without even a second's tribute to Voltaire, Rousseau or Jean Jaurès. Roberta fed us on the run, on gyros from rue St.-Séverin. She grilled us about ourselves, our hopes, our dreams, my previous wives, Junko's Japan. She chirped on about her own apartment on rue des Bourdonnais, where certain walls had to be—what else?—knocked down. Occasionally, we would all lurch to a sudden halt and gaze at some Parisian vista none of us had ever noticed before. This brief interlude lasted only 'til Roberta's gears kicked back in, and she was motoring again toward Val-de-Grâce or rue Mouffetard, tugging at Junko as I cantered to keep up, trailing *frites* and bits of lamb.

By the second day of Roberta's march through Paris, we had seen the worst that the local realty market had to offer, but we had also glimpsed, thanks to Roberta's refusal to pause and let us think too much about what we were doing, some glimmers of hope. We'd peeked into a few places with curious charms, where the bathrooms could stay where they were and no walls need be sledgehammered. We sensed that if we kept on trucking, then maybe.

Benjie's Diary, 20 June '95, Eindhoven: "Life was a blur of apartments. As follows:

"1) The dreary place near St.-Placide.

"2) A fifth-floor walkup on rue Mouffetard. We love rue Mouffetard. This one, forty-five square meters, had a long hallway wasting a lot of space, and it reeked of cigarettes. It was restorable and had a good kitchen. Good ventilation. Noisy. Crappy toilet. Overall, no good. The thing is, we love rue Mouffetard."

The steep, narrow and bustling rue Mouffetard, running down to the Church of Saint-Medard is, alas, every year losing some of its old character. The pick of the housebreaker has been busy hereabouts in recent years, a pick wielded sometimes with curious results, as when a hole pierced in an old wall began to spurt gold pieces on to the astonished workmen on 25th May, 1938. The housebreakers did not at first recognise the coins and tried some of them in penny-in-the-slot machines. The treasure was walled up sometime between 1750 and 1756 by one Louis Nivelle who, having the police after him, decided to stow away his money in a safe place. He chose the chimney of a room he rented on rue Mouffetard, but he died without digging out his money or revealing where it was, and his heirs were never able to find the hoard.—Alan Houghton Brodrick, ed., *The People's France: Paris*, 1950

Benjie's Diary, 20 June '95, Eindhoven: "3) A dump behind Val-de-Grâce. Suffice to say that the shower was in the kitchen. A BU student, among the most resilient New York transplants to Boston, would have been grossed out.

"4) Back to rue Mouffetard, where we looked at our first 'fully remodeled' unit. About forty-five square meters in three rooms, including a generous, well-lit kitchen. The floors were concealed by a carpet that didn't quite match up with the walls. It looked as though it had gotten rained on and shrunk inward. It was also frayed and light gray, easily soiled. The walls had been painted without preparation. A pasty white that had already begun to swell, buckle and crack where it lacked the gumption to contain the moisture and the warped superstructure underneath. By far, however, the stupidest feature of this inadequate apartment was the bathroom, whose only access was through the kitchen … Conceived and designed by the architect from Hell. On to …"

In a few paces we are at the corner of the rue Dauphine, where on Thursday, 19th April, 1908, in the early afternoon Pierre Curie (the discoverer with his wife of radium) was caught by a six-ton dray and was killed, his head being crushed by the left back wheel of the vehicle.—Alan Houghton Brodrick, *ed., The People's France: Paris,* 1950

Benjie's Diary, 20 June '95, Eindhoven: "5) rue Dauphine, where we saw two places. The first, a charming but dark closetless forty-five square meters on an ancient second-story courtyard, was the first place we considered actually buying. This was our first viewing with exposed beams, a sort of signature of vintage Paris. They were beautifully integrated, dividing two interior rooms without need of a solid wall. I tend to see exposed beams as great for attaching things to. I don't know how Junko views them.

"6) Another place on rue Dauphine was interesting because there was a mezzanine. But the kitchen was wretched, the bathroom a shambles.

"So ended Day One. We started late on Day Two because Junko had to file copy with *EE Times* [28]. Roberta and I got stood up at an apartment on boulevard St.-Marcel. Then Roberta, without us, checked a *viagère* [29] on rue de l'Université. It turned out to be N.G.

"7) So, we met Roberta at rue de Montmorency in the Marais, where we found something better than rue Dauphine."

In the rue de Montmorency ... at No. 51 is the house of Nicolas Flamel, scrivener and bookseller and reputed alchemist, who died in 1418, and whose wealth (evidenced by his many benefactions) seemed so inexplicable to his contemporaries that he was thought to have possessed the Philosopher's Stone ... Flamel seems, indeed, to have been a worthy and honest citizen as well as a philanthropist, but in the Middle Ages anyone who gave anything away except to a religious foundation was liable to be accused of the black arts.— Alan Houghton Brodrick, ed., *The People's France: Paris,* 1950

Benjie's Diary, 20 June '95, Eindhoven: "It was fifty square meters in a single rectangle, so it seemed bigger. It had a bad carpet, badly painted beams but vast amounts of storage and a superior kitchen, including a breakfast bar. The bathroom was complete and good enough. We liked it enough to think about making an offer. It was on the first floor with a view of rue de Montmorency and the courtyard in a cut stone building. Nice but kind of dull.

"8) Rue du Bac, not far from the Hotel de Nevers. This was a place with good floors and tall ceilings, with the odd feature of a spare room across the hall. The bathroom was odd, the kitchen small and grubby. Forgettable."

Victor Hugo got the news of Chateaubriand's death at the Palais-Bourbon, and at once set off on foot to the rue du Bac:

M. Chateaubriand lay upon his bed, a little iron bed ... his face was uncovered ... and he bore that expression of nobility he had in his lifetime, mingled with the grave majesty of death ... at the feet of M. Chateaubriand ... were two wooden boxes, one placed upon the other. The larger contained the complete MS of his Memoirs *in forty-eight volumes ... so great was the disorder in which he lived that one of the volumes was found ... in a dirty little closet where the lamps were cleaned. Some tables, a wardrobe, a few blue and green upholstered armchairs cluttered up rather than furnished the bedroom.*

—Alan Houghton Brodrick, ed., *The People's France: Paris,* 1950

Benjie's Diary, 20 June '95, Eindhoven: " 9) A seductive visit. Our first loft. Its only disadvantages were a minuscule but funky (and spotless) kitchen and the funky toilet, the *broyeur*. The place had low ceilings, a host of skylights, lots of clever storage in the slant of the wall and a pregnant owner who speaks American English. It was still being lived in by people who love writing desks and bookcases. Alas, it's overpriced … Junko and I have designated it as our runner-up.

"The hitch, for the seller, is that they claim fifty square meters, but that area has to be space with headroom of at least 1.8 meters. No way. We can beat them down in price with a) the toilet, b) the kitchen, c) the headroom, d) the climb—it's a fifth-floor with no hope of an elevator—and e) their urgency. They want to move to America before the pregnant woman pops.

"We are still charmed by this place.

"End of Day Two."

There is a common French phrase monnaie de singe, *or monkey's money, meaning worthless reward.* Payé en monnaie de singe *is said, for instance, of a hearty handshake instead of hard cash. An amusing, if untrustworthy, legend would have it that jugglers, mummers, strolling players and other 'vagabonds' could get across the Petit-Pont without paying the toll, provided they did a tour de singe or gave an exhibition of their art. Hence such tricks were known as* monnaie de singe.—Alan Houghton Brodrick, ed., *The People's France: Paris,* 1950

Benjie's Diary, 20 June '95, Eindhoven: "10) Never mind. 11) We met Roberta at her place, did a lot of strategy and ad-shopping, then headed to rue de Petit Pont to look at Remodeling Disaster #3. The staircase was rickety and smelly, the cosmetic work inept. If we hope to rent this place to American or Japanese tourists while we're not living there, this locale, across from Notre Dame and overlooking Elliot Paul's rue de las Huchette, is heaven.

"12) We legged it next to rue des Écoles, to look over a classic ... Fifty dirty square meters, with elevator, fifth floor. A solid nineteenth-century building where one dirty old woman had subsisted 'til she died, in a squalid kitchen, two dusty rooms and a toilet the size of a broom closet. She apparently washed by splashing water from the sink. The space was fine, the floors oak. It needed a lot of work, but it wasn't bad if we can knock the price down.

"13) Rue St.-Séverin. Later."

The Frankish assassin and bandit Clovis marched into the city in 486. His name, pronounced with a hiss, is a contraction of "Chlodovech," later to become "Louis."—Andrew Hussey, *Paris: The Secret History*, 2006

The Paris of Louis XIII at the Val de Grace—a squat, clumsy style with basket-handle vaults, big-bellied columns, and a hunchbacked dome.—Victor Hugo, *Notre-Dame de Paris,* 1831

Benjie's Diary, 20 June '95, Eindhoven: "14) We grabbed a *sandwich grec* (great!) and hoofed to place Alphonse Laveron, facing the magnificence of Val-de- Grâce. Alas, the apartment was a stinky, drab, filthy ground-floor fifties excrescence.

"15) The next day, Saturday, Roberta checked out a place on rue d'Assas, then met us at 127, rue de Rennes. This was a very good fifth-floor older apartment (*ascenseur* pending). The owners were well-prepared, gracious and helpful. Sweet old folks. They had a good kitchen and a salvageable bathroom, some decent features, good old-fashioned windows and a great view, but ...

"Rue St.-Séverin is our baby."

Rue Saint-Séverin (parallel to the Huchette on the south) is interesting for its church, one of the most curious in Paris. All around the streets are sordid and dilapidated, though here and there a fine old façade of the grand siecle *peeps through the grime.*—Alan Houghton Brodrick, *The People's France: Paris,* 1950

Benjie's Diary, 20 June '95, Eindhoven: "Its only flaw is that it's a fifth-floor with no elevator. But the entry is immaculate, completely redone, and the staircase is wide, gentle and clean. We're deep in an inner courtyard, so there's no noise at all. It is church-silent. There are fifty square meters of superbly remodeled space with two mezzanines that add as much as thirty square meters. The kitchen is new and beautiful, with a long breakfast bar and tons of storage. The toilet and *salle de bain* are separated, new and modern and perfect. There are windows on the courtyard, a skylight on the mezzanine, a cross-draft, a wealth of solid, dark oak exposed beams, a view of the steeples of St.-Séverin.

"Boy, do we want this place!"

After World War I, the list of ilots insalubres *was expanded from six to seventeen. These included ... a major portion of the most ancient part of the Fifth, a quartier once called Saint-Séverin, which comprised the area around Saint-Julien-le-Pauvre, directly across the river from Notre Dame.*—Luc Santé, *The Other Paris,* 2015

ALBERT
July 19, 2003
Rue Maitre Albert

5

Elliot Paul and Xavier Privas

The peace of great churches be for you,
Where the players of loft pipe organs
Practice lovely old fragments, alone.
—Carl Sandburg, *Smoke and Steel*, 1920

Junko and I fought like cornered weasels against shlepping up five stories to see the presumed dump on rue St.-Séverin. Seemingly, we had found the ideal location, two minutes from place St.-Michel, two minutes from the Petit Pont. But the fool's gold of location, after a dozen disappointments, had jaded us. We had seen, and recoiled from, apartments in the same *quartier*—a Naked Derelict on rue des Écoles, a Counterfeit Renovation on rue Petit Pont. We suspected our Parisian realtors of operating under the assumption that, in this coveted corner, convenient to almost every flashbulb-bleached tour stop in the city, they could wangle a million francs for little more than a two-ply refrigerator carton.

Besides the suspiciously irresistible location, we were dubious about how this joint had been advertised. Roberta found the ad lurking furtively in a one-inch box, in seven-point Times Roman, at the bottom of the realty notices in the conservative *Le Figaro*. The ad lasted but a day. Whoever owned the apartment seemed almost ashamed to admit it.

What was wrong here?

And then there were the stairs, five flights. We had seen too many fifth-floor walkups. In every instance, the result was a long climb to a close-up tour of eighteenth-century amateur plumbing and geriatric squalor.

Nonetheless, so as to leave no hovel uninspected, Roberta made a date with the agent, a woman elegantly named Madame de Gaillande. We demurred the date. Roberta called back and canceled. Mme. de Gaillande called Roberta back and said, "Please." We said no. Mme. de Gaillande, swallowing her elegance, uttered whatever is the French equivalent of "pretty please." We sighed. The woman was begging. This was hard. We had a Frenchwoman with a *"de"* in front of her surname virtually groveling at our feet. Here was a Marxist-Leninist dream come true. Dare we forgo so rare a moment of proletarian vindication?

"Whaddya think?" I said.

"It's a lot of steps," said Junko.

"It's a lot of steps," I said to Roberta.

Roberta's eyes pleaded. This was her third or fourth conversation with Mme. de Gaillande. Roberta, notwithstanding her original standoffishness toward Junko and me, was a soft touch. She had bonded with the Frenchwoman.

"It's gonna be another dump," I forecast.

"All you have to do is look," said Roberta.

"No, first we have to climb," said I.

Roberta was reproachful. Our ascent into Parisian residency and all its attendant prestige was what we had come to Paris to do. To climb stairs. To look at dumps.

"Well," said Junko.

"Well," I said.

Roberta sighed with relief and told Mme. de Gaillande that we'd be there, by golly.

When I was a student, the Saint-Séverin quarter was deserted in the evenings, and there were only two places open to eat, one on the Rue de la Huchette, which I believe was called Chez Papille, and the other on the Rue des Prêtres Saint-Séverin, run by Yugoslavs and decorated with large photos of Mihailovic, head of the Serbian resistance and Tito's rival.—Eric Hazan, *A Walk Through Paris*, 2016

An hour or so hence, we met Mme. de Gaillande at the building's door. Slipping past middle age and tall to the point of awkwardness (picture Allison Janney in *Primary Colors*), she looked like the backup center for the French Toute-Étoile Menopause Basketball Team. She was polite, talkative, gracious and vaguely preoccupied, like a stork who had reluctantly left her nestful of eggs in the care of a magpie.

The location was both awesome and troublesome. Across from the doorway on rue St.-Séverin was the rambling mass of the *église* St.-Séverin, most of it a little over eight hundred years old. Across from the church was a café named for the church. The doorway to the building was in a narrow façade between a Greek restaurant called Knossos (next-door to a Greek restaurant named Biblos) and a convenience store. Ominously, several doors west, toward place St.-Michel, was a Japanese restaurant. Junko looked mistrustfully at a sign in the window:

"KARAOKE NIGHTLY"

"Oh, shit," she said. "What if you can hear it?"

Mme. de Gaillande understood the term, "oh, shit." She

smiled tightly and shooed us inside.

St. Séverin dates back to the sixth century. Severinus was a hermit who sheltered Clodwig, son of Clodomir, who lives in history as St. Cloud. Severinus was buried near the cell where he had lived, and Clodwig built a chapel in his memory. The church was rebuilt in the time of St. Louis and is today famous for its wonderful glass—the subject of one of the windows is the martyrdom of St. Thomas of Canterbury—and for the appeal written on the tower: Bonnes gens qui par cy passez, priez Dieu pour les tréspassés. *The dedication of the church has a curious history. In the fifteenth century the hermit was forgotten, and the patron-saint became another Séverin, who was also the patron-saint of travellers. In his honour, horseshoes were nailed on the church door. But in 1753 the hermit was again remembered, and the church is now under the patronage of both the Séverins.*—Sidney Dark, *Paris,* 1936

A long hallway led us toward the courtyard. This was the pleasantest surprise on all our Paris house hunt. Unlike almost every other corridor we had traversed until then, this one was restored and clean, with scrubbed limestone walls and new light fixtures hanging from a ceiling fashioned of hardwood lathe. The smell of urine was nowhere to be whiffed. Junko and I allowed ourselves a frisson of hope. Here was a seventeenth-century pile whose owner had taken the exceptional trouble to renovate everything on the premises—corridors and courtyards included. He had evidently employed conscientious, capable craftsmen to carry out the rehab.

Yeah, but how far up did these craftsmen climb before they slacked off?

We passed an elevator on the way to the courtyard. I asked about it. Mme. de Gaillande explained that it served only Escalier A. Escaliers B, C and D were not wide enough to accommodate an *ascenseur.*

We passed through a tidy *cour* and started up Escalier D.

In the back of my mind lurked the dangerously romantic perception that we were in the heart of Elliot Paul territory. To live in Elliot Paul's neighborhood! Here was a temptation to shred my bargaining position into tricolored tatters. In two memoirs, *The Last Time I Saw Paris* (1942) and *Springtime in Paris* (1949), Paul had immortalized rue de la Huchette, which runs parallel to rue St.-Séverin, one block nearer the Seine. Paul had come here in the twenties, when this pocket of Paris was little more than a blue-collar slum too far from the Right Bank to be fashionable and too far from the Sorbonne to be bohemian.

My first encounter with Paul was through the best of his madcap Homer Evans murder mysteries, *Mysterious Mickey Finn*. Homer Evans, a sort of cross between Sherlock Holmes and Jay Gatsby, was suave, imperturbable, encyclopedically erudite and sexually blasé when James Bond was still wearing nappies.

James Joyce was making the sixth revision of page two thousand and forty of his magnum opus called "Work in Progress"*; Harold Stearns [30] was sitting at the Select bar, murmuring that murders were unusual, therefore banal, consequently uninteresting; Gertrude Stein and Alice Toklas were drinking brandy and soda; Ernest Hemingway was in the Bois thinking what he would do if the Bois was Wyoming, the swans were wild ducks, and he had a gun.*

Homer Evans and Miriam Leonard, however, were sitting on a Han stone slab, 202 B.C.–220 A.D., in the Cernuschi Museum where the single attendant still slept at his desk.

"Are you going to be reticent and mysterious, or shall your helpers be enlightened from time to time?" Miriam asked. "You said you got exactly what you wanted in the library," she continued.

"If that is true, your wants verge on the eccentric. I got one of the principal frights of my life. My old dad may not have struck oil, but he'll cut off my allowance and beat hell out of me if I figure in the police news."

"We shall spare your parent any undue alarm," Evans said.—Elliot Paul, *The Mysterious Mickey Finn*, 1939

Not all our Montparnasse characters were picturesque or fantastic ones. Some were tragic: fine lives that had somehow been strangely twisted out of shape. I think of Homer Bevans—Homer, who would sit all day long on the terrace of the Dôme, a highball in front of him, staring off into space across the boulevards as though they were some illimitable plain, and then, when night came, would move around the corner to the Dingo to stand for long hours at the bar and be jostled by a crowd of strangers with only now and then some acquaintance to nod to him. Get to know him, as a few of us did (everyone knew him by sight), and you would find him to be gentle, generous, lovable, cultivated and urbane; and this was the man Elliot Paul was later to take as the prototype for his detective story hero, Homer Evans.—Samuel Putnam, *Paris Was Our Mistress*, 1947

Perhaps the only member of the so-called "Lost Generation" of foreign (mostly American) writers in Paris in the 1920s and '30s more lamentably forgotten today than Elliot Paul is Robert McAlmon. McAlmon, who feuded with Hemingway and found T.S. Eliot irretrievably bourgeois. He wrote excellent prose in inverse proportion to his ingestion of second-rate alcohol. He published many of his peers and is unpublished today, probably justly so. Less just is the current obscurity of the far more sober Elliot Paul. He was too modest, amiable and playful to be regarded as belonging to that temperamental company that included Joyce, Hemingway,

Gertrude Stein, Man Ray, George Antheil, Djuna Barnes and Wyndham Lewis. One of Paul's curious and uncharacteristic collaborations was the "proclamation" published—like the better-edited manifesto of Charles Foster Kane—in *transition*'s most famous issue. *transition* (lower case) was an "international" literary journal founded in Paris by Paul and sidekick Eugene Jolas to herald the arrival of a transitional moment in modern arts and letters.

Tired of the spectacle of short stories, novels, poems and plays still under the hegemony of the banal word, monotonous syntax, static psychology, descriptive naturalism, and desirous of crystallizing a viewpoint ...

We hereby declare that:

1. THE REVOLUTION IN THE ENGLISH LANGUAGE IS AN ACCOMPLISHED FACT.
2. THE IMAGINATION IN SEARCH OF A FABULOUS WORLD IS AUTONOMOUS AND UNCONFINED. *(Prudence is a rich, ugly old maid courted by Incapacity ... Blake)*
3. PURE POETRY IS A LYRICAL ABSOLUTE THAT SEEKS AN A PRIORI REALITY WITHIN OURSELVES ALONE. *(Bring out number, weight and measure in a year of dearth ... Blake)*
4. NARRATIVE IS NOT MERE ANECDOTE, BUT THE PROJECTION OF A METAMORPHOSIS OF REALITY. *(Enough! Or Too Much! ... Blake)*
5. THE EXPRESSION OF THESE CONCEPTS CAN BE ACHIEVED ONLY THROUGH THE RHYTHMIC "HALLUCINATION OF THE WORD." (Rimbaud)
6. THE LITERARY CREATOR HAS THE RIGHT TO DISINTEGRATE THE PRIMAL MATTER OF WORDS IMPOSED ON HIM BY TEXT-BOOKS AND DICTIONARIES. *(The road of excess leads to the palace of*

Wisdom ... Blake)

7. HE HAS THE RIGHT TO USE WORDS OF HIS OWN FASHIONING AND TO DISREGARD EXISTING GRAMMATICAL AND SYNTACTICAL LAWS. *(The tigers of wrath are wiser than the horses of instruction ... Blake)*
8. THE "LITANY OF WORDS" IS ADMITTED AS AN INDEPENDENT UNIT.
9. WE ARE NOT CONCERNED WITH THE PROPAGATION OF SOCIOLOGICAL IDEAS, EXCEPT TO EMANCIPATE THE CREATIVE ELEMENTS FROM THE PRESENT IDEOLOGY.
10. TIME IS A TYRANNY TO BE ABOLISHED.
11. THE WRITER EXPRESSES. HE DOES NOT COMMUNICATE.
12. THE PLAIN READER BE DAMNED. *(Damn braces! Bless relaxes! ... Blake)*

The *transition* Proclamation is notable for many reasons, not the least of which is proof that grandiose postgraduate gobbledegook was a phenomenon not exclusive to the sixties. Outraged critics, particularly Harry Hansen of the *New York World-Telegram*, noted that despite its strident iconoclasm, the Proclamation was carefully composed in standard, coherent, non-revolutionary English (rather like the man taking a vow of silence announcing that he's gonna clam up right after this).

I would judge that it was transition, *under the editorship of Eugene Jolas, Elliot Paul, and Robert Sage, which exerted the most influence on writers whom they considered worthy of the name. It was a constant example of how not to write.*—Robert McAlmon, *Being Geniuses Together, 1920–1930*, 1984

More significant, however, is that Elliot Paul, in a prolific and mischievous career of journalism and literature, barely adhered to a syllable of *transition*'s grave and tendentious magna carta. Unlike his fellow signatories, Paul was a fountain of humor and goodwill who loved the "plain reader" (whatever that might be) and the common man more dearly than he loved either fame, critical approval or foolish consistency. Paul was a prolific yarnspinner whose richest contribution to twentieth-century literature was the clarity and affection with which he evoked Paris behind the scenery—humble streets like rue de la Huchette and "people's churches" like St.-Séverin—from the twenties all the way to the sixties. While his peers, Hemingway, Joyce, Fitzgerald and Stein used the city as a backdrop for their social displays and autobiographical effusions, Paul plunged into the lives of actual, non-fictional Parisians, describing and chronicling them lovingly while receding into the wings as a narrator less visible and definable than Nick Carraway. If Paul had been true to the *transition* manifesto—which was too badly written to have been his work—we would have never seen his orderly, traditionally structured and lyrical masterwork, *The Life and Death of a Spanish Town*, nor would we have enjoyed such endearing characters as Hyacinthe Goujon (*The Last Time I Saw Paris*), Marthe Doucet and Bobo Gillotte (*Understanding the French*), or, of course, Homer Evans and his menagerie of cohorts, foes and foils.

A grateful Gertrude Stein wrote that it was Elliot Paul who had expressed the "first seriously popular estimation of her work." In The Autobiography of Alice B. Toklas, *she said that Paul "was a new englander," but he was a saracen, a saracen such as you sometimes see in the villages of France, where the strain from some crusading ancestor's dependents still survives. Elliot Paul was such a one. He had an element not of mystery but of evanescence, actually little by little he appeared and then as slowly disappeared.*—Waverley Root, *The Paris Edition: The Autobiography of Waverley Root 1927–1934*, 1987

Escalier D, like the entryway, was neat and expressive. The walls were yellow stucco, veined with oak beams in burnt umber. The steps, broad and shallow, were unplaned oak, three hundred years old, worn to a smooth dark finish by millions of footsteps. The handrails were carbon steel the color and texture of a cast-iron skillet. When we paused, anaerobic and gasping, on the fourth landing—one flight to go—we could see, through the window and above the roof, the modest steeple of St.-Séverin.

No ambitious ornament intrudes as one stands before St.-Séverin. The carvings of the arch at the entrance are integral parts of the whole; the gargoyles have less literary taint than those of Notre Dame. The little church does not dominate the scene but rests among secular buildings with modesty and restraint. I was to learn that, while in other localities the Church of Christ had wandered far afield, St.-Séverin had remained truly the refuge and consolation of the poor. Its congregation consisted of workmen and their families, and its priests had no bank accounts, were never known to publish books, or mix in politics. Three of them, I was to learn, played the neatest game of bridge I have yet encountered. At the end of each session, they dropped my money into the poor box.—Elliot Paul, *The Last Time I Saw Paris*, 1942

When we finally reached the *cinquième étage* and caught our breath, the apartment into which Mme. de Gaillande led us was the shocker of the week. Despite its age, it was unfilthy. It held no hint of decrepitude, no discernible aroma of mildew or ratscat. Its just-finished renovation looked neither hasty nor haphazard. The work appeared—be still, our hearts!—competent.

Its contour, seen from the entry, was a right triangle. On our left, one wall soared higher than fifteen feet. The ceiling was the hypotenuse, losing altitude precipitously as it crossed the room toward the courtyard. On our right—where three dormer windows intercepted the ceiling and poked out toward the courtyard below, St.-Séverin beyond and a matching row of dormers across the way—the foot of the triangle had been beveled off, leaving a vertical wall about three feet high. The apartment's main room extended back thirty feet from the entry. It was filled with light from the south-facing dormer windows and two skylights high in the hypotenuse. Against the tall wall, our designer had installed a kitchen island fenced by a tile-topped breakfast bar. Above the kitchen hung a roomy loggia, attached to an artful arrangement of mighty gnarled ancient timbers and fresh uniform new beams, plus a few strategically placed I-beams and wires. The loggia alone was sufficient to steal our hearts. It was an indoor treehouse. You reached it by stepladder. You climbed into a sunny aerie, like a child clambering to the top bunk, while the room spread out below, with a window to the sky and a corner where, if you crawled into it and scrunched, no one below would possibly know you're up there, listening and lurking.

In a moment, we had discovered a matching loggia in the apartment's other room. There was a miniature mezzanine above the toilet—adjacent to the entry—and another above the bathroom (a modern, American-style *salle de bain* with double sinks and Hollywood lights), which occupied the deepest extremity of the apartment.

All the solid features aside, the difference here, distinct from every other place we had visited, was intangible. It was sunshine. For days, we had prowled the realty of the City of

Light, but almost every old or renovated apartment we had thus far seen was dim, dingy or outright dark, closed to the sky, hunkering from the sun. Now, here, climbing five flights one more time and entering this intelligently reshuffled loft, we had reached at last the place where Paris converges with the sun. Thanks to the skylights and windows that opened toward the east from the bedroom and bathroom, this Euclidian kaleidoscope collected sunlight all day. Once, later, we stood together in the skylight above the loggia, watching dusk throw Paris' skyline of distant steeples, jumbled tile roofs, crooked chimneys and TV antennas into a jagged silhouette of black-on-orange.

The churches—which were numerous and splendid in the University and which represented every architectural era, from the round arches of Saint-Julien to the Gothic ones of Saint-Séverin—rose above all; and, as one harmony more in that harmonious mass, they accented in close succession the indented outline of the roofs, with their boldly cut spires, with their perforated steeples, and slender needles, the lines which were themselves but a magnificent exaggeration of the acute angle of the roofs.—Victor Hugo, *Notre Dame de Paris*, 1831

It wasn't much of a decision, after all, to covet this garret. It was equal parts a romantic consummation and a practical conclusion. Romantically, the place was ideal. I write, Junko paints, and every writer/painter/artist blowhard in Paris has to live not just anywhere but in a loft, appreciating the texture of the light, watching naked ballerinas framed by the windows across the courtyard brush their hair, and—when it rains—brooding by the window as rivulets truckle down the panes. Here, in this apartment, all this good stuff was built in, plus treehouses!

Paris. There you can be whatever you want to be. Totally yourself.—Langston Hughes

In the practical sense, we had found an eminently rentable *pied-à-terre* in Paris' most popular tourist district. People would be beating down our doors to *louer* the apartment and pay our mortgage for us (if we could float a mortgage). To our fiscal advantage, we had gone apartment-hunting in Paris during an economic slump. Monsieur Lafitte [31], our building owner (we learned eventually), was eager to sell because he was paying alimony, supporting a mistress and repaying a loan while renovating a *chateau* somewhere south of Paris. And he preferred foreign buyers. It is apparently common among Frenchmen, in property matters, to distrust other Frenchmen. This realization came home to us when I first met our *notaire*, Maitre Pedinielli, who wanted to know if the *comble* came as part of the apartment. Perhaps, she asked, it belonged to the *syndic* (the building association)?

"Comble?" Roberta and I said in unison. "What the hell is a *comble*?"

Maitre Pedinielli smiled her Franco-Mediterranean smile. The *comble*, she explained, is pretty darn critical. It's the triangular area below the ceiling, which was probably an attic before M. Lafitte tore out the attic floor and put in the loggias. For three hundred years, our apartment had been low-ceilinged, shoebox-shaped and Sartreanly gloomy. M. Lafitte had transformed it into a light-drenched *atelier* by ripping away ceilings and punching holes in his building. But had he remembered to include the *comble*, that sunny upper triangle, in the dimensions of the reborn dwelling? If he had neglected this, we might end up buying only the lower portion of the space, while the very air above us belonged collectively to the owners of the apartments around and below—sixty-four prickly, proprietary Parisian roommates. We trembled at the prospect.

Feverishly, we studied the specifications. It was all in French, which meant that Junko and I didn't understand any more than two words in a row. It was mostly legalistic, which excluded Roberta (although she was the widow of a lawyer).

Maitre Pedinielli remained serene. She perused.

"Ah, here," she said, caressing a paragraph. "Yes, the *comble* is yours."

"Whew," we chorused.

Our moment of *comble* consternation, of course, occurred later in this saga. It was one in a series of steps that consumed most of the summer of '95. The first of these was making an offer that M. Lafitte would accept. Almost as immediate was the psychic trauma.

Benjie's Diary, 21 June '95, Eindhoven: "With the plunge into Parisian realty, about which we've been talking for probably five years (more?), we're moving into another enormous change of life. In ten years, we've done a lot of that.

"Meeting Junko wreaked huge change in both our lives. I spent two years getting a divorce, cutting myself off from America, leaving my job [as "principal writer" at Arthur D. Little, Inc.], starting another book. Then the big leap to Tokyo. Where Junko had to break to her family that a crazy *gaijin* was moving in with her. A year later, we got married.

"More big changes. I finished my book, went to work at *Tokyo Journal* [as editor-in-chief].

"A year later, out of *TJ*.

"I got a book published, *The Joy of Sumo* [Tuttle Publishing, 1990]. Junko left JVC after eleven years and went to work for an American company, in a job [Tokyo correspondent, *EE Times*] she had never tried before: journalist.

"Neither of us, anymore, was what we had been when we met.

"And then we were out of Japan, in a place neither of us had ever been before: California.

"Two years in California. Time for another wholesale life change. On to Paris, at least as landlords.

"We always get scared and contentious in the throes of these big upheavals. We suffer ambivalence. On one hand, we excite ourselves with dreams and the prospect of adventure. On the other hand, our innate conservatism, the desire to leave well enough alone, retaliates. We ponder the consolation of postponement.

"In this case, we're motivated as much by Roberta as our urge for a place in Paris. We made a commitment by hiring Roberta to help us. Now, we've found the damn place, a place better than we had envisioned. We've found a jewel. Now, we have to fulfill our expectations of ourselves and finish the deal with Roberta. Certainly, we're not doing this for *her*. But without Roberta and her energy, we would have failed on this trip and would be, probably, no closer to a place in Paris than we were a year ago.

"In our other big changes, we were each other's catalyst. I had to move to Japan or betray Junko. She had to change jobs or—well, I don't think I pushed her, but I convinced her that she could succeed in a much more challenging, rewarding job. In this case, we had each other, but we also had Roberta challenging us, at every turn, to put up or shut up.

"We're doing an interesting, risky, scary, exhilarating thing. We owe Roberta for making us stick it out."

Delacroix confided one day that he had in his heart "something black to satisfy." That blackness is the substance of Paris, the city which makes the will infinite and gives to one's fancy inexhaustible forms.—Etal Adnan, *Paris, When It's Naked,* 1993

The deal moved frighteningly fast. By the time Junko and I had finished the last leg of her business junket to Eindhoven and landed in San Francisco, we had exchanged offers twice with Mme. de Gaillande. By this time, we still didn't know the name of the person who owned the apartment.

While discussing price, we also had to find financing. Experts warned us that American banks were reluctant to mortgage French apartments and that the French government preferred French mortgages. We flirted with a big French mortgage company called SOVAC but then switched our interest to a source a little more familiar. We had used Citibank for international transactions in Tokyo, so we tried Citibank in Paris, eventually cornering—by phone, fax and letter—a bilingual phantom (we never met him), Monsieur La Cotte. M. La Cotte steered us to a British lender with French offices called Abbey National. I began then a fax relationship with another phantom named Marie-Odile Pauchet. I pictured a prim spinster, about thirty-five, in a severe suit and lace underwear, quietly filing forms and checking boxes while seething with Gallic sensuality. Over a month's time, while Junko and I negotiated with Mme. de Gaillande, I filled out a heap of Abbey National mortgage forms and sent them off to my sweet, secret Marie-Odile in Cambrai.

Benjie's Diary, 4 June '96, rue Montorgueil, Paris: "There's nothing quite like it: A Parisian woman gliding into a café, taking a seat, lounging silkily with a thin cigarette and a disdainful air, shedding her wrap, crossing her legs, warming her nude shoulders, staying just long enough to draw a dozen furtive gazes and plant a scarlet stain on the rim of her coffee cup and, finally, departing in sinuous dignity. Someone should applaud."

No sooner has the early autumnal twilight begun to tinge the Parisian sky with rose and silver, no sooner has dusk shaded the sharp outlines of tree and monument, obscuring the Tuileries with a lacy veil, and awakening sad and steely lights in the green lake, than the aspect of the Frenchwoman undergoes a subtle change. Her cheeks are tinged with a more vivid rose. Her eyes, cool and faintly mocking in the daylight, become warm shadows, dark and mysterious. Her very profile alters; its angular outlines are softer, more rounded. Her very carriage, her nameless allure, the slight swaying of the hips, the light deliberate walk, the poise of the graceful little head, the delicate rigidity of the shoulders suggest a new assurance.—George Slocombe, *The Heart of France: Parisian, Provincial & Peasant*, 1934

While Marie-Odile tapped her pretty foot patiently, the mortgage numbers kept changing. This continued for months because of Junko's father in Chigasaki, who was busily bailing himself out of the post-bubble Japanese economy. Within a week of our mentioning to Pa Yoshida an apartment in Paris, he began to see it as a better investment than a Japanese postal savings account paying a half-percent interest a year. So, we had financing from Japan. We still needed La Belle France to come around.

And there was the inspection. The apartment had been renovated. It looked wonderful. But the building was three hundred years old, and we had already seen a half-dozen preposterously bogus renovations. Had they passed the inspection? If so, we must be safe. But if not ...

Moreover, a few decades before, the Ville de Paris had dug a new tunnel for the RER subway line directly beneath our foundation. Roberta hastily made contact with an engineering company called AFITest and enticed its weighers and measurers to rue St.-Séverin with plumbob, stethoscope, astrolabe and ouija board to determine whether our yearned-for quarters would withstand the rumbling of the trains, the onset of the monsoon season and/or another eruption by Vesuvius.

Meanwhile, Junko left on a long trip to Japan. Simultaneously, I was abandoned by Mme. de Gaillande, who was going on vacation, and by the owner, M. Lafitte (we knew his name by now), who was nowhere to be found (except by Mme. de Gaillande). I didn't even have Roberta, who was shuttling somewhere among Paris, Luberon and Glendale, California. I alone was fixed and steady, at home, with a French mortgage application, incomprehensible French letters from two mildly adversarial *notaires*, a building engineer named Hoang, several bankers at Citibank Paris and a copy of Larousse.

I started to sweat after our (sort of) final offer had been languishing unanswered for almost ten days. At first, the only issue seemed to be the "real" price of the apartment versus the price M. Lafitte and his *notaire* disclosed to the Trésor Public. Traditionally, the amount paid for a Paris apartment (the real price) is ten to twenty percent higher than the amount submitted for perusal by the tax authorities (the stated price). In the first several exchanges, we had dickered the real price down slightly while fattening the under-the-table bonanza for M. Lafitte. Since the buyer pays the full freight in any case, I ceded this part of the negotiation entirely to Roberta and Mme. de Gaillande. Roberta, who didn't want us to run afoul of the taxman, strove to keep the stated price as close as possible to the real price. This was good strategy, I thought.

Until I hypothesized Hal and Mitzi.

Through the end of June and into the first week of July, Junko and I had nursed the delusion that we were the only bidders for our sun-splashed hypotenuse on rue St.-Séverin. But as our fantasy crept toward reality, as the mortgage evolved into a genuine possibility, as the difference in offers boiled down to barely a fistful of *sous*, as our hopes soared, I decided there must be a hitch. Someone else. Turds in the punchbowl. Fifth columnists. Counterbidders.

These opponents began to assume shape, identity and a fearsome avarice. Likely, they were foreigners like us because M. Lafitte preferred foreigners. Americans probably. Worse: Republicans!

Suddenly, looming before my mind's eye, like Godzilla from the sea, there they were.

Harold and Mitzi Ninneman of Willoughby, Ohio.

Classmates at Ohio State, where Hal had been a scrappy but undersized reserve tackle on the Buckeye football team, they had met in a required freshman French class. Hal had gone on to graduation and a successful insurance career, with Mitzi serving loyally as his crackerjack receptionist and office manager, all the while raising their children: Connie, Hal, Jr. and Moira. Meanwhile, an incurable romantic, Mitzi had diligently persisted in her French studies. She took night courses at the community college in Kirtland, subscribed to *Paris Match*, talked Moira into becoming an exchange student and joined a little French conversation club in Willoughby.

Their fourth trip to Paris was in June 1995. This was just after Hal had semi-retired and turned the reins of the Ninneman Agency over to Hal, Jr. One morning, Mitzi was slogging through a day-old copy of *Le Figaro* over croissants and *café crème* on the storied *terrasse* of La Rotonde.

Legend has it that the shift from the Rotonde to the Dôme occurred one day when the manager of the Rotonde refused to serve a young woman who was sitting at this café terrasse *without a hat (gasp!) and smoking a cigarette. When she walked defiantly across the boulevard, the Dôme manager tipped the tide of history with his leniency. Whether the story is true or not, many patrons of the 1920s, including Malcolm Cowley [32] and Peggy Guggenheim, record that they and their friends denounced the intolerance of the Rotonde and quarreled with the owner. On Bastille Day 1923, Luis Aragon, Lawrence Vail and Malcolm Cowley were sitting at the Dôme discussing the rudeness of the owner of the Rotonde and the possibility that he was a police informer who had betrayed several anarchists. They crossed the street and made loud demands; finally, Cowley took a swing at the patron, catching him in the jaw—a blow that ensured Cowley's immortality in the history of Dada. But the incident got him arrested in the street later, after they had fled the Rotonde. Friends insisted that he was not in the café, which gave him time to catch his ship home.*—Noel Riley Fitch, *Literary Cafés of Paris*, 1989

Hal Ninneman might have been hoping for ham and eggs, or recalling his days of gridiron glory as fullback for the Fighting Wallabies of Willoughby High, but Mitzi had insisted on the "classic Parisian breakfast" before tuning out her spouse and immersing herself in *Le Figaro* and straining her eyes over minuscule items in the classified section.

"This might sound silly, Hal," she probably said.

"What?"

"Well, just for fun, why don't we answer one of these ads for an apartment in Paris?"

"An apartment in Paris? What the hell, Mitz?"

"Well, Hal, my goodness, haven't you always said the only investment worth a tinker's dam is real estate?"

"Real estate in *Ohio*, hon. Not France! Jesus Christ in a fruit jar, Mitz! France?"

"Well, I'm not saying we should *buy* anything, Hal. I just thought it might be fun to take a peek. Maybe just one listing. For fun."

"Don't be a goddamn fool, Mitz."

"It was just an idea, Hal."

"A damn fool idea. Forget it."

"Well, then ..." Mitzi shrugs. "... It's off to that exhibition of thirteenth-century Parisian door knockers at the Musée Carnavalet."

"Door knockers?"

"Oh yes, hon. You wouldn't believe how many different—"

"Er, wait a minute, Mitzi."

Maybe they were noncommittal, even playful, at first. But they climbed the stairs. They looked at the apartment. Mitzi gushed. Hal grunted. And they went back down the stairs. A week passed without a word. Mme. de Gaillande wrote off Hal and Mitzi Ninneman as mere realty voyeurs.

But back in Willoughby, Mitzi kept chipping away at Hal. That pretty loft in the Latin Quarter would be perfect for Moira while she finishes her postgraduate thesis on medieval French pottery. Wouldn't it also, Mitzi asked, be a wonderful vacation spot for Connie and Ray and the grandkids? Even Hal, Jr. chimed into the conversation, mentioning that, with the French real estate market in a slump, this was the sort of investment that could amortize itself in jig time. And so, by and by, Mitzi minced over to the phone, spread her *Petit*

Robert on the kitchen counter and put in a call to that nice, tall Madame de Gaillande.

I could almost hear her, the acquisitive bitch, Speaking French in that tinny Ohio accent but—let's face it—better French than mine.

How could Junko and I hope to compete against the Ninnemans? Hal was the insurance baron of northeastern Ohio. He could literally dole out cash in carpetbags and, without batting an eye, slip M. Lafitte an extra quarter-mil above the stated price. And who were we? A cute Japanese reporter and her husband, the ne'er-do-well literary poseur.

I despaired. We were losing our garret in Paris. I tried to call Roberta to see if she could suss out the latest sally by the dread Ninnemans, to see if we could inch up our offer just a few thousand francs, to see if we could convince Mme. de Gaillande that even if the stinking Republican interlopers from darkest Ohio were richer than we were, we deserved Paris more than they did.

Who did these Buckeye bastards think they were? They'd only read one ad. They were doing this "for fun." Amateurs! They had only climbed one staircase.

The staircase! That was it—our last hope. Hal had played some football when he was young. But those days were forty years of ribeye steak, sixers of Schlitz and deep-dish apple pie ago. Old Hal had filled out a mite. His knees were scarred and wobbly. His wind was gone and his blood pressure in the danger zone. A staircase like this one could land him in a plot at Père-Lachaise [33] before Christmas, leaving Mitzi to enjoy *our* Paris loft all by her lonesome, maybe entertaining the occasional slick boulevardier with champagne and candlelight in the bedroom loggia.

Jezebel!

Maybe if I could get Hal's phone number from Mme. de Gaillande, I could tear the scales from his eyes. Why, after all, did Mitzi persevere with all these French magazines and conversation classes? Why did she hum the theme from *A Man and a Woman* every time she got tipsy and amorous? And what was so bad about Willoughby, anyhow? What was she trying to get away from? *Who* was she trying to get away from?

But I couldn't reach Mme. de Gaillande. Roberta was missing in action.

The Ninnemans haunted my lonely vigil. I pictured them hitting the Ohio lottery for $10 million, after which they put in a call to Paris. Flush with windfall, they tell Mme. de Gaillande, "Cost is no object. Double the price! Triple it! What the hell? We're rich, rich! *Rich!*"

I despaired. We had lost our loft. I didn't tell Junko. It would have broken her heart. However, I started composing a fax to Roberta, telling her we had no hope. We would have to start all over. We would make reservations for a return to Paris in the fall. Roberta would have to draw up a new list of cellars and hovels to inspect. More stairs. More pee-stained corridors. More catastrophic plumbing ...

Damn those Ninnemans.

But, maybe this defeat wasn't as bad as it seemed, I consoled myself. Paris wasn't so hot. Paris can be a real dump. Right?

It is not a figure of speech, it is a mere statement of fact to say that a French cook will spit in the soup—that is, if he is not going to drink it himself. He is an artist, but his art is not cleanliness. To a certain extent he is even dirty because he is an artist, for food, to look smart, needs dirty treatment. When a steak, for example, is brought for the head cook's inspection, he does not handle it with a fork. He picks it up in his fingers and slaps it down, runs his thumb around the dish and licks it to taste the gravy, runs it round and licks it again, then steps back and contemplates the piece of meat like an artist judging a picture, then presses it lovingly into place with his fat, pink fingers, every one of which he has licked a hundred times that morning. When he is satisfied, he takes a cloth and wipes his fingerprints from the dish, and hands it to the waiter. And the waiter, of course, dips his fingers into the gravy—his nasty, greasy fingers which he is forever running through his brilliantined hair. Whenever one pays more than, say, ten francs for a dish of meat in Paris, one may be certain that it has been fingered in this manner. In very cheap restaurants it is different; there, the same trouble is not taken over the food, and it is just forked out of the pan and flung onto a plate, without handling. Roughly speaking, the more one pays for food, the more sweat and spittle one is obliged to eat with it.—George Orwell, *Down and Out in Paris and London*, 1933

Syphilitics, madmen, kings, puppets, ventriloquists,
What can you matter to Paris the whore,
Your souls or your bodies, your poisons or your rags?
She'll shake you off, you pox-rotten snarlers! ...
When your feet, Paris, danced so hard in anger!
When you had so many knife wounds.
—Arthur Rimbaud, *L'Orgie Parisienne*, 1871

Desolate in California, haunted by the specter of Hal and Mitzi Ninnemans' unbridled avarice, I cultivated a protective contempt for Paris and sneered at the imminence of Bastille Day.

The ensuing shock, triggered by a phone call from Paris, was almost hallucinogenic.

Fax, Benjie to Roberta, 13 July '95: "According to Mme. de Gaillande on the phone today: 'Zee flat eez yours!' She promised a fax thereafter and it has arrived—not only in French, but in French cursive, which is harder for me than Cyrillic! However, I'm struggling to translate the details. Your copy follows."

Junko was still in Japan. I called her in the seaside village of Chigasaki, where resided her parents, and told her that our offer, incredibly, had been accepted. I didn't mention the buttinsky Ninnemans. If I can't shield my true love from people like that, well, what's a husband for?

Junko and I were, in principle at least, French property owners. We exulted briefly and unsatisfactorily across the Pacific. Junko's father was so juiced at the news that he immediately transferred another packet of yen to our new bank account in Paris. The thrill, of course, was transitory. We still had lots more temperamental bears to cross.

If you go down in the woods today, you're sure of a big surprise.
If you go down in the woods today, you'd better go in disguise,
For every bear that ever there was
Will gather there for certain because
Today's the day the teddy bears have their picnic.
—Jimmy Kennedy, "Teddy Bears' Picnic," 1932

Fax, Benjie to Roberta, 26 July '95: "While you proceed to get the engineer's report, we will complete the mortgage forms and send them tomorrow to Ms. Pauchet at Abbey National. In doing so, we will provide all the information we have regarding the property, the owner and the owner's *notaire*. Please fax us, ASAP, the name of our *notaire*, so we can add that to the info. I'll tell Ms. Pauchet that we are seeking both a *promesse* and/or sales agreement but must await the engineer's pleasure and the assurance that our deposit is returnable, in case the mortgage is somehow (unlikely!) unattainable.

"I'll also tell Ms. Pauchet that copies of all agreements stabilizing the deal—from us, from the owner, from the broker, from you, from the *notaires*, from lawyers, from Judge Crater [34] and Ambrose Bierce—will be forwarded to her, to show that we're dealing with a real apartment and not a frigging cabin in the sky. In return, I'll ask that she strive to forge an Abbey National Agreement in Principle, promising to lend us money so that all and sundry parties can rest a little easier as August slowly grinds France to a sweaty halt."

In summer there are several days when the sun sits in the center of the Arc de Triomphe on the Étoile, if you look from the place de la Concorde. The gardens of the Tuileries are the most beautiful in Paris because they are part of the ensemble, and anyone who stands and looks at the red sun pouring onto the stone of the Arc on the Étoile also becomes part of the ensemble, as in front of "Aristotle Contemplating the Bust of Homer" you "contemplate" Rembrandt and feel alive.—Nina Berberova, *The Italics Are Mine*, 1992

After two hot months of filling out mortgage forms, *réléves du bancaires* (whatever they are), and French letters I could barely decipher, I had to go back to Paris in September by myself to meet the woman in charge of our Parisian bank account, make a down payment to M. Lafitte via his *notaire*, Maitre Jacheet, confirm my mortgage with Abbey National and meet for the first time with the *notaire* Roberta had found for us, a formidable cupcake named Nicole Pedinielli.

In France, full-blooded lawyers are too exalted to soil their hands with mere property deals. Such duties fall to notary publics, whose aegis dwarfs that of their U.S. counterparts. In France, *notaires* like Maitre Pedinielli handle virtually all routine legal matters not subject to courtroom litigation. The typical office of a Paris *notaire* is a whirlpool of arcane activity, hip-deep in the intricacies of Gallic property laws and sticky with the medieval muck of primogeniture. In the midst of this, when first I met her, Maitre Pedinielli was tousled but unsoiled and unflappable. She slipped sinuously between several rowers of paper to her chair, brushed a black tress away from her eye and sat, regarding Roberta and me with a suggestion of omniscience, pity and haste.

She had all the paperwork from Maitre Jacheet, more or less in order. Compliant with French law, M. Lafitte had bared his entire life in a veritable tome of private disclosures, all meant to demonstrate that he was the true owner of the joint and that no mortgage mill, loan shark or lien-holding ambulance chaser secretly held equal dibs on our dream home.

As Roberta had warned, Maitre Pedinielli proceeded to explain French inheritance, a legacy of agrarian monarchy that situated men above women, children above moms, sons above daughters and firstborn sons above subsequent sons, thereby shipping second (and third) wives up shit creek without means of propulsion while the Catholic church lurked constantly in the background ready to snatch up the whole enchilada and hand it over to Claude Frollo if anyone in the extended family made a false move.

Unfortunately, we needed this disquisition because I am, to my personal mortification, a twice-divorced, thrice-married foreigner with two sons by two marriages and a daughter in-between. I was The Thing That Came from Probate Court. Maitre Pedinielli asked pointedly what were we going to do about this?—well, yes, pointedly, but with an air of ironic bemusement that veritably vibrated with sex.

I loved her. She was better than Marie-Odile Pauchet. I was ready to do whatever Maitre (which means "master") Pedinielli told me and follow her home.

Gringoire, a practical philosopher familiar with the streets of Paris, had observed that nothing is more conducive to reverie than following a pretty woman without knowing where she was going.

There is in this voluntary abdication of free will, in this submission of one's fantasy to another's, a mixture of fantastic independence and blind obedience, a certain intermediate between slavery and freedom.—Victor Hugo, *Notre Dame de Paris*, 1831

"The solution," I said to Maitre Pedinielli, "is easy. Put the entire property, every beam and carpet tack, in Junko's name. Write me out. That way, it doesn't matter who dies first."

Maitre Pedinielli smiled. "This is all right with you?" she asked.

"I'm a slave to women," I confessed.

"Get that in writing," she said.

"Along with everything else," I said.

"*Bien sur*," she said. And crossed her legs. And reached for a cigarette.

Whereas the women of other nations are strictly national, as a general rule preferring the men of their own country to all others, the Frenchwoman alone is universal. She has no preferences in her unique passion. She has neither preference nor prejudice. She is not in love with Frenchmen. She is merely in love with love. And under this softy dominance she changes visibly. The very inflections in her voice echo her secret. Her eyes grow eloquent with hidden speech. At the dimpling corners of her mouth there plays a mutinous, a secret smile.—George Slocombe, *The Heart of France: Parisian, Provincial & Peasant*, 1934

Letter, Benjie to M. Lafitte, 22 September '95: "Comme convenu, je vous confirme bien volontiers vouloir substituer dans le bénéfice de la promesse vente que vous m'avez consentie suivant act reçu par Me. François JACHEET, notaire a SAINT ARNOULT EN YVELINES le Septembre 1995, mon épouse,

Madame Junko YOSHIDA, sous les charges et conditions de ladite promesse."

Fax, Benjie to Roberta, 22 September '95: "We've had no response from Abbey National. I have no idea what their usual pace is ... one nagging item in the back of my mind. If memory serves, *notaire* Pedinielli was sending a copy of the *promesse* to Abbey National ... Am I right about this, or was I supposed to send the *promesse* to Abbey? ...

"Junko makes a good point on the issue of repairs ... She assumes that these will be complete before we close ...

"• the leak in the roof

"• water hookups for the washing machine and dishwasher

"• shower hardware in the bathroom

"• a cover over the electrical box ...

"I've reached a lawyer named (no kidding) Jesse Jack, who is—as we speak (I hope)—drafting a letter for Me. Pedinielli waiving my claim to community property on the Paris apartment. As soon as I have it in hand."

When Junko and I reviewed the legal document placing the apartment on rue St.-Séverin totally in Junko's hands, we noticed a mistake. The address was listed as located both on rue St.-Séverin and rue Xavier Privas.

"Xavier Privas? Who the hell is Xavier Privas?"

Xavier Privas quite evidently was a man's name, and it is not the custom to name Paris streets for men until after they are dead. Usually, unless the street's namesake is a saint, the honor is bestowed because the party in question had distinguished himself on one of the sciences or arts or had served France in some important civil or military capacity. So, when I noticed the two new and strange street signs on the short southern stretch of the tiny cross street, I asked my old friends and new acquaintances who Xavier Privas was, and what he had done to deserve a memorial in our quarter. Nobody could answer me, or had thought much about the subject.

St.-Cricq, the shoemaker at No. 9 [rue de la Huchette], had the idea that Xavier Privas had been a poet, and not a particularly good one. The Satyr, a professional cook, was of the opinion that Privas had been a composer of music. I consulted Anatole, the clerk in the large bookstore on the quai, who knew the names and works of nearly all the French poets. He had never heard of Xavier Privas, and could find no record of his writings. There were two fairly well-stocked music stores between the place St.-Michel and the rue du Petit Pont, one of them situated on the corner of the rue Xavier Privas. None of the clerks could find on the shelves any published music attributed to Xavier Privas, or give me any information about him.—Elliot Paul, *Springtime in Paris*, 1949

Having never heard Xavier Privas' name mentioned by either Roberta, Mme. de Gaillande or Maitre Pedinielli, Junko and I went to Jesse Jack and berated him for tossing a superfluous street name into my disclaimer of proprietorship. We didn't learn 'til later that our building formed a sort of coiled snake lurking behind the numerous addresses on rue St.-Séverin. Its little head poked out onto rue St.-Séverin at the doorway of No. 16. Its body was unseen from the street. But the tip of its tail eventually emerged onto rue Xavier Privas by way of the entrance to a couscous bistro. Our top-floor nook made no contact with rue Xavier Privas, but our building, in the strictest legal sense, had a sliver of frontage there that merited passing mention in our legal documents.

Then I encountered an oddity. Checking my favorite local map, which is printed on the flyleaves of Elliot Paul's two charming books about our neighborhood, I noted that rue Xavier Privas had a different name on each flyleaf. Before

World War II, in *The Last Time I Saw Paris*, it was called rue Zacharie, which—it turned out—was not its real name, either.

It was around Saint-Séverin, rebuilt since 1230, that the activity of the left bank was most intense. The names of the streets speak for themselves: Rue de la Parcheminerie (parchment-makers), with its public scribes, copyists and parchment-vendors; Rue des Enlumineurs (illuminators), now Rue Boutebrie; the Rues de la Huchette-d'Or (Golden Bin), de la Bucherie (woodmen), and des Sacs a Lie (lee sacks, i.e., winelees for treating skins), which has since become the rue Zacharie.—Robert Laffont, *The Illustrated History of Paris and the Parisians,* 1958

Fine. We knew that rue Sacs a Lie had morphed into rue Zacharie (much the way rue St.-André des Arcs had become rue St.-André des Arts), after which it was recruited as the most modest possible memorial to somebody named Xavier Privas. But this tidbit of etymology did not solve the prevailing mystery: Who the hell was Xavier Privas?

"Taravel, Antoine-Paul, called Xavier Privas," Mainguet began.

"It takes our visitors to get to the bottom of things Paris," said Noel.

Mainguet continued. "Born at Lyon in 1863. Died 1927. He was a graduate of the Lycée St.-Chamás, a bachelor of science. Xavier Privas organized the entertainments known as 'Evenings of the Pen,' later the Soirées Procope, apparently at the Black Cat, was featured at the Cabaret des Quat'z'Arts ..."

Therese began to laugh. "Not even a war hero," she said.

"A hero of the night," said the American delegate.

"Xavier Privas was a founder of the Cabaret des Arts, then of the Noctambules," Mainguet continued.

"Now we're getting somewhere," said Mme. Swallowtail. "The Noctambules is not far from here."

According to L'Humanité's files, Privas had for a collaborator in 1903 Madame Francine Lorie, who became his wife in 1913.

"High time," remarked the Satyr.

Privas' inspiration, as set forth in his obituary notice, was "idealistic, charitable, patriotic and sentimental." Among his best known songs were: Les Thurifieres, Song of the Hours, Human Songs, Songs Lived, Sentimental Songs, Children's Songs, Sweet Songs, dating from 1897 through the volume called "French Songs" published in 1919.—Elliot Paul, *Springtime in Paris*, 1949

Xavier Privas, whose light burned brightly before the First World War, was forgotten almost within his lifetime. This seems a sort of fateful destiny because he was a party animal, not a statesman, philosopher or divine. His immortalization on a scrawny Left Bank street infested with couscous panders probably came about in a fit of nostalgia by a fellow roué who, in his dotage, had wormed his way into Paris' city government. Privas was a man, indeed, best remembered by gourmands, night owls and sentimentalists.

I remember the tender reverence with which I heard Xavier Privas, the Roi des Chansonniers, a beautiful old man with a white spade beard, intone, at the tiny Théatre des Noctambules, in the Quarter:

"Pour qui sait aimer, les heures son roses."—A.J. Liebling, *Between Meals: An Appetite for Paris*, 1959

As events turned out, the inclusion or absence of rue Xavier Privas from the eventual document assigning ownership of the Paris loft to Junko was insignificant, just as the street itself—

except perhaps for budget tourists with debased palates—is one of Paris' least relevant passages.

"Let's search the Left Bank," I proposed to a friend. "Let's try to find a bad meal."

We succeeded. It was an Algerian restaurant on the rue Xavier Privas, because we wanted couscous, that North African specialty of grains and vegetables and spices and various meats. But we cheated. It was a restaurant aimed like a missile at tourists, with a barker outside; and even here the food was merely mediocre, perhaps even interesting, *which is not a word of great commendation for food. One can eat poorly only with the greatest difficulty in the myriad small restaurants of the Rive Gauche.*—Herbert Gold, *On the Left Bank*

By the end of September, Junko and I in California had filed most of our papers and gotten our mortgage. M. Hoang, the house inspector, had given the joint a clean bill of health and sent us an invoice big enough to underwrite a family meal at La Tour d'Argent. We had a banker, to nurse our money, on rue de Beaubourg. We started figuring out when we might go back to France, meet the mythic M. Lafitte and close on our apartment in Paris.

Our apartment in Paris.

We proposed late October. Roberta said that might be okay. We sent word to Maitre Pedinielli and Mme. de Gaillande that we'd be there, with pencils sharp and lead ready to lick, before Halloween.

The worst was over. Sure ...

One glory of the narrow Rue Champollion in which, some forty years ago, flourished so many waitress-brasseries, is the Cabaret des Noctambules, as who should say, "the Nightbirds." It is installed since 1904, in one of the very dens—artistically adapted and considerably enlarged, where daughters of Eve used formerly to serve beer and liqueurs—*for preference the latter, more profitable for the retailer.*

M. Martial Boyer guides the fortunes of this amusing cabaret-theater of which the patrons—select, like the refreshments—applaud the gaiety and pungent sallies of the Chat-Noir, now back on the Left bank.—Jean Émile-Bayard, *The Latin Quarter Past and Present*, 1921

RuE du Petit Musc
June 27, 2015

6

The Strawberries of November

The last time I see Paris will be on the day I die. The city was inexhaustible, and so is its memory. I can stand in a dazzling sunshine and experience an eclipse all my own, with Paris in dim blue lights and shrieking sirens between me and the sun and the landscape. I can recall the first moment I realized there was moonlight on the dingy old Gare St.-Lazare and the surrounding streets and buildings.

—Elliot Paul, *The Last Time I Saw Paris,* 1942

Cocooned in ignorance, buoyed by optimism, Junko and I flew to Paris at the end of October. We had set a date for closing the deal on our apartment and had faxed Roberta accordingly. We strode the labyrinth of Aeroport Charles de Gaulle at the head of a veritable convoy of metaphorical ducks, all waddling behind us in an obedient V-formation. We had concluded our negotiations with Abbey National, we had forked over the francs for our *frais d'acte, frais de dossier* and *frais du prêt*—why are French realtors so obsessed with strawberries?—and we had our *assurance des emprunteurs* firmly in hand. We had received an imprimatur from the engineer and paid him exorbitantly. We had delicately spliced relations between Citibank U.S. and Citibank France—who normally hate to admit they have anything to do with each other—so as to place all the necessary simoleons expected by numerous parties at our very fingertips at an instant's notice. We carried several copies of the legal papers waiving my share of the quarry and assigning it entirely to Junko's tender mercies. Through Roberta, repeatedly, we had issued fair warning—to Mme. de Gaillande, M. Lafitte, Maitre Jacheet and Maitre Pedinielli, Mme. Masselot (Marie-Odile's successor) of Abbey National and the whole Parisian shootin' match—that we were hell-bent for La Belle France and loaded for bear.

Fax, Benjie to Roberta, 11 October '95: "I've figured out most of the mortgage language now, except for the impenetrable legalese, which nobody ever figures out. Our official receipt date on the *offre de prêt* is 4 October, which makes Junko's signing date 15 October. We'll have the response on route to Abbey National promptly on Monday the 16th, with a check ... We don't have our French Citibank checkbook yet. I suspect it's been sent to rue St.-Séverin. But we will draw a franc cashier's check here to cover the *frais du prêt*. No problem. We have found the error in Junko's insurance form and revised it.

"I have yet to fax Mme. Masselot to inform her of these matters but I will today. I'll also fax Mme. de la Salle at Citibank to rattle her cage about the wandering checkbook—which we'll need for the closing! Right?

"We have reservations to fly to Paris 27 Oct., arriving 28 Oct., hoping to be able to occupy the apartment soon thereafter. But I'll be making a reservation at the Hotel de Nice just in case. Our departure is Sunday, 5 November, which gives us a week for maneuvering the closing."

As we blithely commuted from CDG to the Hotel de Nice, above a biker bar on the rue de Rivoli, there was much that Junko and I didn't know, hadn't anticipated and saw but through a glass, darkly.

Some rules had gone unexplained, like French arrival regulations. Everyone, of course, knows that in France a dinner date for eight o'clock is not an eight o'clock rendezvous. If you arrive "on time," you have trashed every tenet of civilized social intercourse. Your host and hostess are still in the shower or rummaging through the socks drawer, feeding *les enfants* or dallying with the upstairs maid—and the calf's brains have barely begun to marinate in the Côte de Nuits. You are not guest, but intruder. What Junko and I didn't know was that the one- to two-hour delay customarily assigned to dinner dates also applies to real estate closings, except that it's a week—at least.

Plus, there was All Saints' Day. In America, All Saints' is the day after Halloween. It's indigestion for kids, it's soap on the bay window, it's the fence gate hanging from the weather vane. It's anticlimax. At its very best, it's a day off school for kids in Catholic schools. In France, still Catholic after all these revolutions, it's damn near Christmas. Who knew?

Every nation on earth has its irrational periods of mass human dispersal when, suddenly, perhaps prompted by a dormant gene that has passed into the higher primates by some Pleistocene congress with a giant saber-toothed lemming, everyone in the country just up and splits. They react to an urge to go someplace, anyplace, all on the same day, in such flaming haste that steam irons are left steaming, and no one is sure whether the garage is locked. In America, the foremost of these exodi are Labor Day, Thanksgiving and the Fourth of July. The Japanese equivalents are Golden Week, *Obon* and *O-Shogatsu*.

In France, to our dismay, one of the days when no one's home and they're not expected back until it's too late for you, dummy, is *le jour de la Toussaint*. We flew into Paris on the All Saints long weekend. The city's aspect was vaguely reminiscent of a scene in *The Omega Man* [35]. M. Lafitte had dematerialized into the vast, verdant, anonymous *terroir*. Mme. de Gaillande was little more than a lanky rumor. Roberta was present, but she looked incongruously surprised to see us, and excuse her, she had a Halloween party to hostess. Maitre Pedinielli was just leaving. Everyone we could find, acquaintances and strangers alike, shared a universal, slightly indignant sentiment:

"What the hell are *you* doing here?"

Dulled by jet lag, however, we took this setback with uncharacteristic aplomb. We inhaled damp autumn air spiced with the aroma of chestnuts roasting on an oil drum. We swilled some wine, fell asleep to the roar of motorcycles and bided our time.

Paris is always beautiful, even in the months when we forsake it. To make this discovery, we have to come back in October, when river and stone are steeped in the splendor of the early autumn sun.

A storm had swept over the city that morning, and large drops of warm rain had washed the gray quays. The trees bending towards the Seine were laden with drops from the purple sky, and the dark ivy carpeting the base of Notre-Dame gleamed as if it had been newly polished.

I went right along the old quays, purposely walking slowly so as to savor the purity of the rain-washed air and the mixed smells of vegetation and tar. This corner of Paris should be the preserve of painters and poets, for this is where the city's essence can best be understood.—Yvonne de Bremond d'Ars, *In the Heart of Paris: The Fabulous Adventures of an Antique Dealer*, 1959

Benjie's Diary, 31 October '95, quai de Montebello: "We're out by Shakespeare & Co., Junko painting a portrait of Notre Dame. I just did a little book shopping and found several small treasures—including the original paperback cover of *The Catcher in the Rye*, marked up from 50¢ to 25f—on the rickety bookrack outside the entrance. I've been inside George Whitman's dusty lair a few times, but I'm disinclined to browse among tourists who normally avoid bookstores and libraries that are not featured in the travel guides found on spinning racks in airport departure concourses. Besides, the dog-eared, marked up and neglected paperbacks outdoors here are the cluttered, non-Dewey Decimal essence of bookselling. In one book, I found a note scribbled God knows how long ago, in red ink, a terse mysterious catalog that reads, 'Pricilla' (underlined), 'Global—Predidactic' (or something like that), 'Tracy' (underlined) and on the other side 'Vascular dementia' (circled!). I could build a whole novel from this list of cryptic clues.

"Our first word off the plane from San Francisco was Roberta with the news that Me. Jacheet (the comic *notaire*) had failed to obtain from the French government something called an *état hypothéquer*, which is the Gallic version of a title search. This misstep was later amended by Me. Jacheet's clerk, Fifi, who said she had the e.h., but with strings attached because M. Lafitte, our *vendeur*, is subject to a blizzard of liens imposed by a former *acheteur* who never received the property he thought he was buying. However, it turns out that our particular apartment is lien-free. This has been attested by a reputable *avocat*, leaving the *état hypothéquer* more or less free and unencumbered—in a French sort of way—as soon as the e.h. traverses its way from the suburbs to Paris and lands in the clutches of Me. Pedinielli (the good *notaire*). All this comes down to: Today's the day after our scheduled signing, but we haven't signed and we have no date to sign because Me.

Pedinielli ain't doing squat 'til she has an *état hypothéquer* in her hot Sicilian hands, and the loan company ain't movin' no gelt less'n they get the word from Me. Pedinielli and, besides, the elusive *vendeur*, M. Lafitte, is on vacation this week (despite our request two weeks ago for a 30 October closing) because this is a vacation week, and you take a vacation on a vacation week, even if your eager *acheteurs* ain't got no idea it's a vacation week.

"So?

"So, there's hope for a signing this week if—

"a) the e.h. lands on Me. Pedinielli's desk, and

"b) she likes it, and

"c) she calls the loan company with a signing date, and

"d) the loan company agrees to release the loan to our bank before the signing, and

"e) since I'm here by myself this week and Junko's in frigging Finland covering telecommunications for *Electronic Engineering Times*, Me. Pedinielli draws up a *procuration* substituting either Roberta or me as Junko's proxy, and

"f) Me. Jacheet and M. Lafitte accept the *procuration* (which they likely will), and

"g) M. Lafitte decides to return to Paris from his *chateau*, and

"h) Me. Jacheet yanks his head out of his ass and shows up at the signing with all the necessary papers, and

"i) some fresh unforeseen hang-up doesn't toss the whole show into a cocked beret.

"And if it does?"

Élan vital, *is it life? No. Life is calm, vast, simple. It is the desire to live in haste, in pursuit; it is the impatience to possess all of life right away, right here. Paris is full of this desire; that is why it is so close to death.*—Rainer Maria Rilke

Ignorance is a dull, two-edged sword. On one edge, we didn't know the normal rules of engagement for real estate deals in Paris. On the other, most of the time, we didn't understand what everybody was talking about. People kept telling us that this meeting or that paperwork was inconceivable within the preposterous timetable we had created by arriving months—*months!*—too soon to receive the sacrament. The oft-uttered word, "Impossible!" we grasped. Most every other utterance flew right past us, faster than tossed *porte-jarretelle* at the Crazy Horse. We responded by cheerily saying, "Well, we're here. Let's go ahead and see what *is* possible."

By and by, the various Frenchfolk conceded that they had to do *something*, if only to get rid of us. Besides, we were the ones distributing francs. Even in France, money has certain lubricative powers. Events speeded up, gradually.

A scholar, one of those rare and tireless souls whose lives are a constant reproach to ambition, has observed of the differences between France and America that whereas the Americans are prodigally spendthrift with materials, discarding recklessly all that is old and worn, the French are equally wasteful of time. They are indifferent to haste. They are uneconomical of labor.

—George Slocombe, *The Heart of France: Parisian, Provincial & Peasant*, 1934

Benjie's Diary, 31 October '95, Paris: "Good news from Roberta. Me. Pedinielli has agreed to see us twice. Our first date is to set up substitution procedures for the signing ... The next time, allegedly, is the actual signing, on Tuesday, 7 Nov. at 2 p.m. Roberta actually got Me. Pedinielli flustered. Apparently,

Pedinielli received the dread *état hypothéquer* and found it acceptable. But then, horrors, she had misplaced her copy of Abbey National's *offre de prét*, an unnerving experience because Me. Pedinielli is a woman who never misplaces anything. During this crisis, Roberta called. Me. Pedinielli could only gibber on the phone until, at the point of panic, to the rescue came her trusty fax machine, Trigger, who started spitting out a new copy of the *offre*, forwarded from Mme. Masselot ... In a trice, Pedinielli had swabbed her fevered brow and determined the crucial dates.

"As it appears to have turned out, our arrival in Paris, followed by Roberta's barrage of phone calls, served to catalyze all the many parties to this *projét* to motivate themselves. Had we not shown up, demanding to know where's our contract and how soon we can move in, they would have all gladly temporized until the first of the year."

To err is human. To loaf is Parisian.—Victor Hugo

We had dates but also the better part of two weeks to kill in Paris (hardly a hardship), which we did by presuming eminent domain in our as-yet unpurchased garret, picking up an *E. coli* infection at a careless lunch, shopping, lounging in cafés, flaneuring hither and yon, and keeping an eye peeled.

People-watching from a café is the national pastime in France as is baseball in the United States. The field for this sport is important: one must choose the ground carefully, seeking comfortable surroundings near a busy street or intersection, just the right amount of sun, and enough loose change for at least one coffee. The best players choose a good sight-line both to pedestrians and to their fellow players. The object of the game is to identify passersby, by nationality and profession. Americans were once the easiest to recognize because of their broad stride and innocent faces. Professional people-watchers can quickly surmise life stories. There is only one rule in this game: never be caught staring.—Noel Riley Fitch, *The Literary Cafés of Paris*, 1989

Benjie's Diary, 31 October '95, Paris: "On the Île de la Cité, we stopped at a tourist trap for soup and *croque monsieur*, which was pleasant and sleepy until the four harridans from Illinois roosted directly in front of us. Without warning, they spent five deafening minutes gathering and comparing their French small change, counting the alien coins and bitching about how many were needed to negotiate the acquisition of two Sprites, a Coke and a glass of orange juice. Typical remark: 'Boy, if you're thirsty, France is the worst place to go!' ... After the two Sprites, the Coke and the o.j. arrived, a cry went up that the waiter had tried to pad the price of the orange juice from 19f to 23f. The waiter, of course, thrives on stiffing bloated church ladies from the Midwest at eighty cents per swindle. Fortunately, it turned out that Heartland Harpie #3 had mistaken the price of a Coke for the price of an o.j. So, the foursome retreated from scratching out eyes of the avaricious *serveur.* At which point we had enjoyed enough proximity to the Moose Lodge Ladies Auxiliary and took flight."

After a weekend in the cozy but noisy Hotel de Nice, overlooking the lively *terrasse* of the Low Rider Café, we boldly invaded our incipient quarter above rue St.-Séverin. No one objected. No one dared. There were no other *acheteur*s on the hook—my Ninnemans had dispersed into a cloud of neurotic fantasy—and we had to be indulged. Our first days at rue St.-Séverin were bleak. The place was barren and chilly. Still, the taps ran, the toilet flushed and—when we figured out how to turn it on—the heater worked splendidly until the moment it went on strike without a gaseous syllable of explanation. Actually, the abrupt and mysterious absence of warmth wasn't our big worry. This was only autumn, after all. Far more fretful was the prospect of making a phone call, in broken French, to the heating company to explain, in broken French, that our *chaudier* was pfft, the gas wouldn't flow and the pilot wouldn't ignite. What was French for "pilot light"? *"Le pilote de la lumière?"* Was it a "light" at all?

We advised Roberta of the *chaudier* dilemma and, meanwhile, began our quest for enough bedding to survive a week or so of brisk nights in a cold-water flat. Thus began what we came to regard as our "Samaritaine Period."

***La Samaritaine** (grand magasin), between rue de Rivoli and the x, rue de l'Arbre-Sec, rue du Pont-Neuf, and rue Boucher.* ***Frantz Jourdain**, 1906.* ***Frantz Jourdain and Henri Sauvage**, 1928 and 1930.*

La Samaritaine (the good samaritan) was the name of the water-supply pump erected at the Pont Neuf in 1605, one of the city's earliest public utilities. Ernest Cognacq [36] borrowed the name in founding his shop at the corner of rue de la Monnaie and the rue du Pont-Neuf in 1869.—Norval White, *The Guide to the Architecture of Paris*, 1991

I've decided that one of the sure measures of greatness in a city is its department stores—not just their existence but their variety, size, centrality and demeanor. Consider Los Angeles, a city absent a grand throbbing department store at its center, a city that farms its prestigious shopping out to a veritable suburb. And even in that adjunct enclave, Beverly Hills, this commerce is dispersed haphazardly among a string of rhinestone storefronts on Rodeo Drive, none with altitude sufficient for an escalator. Even J.C. Penney's has escalators, for Pete's sake.

If rail lines are the blood vessels of a classic city, its department stores are its heart, pumping the nutrition of staple goods and household necessities to those denizens who would rather die than move beyond the Périphérique. Hardcore urbanites gladly pay for their Milk Duds and diamond tiaras the premium exacted from a captive audience. The alternative is to buy a car and billet outside the city walls, where brigands and Visigoths prowl the hedgerows, where strip malls kill the joy of shopping, and farmers in pickups outnumber Bickles in taxis. A department store identifies a city as a city, as a bastion against frontier barbarity, as an oasis of law and growth and gentility. When I was a boy, growing up in western Wisconsin, I distinguished my town, which called itself a city, from real cities by its absence of a department store. In Tomah, we had the Cash Store, a sort of overgrown trading post. In La Crosse, forty-two miles west and ineffably larger, there was a Sears Roebuck, a Montgomery Ward and a native emporium called Doerflinger's. Each was a department store, with escalators. Each was layered floor by floor, with the myriad dry goods that bespoke sophistication, modernity and the faint hope of human evolution. Doerflinger's even had revolving doors. Here, truly, was a city.

In a way, the French have taste the way other people have gods or despots. The fact of an unauthorized, official good taste reassures them. They would be anxious without it, because their articles of taste are like articles of faith—not meant for improvisation but firm and aggressive, like good haircuts or well-cut suits or the right flowers on the table. They are a kind of controlling principle in most Frenchmen's lives, emblems of Frenchness that unite and identify a people.—Jane Kramer, *Prisoners of Taste*, 1989

Department stores bring more to a city, of course, than stability and legitimacy. They are style. The boutiques and opulent shopping streets, Bond Street, the Ginza, Michigan Avenue, the rue du Faubourg St.-Honoré, bestow prestige on the city and draw the dropjaws and out-of-town spendthrifts. But Tiffany, Armani and Kenzo are, after all, just chain stores. Department stores are singular and particular to the city. They carry the same brands as the boutiques but all in one place and mixed with store brands selected by buyers and managers who share some abstruse and indefinable unity of taste. City dwellers emerge from their department stores with a sartorial panache unique to the city, sometimes even to that particular store. Doesn't a Macy's patron look subtly different, although you can't put your finger on it, from a Bloomingdale's loyalist?

Surely, we know a great city by its great stores and a great store by its birthplace, regardless of any subsequent branching out into satellite cities and suburban malls.

New York is Macy's and Bloomie's. Chicago is Sears, Marshall Field's, Carson Pirie & Scott. San Francisco is Nordstrom. Moscow is GUM. London: Harrods and Marks & Spencer. Tokyo is the world capital of department stores: Mitsukoshi, Matsuya, Takashimaya, Matsuzakaya, Seibu, Isetan ...

And Paris. For the profligate, there is Galeries Lafayette, for the encyclopedic, the Bazar de l'Hôtel de Ville (BHV), for the fashionable, Printemps and Le Bon Marché. And for the masses, the hulking three-store maze of Samaritaine sprawling between the rue de Rivoli and the Seine. Oak floors. Wrought-iron banisters, steel gingerbread.

Cognac hired Jourdain in 1883, but site assembly and clearance delayed construction of the vastly expanded store across the street (between rue de l'Arbre-Sec and rue de la Monnaie) until 1900, then built only in increments, culminating in 1906. This was a loveliness in steel—hard, crisp and ornamented with tile—which you still find on the side streets (rue de l'Arbre-Sec, rue Baillet, and rue de la Monnaie). Unfortunately, La Samaritaine was such a resounding success—commerce consummated by and within the architecture of Jourdain—that Cognac sought bigger and better facilities. The result was the demolition and surelevation *of the Seine end of Jourdain's greatest work; Henri Sauvage, younger at the time (1928), became his partner. The result is an architectural historian's special example of Art Deco—but a disaster for lovers of steel and glass.*—Norval White, *The Guide to the Architecture of Paris,* 1991

Junko and I chose Samaritaine practically. It was walkable from rue St.-Séverin, walkable, that is, with bulky packages—notwithstanding the inevitable aching arms and collisions with inattentive tourists. The alternative venues were worse. Galeries Lafayette, Printemps, even the Habitat housewares cornucopia at Les Halles, required Métro journeys.

We were not, however, entirely true to La Samaritaine. Although costlier, BHV was roughly equidistant and a lovely stroll past Notre Dame, across the Pont Notre Dame and through the glorious bloodsoaked plaza at the great wedding cake of Hôtel de Ville.

The avenue Victoria ends eastward in the huge place de l'Hotel de Ville, that is, the old place de Grève or Strand Square standing back from the grève *or strand of the Seine, where malcontents and disgruntled workmen would assemble. Hence the word* grève *for "strike." From 1310 until 1830, the Grève was also the site of public executions—except for those of the Revolution. Here, Montgomery [37] (the unwitting killer of his king ...) was tortured to death, not for his mischance, but as a rebel, years after the accident of the place des*

Tournelles. Here, Ravaillac [38], the assassin of King Henry IV, was broken on the wheel; here Leonora Galigai, the confidante of Marie de' Medici, was burned alive. From 27th August, 1792, the guillotine was set up here for the execution of common-law criminals. After the 9th Thermidor, political victims were also here decapitated.—Alan Houghton Brodrick, ed., *The People's France: Paris,* 1950

We found our sofa at BHV—that's another story—and some ostentatious linens. But Samaritaine was our anchor and Habitat our backup source, for the basic items of a Parisian novitiate. We spent a half-day roaming between Samaritaine's four clustered stores, finding the departments most useful to our needs—lighting, tools, draperies, cleaning supplies, bathroom fixtures, bedding, kitchenware, appliances, electronics and *bricolage*. Intricate, intimidating, irresistible, indispensable *bricolage [39]*.

Our initial purchases at Samaritaine—before even considering the intricacies of *bricolage*, the measuring of walls, the laying of wires, the drilling of holes and screwing of screws—were a pair of comforters, which we laid on the floor, one atop the other, to serve as our bed. We might have reverently regarded as momentous a bed of our own in Paris, in a place almost ours, if we had had the leisure to pause and acknowledge the moment.

For that matter, at some point, I should have carried Junko over the threshold. But after climbing five flights of stairs, one doesn't relish the prospect of lifting a woman, even a size-six petite.

Benjie's Diary, 31 October '95, Paris: "Monday, yesterday, we were tired because our second night of jet lag tends to be the most restless. Nevertheless, we moved from the Hotel de Nice to rue St.-Séverin. We had some time with Roberta, but she was frazzled by a friend about to get a divorce, about which the incipient divorcée had yet to inform the affected husband.

"Then, again, Samaritaine. We haven't had a day in Paris without hitting Samaritaine. This time, it was towel hooks and a toilet brush and—aha!—a vacuum cleaner. Philips, 690f, on sale. Cheap!

"Today, Roberta went through an amazing process, entirely by phone, of arranging our telephone service. According to her, it will be installed by Monday.

"Oh, the bed. Monday we bought a futon at Espace Loggia on blvd. St.-Germain. A sweet man, M. David., who spoke no English, who smashed a display to smithereens, who refused to sell us a slightly mildewed floor model—even at a discount—and who taught us how to write French checks, took our money and told us to come back on Friday and collect our bed."

It was a most unParisian week. In previous Paris adventures, we had always withdrawn from the day-to-day grind of our life in America. In France, we morphed into visiting royalty. In the movie, we would have been portrayed by Troy Donahue and Suzie Wong. We meandered from café to café, pondering our options for dinner, dropping in on museums and churches we encountered along the way, rankling our synapses with alternating doses of Beaujolais and caffeine. This trip, however, we became humdrum householders (William Bendix and Thelma Ritter), hurriedly applying for gas, electricity and phone, trudging twixt rue St.-Séverin and rue de Rivoli with no leisure and precious little alcohol. We panicked with every setback, terrified that our Frenchlessness would foment disaster. We were repeatedly surprised by the graciousness of each Parisian clerk and tradesman who got us through the latest anxiety.

In Paris, everybody wants to be an actor; nobody is content to be a spectator.—Jean Cocteau

Benjie's Diary, 3 November '95, rue St.-Séverin: "We got, just after noon today, a visit from a charming French *gaz*-man, who looks like Kolchin, the young sailor (played by John Phillip Law) in *The Russians Are Coming, the Russians Are Coming*. Kolchin fussed over our heater for ten minutes and got it roaring like a blast furnace. Genius. So, at long last, we're warm again and ready for the arrival of Serge, who hates the cold."

Before Serge's impending visit, we had added to our household, besides the comforters and two futon, toilet brush, towel hooks and *aspirateur*, pillows, a washing machine, a kitchen range and range hood, a refrigerator, sheets and a silent phone. Shortly, thanks to Serge, there was also a couch. But that's another story. The trek across the Pont Neuf—usually glorified by the thrill of crossing the Seine and pausing at the views upstream to Notre Dame and the Conciergerie and downstream to the Pont des Arts, Les Invalides, and the Eiffel Tower—had become a burdensome slog. We were either carrying something heavy and drearily utilitarian or remembering something we forgot to buy, goddammit! The Pont Neuf had lost its charm, a seemingly impossible feat.

Over the Seine is a stately bridge called the Pont Neuf, begun by Henry III in 1578, finished by Henry IV, his successor. It is all of hewn freestone found under the streets, but more plentiful at Montmartre, and consists of twelve arches, in the midst of which ends the point of an island, on which are built handsome artificers' houses. There is one large passage for coaches, and two for foot-passengers three or four feet higher, and of convenient breadth for eight to ten to go a-breast ... The confluence of the people and coaches passing every moment over the bridge, to a new spectator is an agreeable diversion.—John Evelyn, writing in his diary, Christmas Eve, 1643

Were we losing the romance of Paris just as we were gaining a foothold in the city of our dreams? Or was this bridge-humping tedium merely a growing pain by which we would become less *les étrangers* and a little more *les habitants*? Mind, we could never really be Parisians. We understood this.

The Pont-Neuf is famous in the folklore of Paris. The bridge was long a-building, but it has lasted long: so they say of a stout fellow,

"Il se porte comme le Pont-Neuf" *("he's in as good shape as the New Bridge," that is, of course, the oldest in the city). The ancient adage is that you can't cross the bridge without seeing a white horse, a pastry cook and a hunchback. Georges Ohnet, the novelist, who was afflicted with what is politely called a pronounced stoop, used to say: "It's very queer. I've often seen the white horse and the pastry-cook's boy, but never the hunchback."*—Alan Houghton Brodrick, ed., *The People's France: Paris*, 1950

Sometime that week, likely during a hasty lunch at one of Paris' several branches of Le Paradis du Fruit, a juice bar/restaurant—probably after bolting a tainted glass of "all-natural" mango squeezings—I picked up an intestinal infection that sent me hourly to the toilet to discharge a mixture of blood and diarrhea. This affliction made me irritable and led to a few clashes with Junko. She wanted to shop for furniture while all I wanted was to hunt for a commodious commode—a quest which, in Paris in the nineties, retained an element of safari. Indeed, most of the world's great cities make scant provision for their visitors' bowels. One learns the protocols of each city's water closets by trial, error, desperation and chutzpah. It helps in Paris to know that, either by law or tradition, no café, restaurant or bar can bar its toilets to non-patrons. Few venues in Paris post New York-style warnings that the "Toilet is for Customers' Use Only." [40] However, even if one is free to breeze unimpeded to the privy, one never knows 'til one opens the door whether it is better suited to an acrobat or an Asian peasant than to a spoiled North American conditioned to expect a three-segment facility composed of porcelain bowl, hinged seat and superfluous lid. In Paris, the facility might feature one, two, three or none of these elements, depending on the provenance of the plumbing and the sensitivity of the proprietor to the delicate foreign *tuchis*.

"But, daddy," I heard a child complain the other day, "there isn't any toilet."

"Yes, there is," the father told him. "The sign says so."

"There isn't though. There's just ... there's just ..."

"That's the toilet."—C.W. Gusewelle, *A Paris Notebook*, 1985

It is also probably in the loo of some café that the toileteer will encounter his first stoop or croucher (or as some call it, squat). This apparatus, little more than a hole in the ground with two foot rests, provides an agreeable change to the usual appointments of the Anglo-Saxon loo, and also one which men of medicine consider far more beneficial to the shape of the human race.—Jonathan Routh, *Jonathan Routh's Guide Porcelaine to the Loos of Paris*, 1966

There were moments during my *E. coli* infestation when, too pressed to be fussy, all I could do was plunge down the stairs toward the lavatory praying for the best. When the *Hommes* facility was too challenging for my purpose, I now and then found relief behind the ladies' door, which, conveniently in Paris, always shares the same foyer as the men's. Although recognizing that the most primitive sort of privy suits women—who must sit, crouch or at least "hover" regardless of the particular operation—as well as men, the more chivalrous among Parisian victualers have upgraded the female facility to provide at least the porcelain bowl if not always a seat (but rarely a lid). Once I had discovered this inequity, I regularly succumbed to my feminine side, even so far as to occasionally respond in Monty Python falsetto if an importunate woman rattled my door-latch.

The option we avoided, after one brave and nerve-wracking experiment in claustrophobia by Junko, was the newfangled unisex toilet cabins installed on main-traveled tourist sidewalks. They are clearly marked "W.C." and only cost two francs. Sleek replacements for the rickety and stinky open-air *pissoirs* that have been banished from Paris, these conveniences are reputedly as sanitary as an operating theater at the Hôpital Saint-Louis. But there is something macabre, even menacing, about these gray, windowless capsules.

My little cousins call them "toilets of death." Legend has it that a woman desperate to use a Parisian pay toilet but lacking the correct change, had dashed in after a previous patron but before the toilet had begun its automatic cleaning cycle. Inside, she was trapped and killed by the fumes.—Arwen O'Reilly, "Paris Vignettes"

Benjie's Diary, 31 August '93, square Samuel Rousseau: "Junko is making an intricate drawing of the basilica of Ste.-Clotilde. It's a splendid church, and this little park is beautiful, local and tranquil. It also features the last extant *pissoir* left in Paris. We noticed it last night on the way to our hotel from a brilliant chicken dinner at La Poule au Pot. As we passed the church on rue St.-Dominique, we saw a taxi driver jump out of his cab and run into the park, apparently to pee in the bushes. But when we passed the cab, we realized he was inside a stall. This *pissoir* should be designated as a national monument. I haven't used it yet, but I feel as though it's my duty."

During our week of waiting to close the deal, Junko and I met with Maitre Pedinielli and signed a power of attorney allowing Roberta to be Hotlips for a day. We spent an evening at our favorite bistro Chez René, with Gene Vricella, a multilingual charmer who was escorting an elderly jazz band from Michigan to Timbuktu for the U.S. State Department. By Friday morning, I was weak with *E. coli* but too busy to crawl into bed and indulge my illness. For one thing, there was no bed.

Boulevard Saint-Germain in these early hours is a majestic artery of the city. It was built with imagination when the French had a sense of grandeur, an inflated one at times, but a real one. They sensed that their citizens needed room around their shoulders when they walked, and a large horizon. The boulevard, in these hours, is an epic road. Trees, on each side, breathe easily, their leaves quivering with the breeze. They make a canopy for glory. In this magnificence I was walking in the middle of the boulevard like someone making a triumphal march.—Etel Adnan, *Paris, When It's Naked*, 1993

Benjie's Diary, 6 November '95, rue Jean de Beauvais: "Friday ... we slept as late as my tummy allowed, then went to Espace Loggia on the boulevard St.-Germain—our futon shop—to determine if they had our new futon which, lo and behold, they did. After ordering another identical futon and a frame (green) to support it, we tested the heft of our new bed and judged that, despite my weakened condition, we could carry it, rather like two native bearers toting a dead bear, the several blocks to our place. The futon was wrapped in a very heavy plastic sheath tied at both ends. The end-knots made good handles. So it was relatively light work to shlep our burden conspicuously along boulevard St.-Germain to rue St.-Jacques and then right at Oysters R Us toward rue St.-Séverin. After wrestling the thing up the steps, the hard part was wedging a double bed through a single-bed opening, up a stepladder, to the mezzanine. This was mostly a one-Benjie job of sheer brute yanking, straining and cussing. But it's there. And it's a wonderful bed. Firm as a meadow. Twice as thick as our Japan/U.S. futon and providing more comfort. Last night, my first without intestinal discomfort, was sublime. We'll look forward to returning to Paris, just to crawl back into this bed."

And then there was Serge, whose bus from Brussels tooled into Paris late on a wet and chilly Friday night.

I had known Serge Levi since the spring of 1986. He befriended me as I was climbing onto a bus in Agadir, Morocco, where I had been sent to capture, in five days, the essence of the Club Med experience. This assignment, which mostly consisted of sitting beside a swimming pool drinking cheap red wine and watching women brown their breasts, was part of my ghostwriting duties for Arthur D. Little, Inc., the consulting company for which both Margaret Orsal and I then worked. I was in mid-life then, between wives and on the verge of parting ways with my alleged "consulting" career to live in Tokyo with my own true love (Junko). Serge was a Belgian university student on spring break. He spotted me in the parking lot of the Agadir airport and attached himself to me like one of those slimy black things on Humphrey Bogart's torso. Serge saw me as his golden opportunity to practice English. We communed for five days around the pool and in the Club Med bar, drinking up our beads and cracking ruthless jokes in *anglais* about our co-*vacancistes*. I taught Serge American idioms, mostly profane, which he wrote on a scrap of paper that stayed in his wallet for a decade. After our Agadir adventure together, we were never long out of touch, especially after Serge had met Junko and—like most men who've ever been introduced—fell in love with her.

Letter, Benjie to Junko, 14 March '87, Agadir, Morocco: "Another observation about the change in Club Med [since its commando-style founding]. Daniela told me I didn't have to bring anything to wear. Shorts, t-shirts, bare feet, bathing suits. That's all. Well, not anymore. Now we have people showing off their wardrobes. Miami Vice pastels. Colored slacks. Dior pantsuits. All the stuff that rich people lug to resorts. Serge calls them snobs. He also told me that 'snob' is from the Latin *'sine nobile.'* "Without nobility." A nice word. Serge is frighteningly bright."

There are, mind you, many trains from Brussels to Paris, but Serge took the bus, fearful of bombs left on trains by the Algerian terrorists who were notably frisky in the autumn of 1995. We met him at the Low Rider Café. I hugged him violently, as is our manly custom. Junko kissed him twice and we went foraging for beer. We shouted and laughed together 'til well beyond midnight, Junko and I rejuvenating ourselves from Serge's inexhaustible vitality. Every reunion with Serge fills me with energy and bombast. I've never made a friend as spontaneously as I had with Serge, nor with deeper certainty that nothing would ever erode our bond, perhaps because each of our names evokes one of Israel's twelve tribes. Serge styles himself as an atheist, but his *joie de vivre* and optimism suggest that he is absolutely certain to be drafted into Heaven, to loll there throughout eternity in the lap of a merry, benevolent and slightly tipsy Almighty.

The next day, we all trooped to BHV, where Serge helped us buy a couch.

Benjie's Diary, 6 November '95, rue Jean de Beauvais: "The evening with Serge, at the Bière Académie on rue des Écoles, and the next two days had their tribulations, but Serge was grand consolation. His best moment was negotiating the discount on our couch at BHV Saturday morning. He charmed and cajoled a young male clerk into the standard discount and then into selling us the floor model at ten percent off. Then the Vulture struck. The clerk who had shown us that very couch on Friday swooped in and, as rudely as possible, stole the sale from our young guy just as we were about to sign. We stood helpless as an entire crew of BHV furniture department staffers sank into a state of whispering apoplexy over the predatory practices of the Vulture. Serge, bless his heart, poked into the huddle and determined that management was on Junior's side. Just like that, the Vulture was in trouble. Word was, as Serge interpreted for us, that the bitch is notorious for this sort of commission poaching.

"The offshoot was that we're taking couch delivery on Wednesday along with our appliances from Samaritaine. The joint is gonna be rockin' and rollin'."

Junko left for a business commitment in Finland that was unshakeable. She had to go. I remained in Paris, still cold—the heater had pooped out again, but M. Lafitte's *plombier* had diagnosed the problem as an ill-designed *tirage*—and forlorn. My assignment was to get to the bank and withdraw a whole mess of francs, then hustle to the closing, hand out the money and sign a stack of papers on the appropriate lines. Easy, mainly because I would have Roberta at my elbow, pointing out the little x's on the forms.

Benjie's Diary, 7 November '95, rue St.-Séverin: "Going to get my bank check today, my fly was open. No one seemed to notice before I did, but people usually pretend not to. Sandrine, the cool girl at the front desk at Citibank, told me my certified check would be ready at two.

"'Two? We close on the apartment at two!'

"Fortunately, the bald guy in the next office said (I'm

paraphrasing here), 'Eh, you don't need a goddamn certified bank check. Just a regular bank check, Sandrine. Chill, sweetie.'

"Sandrine chilled, which she does well, the check arrived and Mme. de la Salle, who was supposedly in a meeting 'til two, appeared as though by magic—somehow sensing danger to a fat transaction. The whole experience was both efficient and suspenseful. No one smiled.

"I collected my check, Junko's French ATM card and a new set of French Citibank checks."

Have you not noticed that the French don't smile, except when they know you, or wish to be charming?—Shusha Guppy, *A Girl in Paris*, 1991

I was too nervous to eat lunch. With victuals in mind, I poked into a few cafés but ended up roaming the streets off the rue du Faubourg St.-Honoré, near which our *notaire* kept her offices. It was just shy of two o'clock when I turned up rue Montalivet, alert for signs of Roberta. She was not in the street, nor in the building lobby, nor on the staircase leading up to Maitre Pedinielli's office, nor in Maitre Pedinielli's office. She was not waiting in the conference room where the principals to the transaction gathered, each of them showing me more deference than a Boys State delegation at the White House. I finally got a load of Maitre Jacheet (the comic *notaire*), who seemed less muddled than he was in my mental portrait. Mme. de Gaillande was steeped in gravity, as befits the middlewoman bent expectantly over her impending percentage. Maitre Pedinielli (the good *notaire*) bustled into the room on her lovely legs, all goodwill and fizzy efficiency.

And here, at last, was the elusive Lafitte, whose history had trickled down to us through capillaries of state-imposed confession footnoted by elliptical references from Nicole Pedinielli. Ostensibly, M. Lafitte was as rich as Croesus, the erstwhile owner of a building situated in one of Paris' most coveted blocks and the landlord of an actual *chateau*, where he kept a crew of workmen on a perpetual payroll as they methodically rebuilt the ancient pile into Lafitte's private San Simeon. And yet, extended to the last measure of his assets and constrained by the Catholic Church of France—who said, fine, you can have your cupcake and eat her, too, but you have to pay the rent and buy the board for the baguette you left behind—he was a man in many respects poorer than me. And me, I hadn't had an actual job since 1990. If he didn't get his money today, from me, for the last salable unit in his building, he was ankle-deep in doo-doo. But did M. Lafitte look worried?

Hah!

M. Lafitte could have been president of the Paris chapter of the Gig Young Club. His aspect was impeccable, in cashmere blazer, slacks, pastel shirt, silk tie and glove-leather loafers, his hair peppery-gray, his smile as genuine and opulent as the grille of a Porsche. His eyes had the soft matte glint of a retired senator poised beside your ear to whisper the right advice after a long string of bum steers. He shook my hand, handling it like the cheek of a grandchild. Here was a guy, I realized, into whom no problem sank deep or lasted long. I felt privileged to be his *acheteur*. I wondered if he had anything else to sell.

Breaking the spell cast by M. Lafitte, I looked around. We were all there.

No, not all.

Like an Eliot cat, Roberta wasn't there.

This wasn't fair. I wouldn't be in this fix, surrounded by expectant Frenchpeople, if not for Roberta. I wondered where …

You may seek him in the basement, you may look up in the air—
But I tell you once and once again, Macavity's not there!
—T.S. Eliot, *Old Possum's Book of Practical Cats,* 1939

Benjie's Diary, 6 November '95, rue Jean de Beauvais: "Pedinielli's office is close to the Élysée Palace and lots of government bureaus. Whenever a minister sits in his chair these days—with Algerian bombers running amok—the cops block the streets and brandish AK-47s. So we had to take a three-block detour, but not before Roberta forced two cops in retro-Gestapo outfits to help her find the way on a map of Paris. They even smiled. She does worm her way under your skin."

The Palais de l'Élysées, now the home of the Presidents of the Third Republic, where Félix Faure [41] died and where Poincaré [42], the Lorrainer with the shrill high voice, lived during the war, was built in 1718, and in 1753, a year before her death, it passed into possession of La Pompadour, the passionless courtesan whose domination over Louis XV lasted long after his passion for her had ceased. La Pompadour was a woman of greed and brains, sufficiently a child of the eighteenth century to favour the philosophers, generally only to be snubbed by them. Voltaire called her "La Pompadounette," Rousseau wrote to her that "a charcoal-burner's wife was more to be respected than a king's mistress."—Sidney Dark, *Paris,* 1936

Two o'clock was behind us. Maitre Pedinielli had another appointment percolating on her agenda. She speared me with her sultry gaze and asked if I was capable of proceeding with the closing in Roberta's absence. I went, sure, hey, yo, what's the big deal? *Pourquoi pas?* We all sat down around the table and got down to *punaises en laiton*. I sat in a haze of French legalese while the natives chattered knowingly. To keep up appearances, I nodded frequently and uttered *"oui"* or *"bon"* whenever the gibberish flagged and more than two people peered at me expecting affirmation. I felt like Colonel Blake of the M*A*S*H 4077th as Radar handed him a clipboard stacked with two inches of forms for him to sign.

"Radar, what the hell am I signing?"

"I don't know, sir. It's top secret."

"Well, shouldn't I read it?"

"If you did, sir, it wouldn't be secret anymore."

Then, a few ticks after the nick of time, Roberta arrived, puffing slightly from her sprint up the staircase. She had suffered—she later revealed—a classic Parisian delay. She'd consumed her lunch (I pictured a *salade Parisienne* with lots of diced ham and Emmental and that piquant house dressing almost universal among the city's cafés), drunk her espresso, laid her napkin on the table, then spent fifteen minutes trying to flag down her artfully dodging waiter and snag *l'addition*. I thought, Wow, if even twenty-five years in Paris and French fluency can't qualify Roberta for a quick waiter when she needs to hit the street, what hope for a hayseed from Wisconsin?

But let him get the idea that you desire his presence in order to pay him, and he will resort to any device to evade the issue. Wave your money in his face as he passes, and he will "toot-sweet" you and promptly forget his promise. Try to catch his eye from a distance, and he will pretend to look elsewhere. There is only one way to bring him to his knees. Get up as though you were going to leave without paying. Then he will dart from his hiding and, model of smiling courtesy, will add up your amount, give you your change, thank you for the tip and bid you au revoir *as if there had been no unpleasantness.*—Robert Forrest Wilson, *Paris on Parade*, 1925

"Roberta," I whispered, "maybe we should think twice about—"

"Sh. This is important."

"Okay, Radar."

Once Roberta had ruined the suspense of the closing ceremonies by arriving, the sale was quicker than a driver's license renewal. When it was over, Maitre Jacheet looked put out, probably pondering his drive back to the 'burbs. Mme. de Gaillande had the look of a well-nourished ostrich. Maitre Pedinielli seemed taken fleetingly by post-partum euphoria. M. Lafitte was, of course, elegantly inscrutable. Roberta and I tucked away our precious paperwork and headed for a celebratory tea at Ladurée.

Junko hadn't missed much.

Benjie's Diary, 7 November '95, rue St.-Séverin: "When Roberta, the repository of Junko's power of attorney, arrived, the *fait* was *accompli*. We all initialed and signed. I gave a check to Pedinielli, who went away and brought back a check for M. Lafitte. We all shook hands. We all split. *Finis.*

"Junko and I are Parisians, of a sort. Or will be ... by the time we're dead."

A Parisian may be born elsewhere, but he dies in Paris. To live in this city, in a voluntary exile, dulcet and compensatory; to live here and die here—there is no other hallmark for the Parisian. He may have been born a provincial, like Balzac; or a foreigner, like Heine: both of whom achieved celebrity as Parisians. But the deliberate act of selection remains for his epitaph. He cannot, your Parisian, by predestination, kick his heels in any other city, however attractive. His fate leads him by land or water to his town between four hills, as it led a Roman Emperor, and after him Napoleon; as it led Dante, and after him all poets. The curious spell of the city is powerful to the grave, as the starving man knows whose weary feet tread its stones, and the beggars sleeping under its bridges.—George Slocombe, *The Heart of France: Parisian, Provincial & Peasant*, 1934

Although the Tuesday of the closing was the day before we left Paris, I had lots of work to do, all of it on Wednesday, all of it simultaneously.

Benjie's Diary, 8 November '95, Hyatt Regency Hotel, Aeroport Charles de Gaulle: "A stirring morning ... I dragged myself up at eight, hoping that the promised morning deliveries might actually begin early. Everything came together. Before nine, the guys from Samaritaine were heaving into sight on the landing, towing the kitchen range. They were a silent pair but strong and professional. They seemed blithely unfazed by the staircase, although the fridge did cause one of them to puff lightly and mop his brow once, delicately. Just as they were finishing up, carrying the range hood, turning off the electric juice and connecting the range to its special socket, M. Lafitte, cheerful and debonair, arrived with the electrician—a jolly guy in his own right—who set eagerly to the installation of the *lave-linge*, He whistled while he worked. It turns out that the washer, like the stove, requires a special supersocket, which we already had, on the right side of the sink. So, the electrician merrily drilled holes to accommodate the wire. While he was down there, he connected all the pipes. While the electrician was humming 'neath the sink, the BHV crew showed up with our new couch about 9:30. Another easy lift for the *livraison* guys. Paris deliverymen are hardier than most ... gorillas ... weightlifters ...

"Before ten, Roberta had joined the party, and then, at 10:15, things hotted up further with the appearance of M. Ganier, the *plombier célèbre*. Well, if not *célèbre*, then *gentil*. A swell guy. He immediately joined with the electrician—actually a jack of all trades—to start work on the new vent in the *chaudier* closet door. This involved a jigsaw and a lot of noise. With everybody gathered and Roberta bending M. Lafitte's ear, I took the opportunity to hit the street—just to pick up a *Herald*, a couple of *pains au chocolat* and a cup of McDonald's coffee. Before eleven, the washer was completely hooked up, the stove in working order, the fridge and couch in place. M. Gagnier had installed our new shower, and the electrician—a workman to shatter the stereotype of the indolent French laborer—was vacuuming the floor. Of course, this was after finishing the vent in the *chaudier* closet. M. Gagnier gave me lessons in the economical use of the *chauffage*, with Roberta doing her usual translation—which is to say, hardly any.

"In two hours, the place had graduated from a campsite to a livable domicile. It was almost miraculous. I was really sorry Junko wasn't there to witness the transformation. But in a way, this is her penance. She's the one who barged into the joint before anything was ready, when we could have been staying in a nice warm hotel.

"Besides (yeah, I know), if we hadn't been there, using it prematurely, we would not have discovered the one crucial flaw—the *tirage* in the *chaudier*! So, next time Junko comes home to Paris, home in Paris will be ready for Junko."

Evidently, the whole outfit had been bought, as a unit, in some second-rate department store like Samaritaine.—Elliot Paul, *Springtime in Paris*, 1949

Arts
La Crêperie
Rue St. André des Arts
Sept. 7, 2015

7
Ikea and Pa Yoshida

Probably one of the dullest stretches of prose in any man's library is the article on Paris in the Encyclopedia Britannica. Yet when we heard the news of the liberation, being unable to think of anything else to do, we sat down and read it straight through from beginning to end. "Paris," we began, "capital of France and of the department of Seine, situated on the Ile de la Cité, the Ile St.-Louis, and the Ile Louviers, in the Seine, as well as both banks of the Seine, 233 miles from its mouth and 285 miles S.S.E. of London (by rail and steamer via Dover and Calais)." The words seemed like the beginning of a great poem. A feeling of simple awe overtook us as we slowly turned the page and settled down to a study of the city's weather graph and the view of the Seine looking east from Notre-Dame. "The rainfall is rather evenly distributed," continued the encyclopaedist. Evenly distributed, we thought to ourselves, like the tears of those who love Paris.—E.B. White, *Liberation of Paris,* 1944

So...

...we had this ridiculous mortgage on a place where we couldn't live, in a city twelve hours from where we earned our daily bread. In a practical sense, by any measure, it was a valuable stake—a sunny pleasure dome in a high-rent neighborhood in a glamorous foreign capital. On the other hand, it was vulnerable to the forces of nature, the possible depredations of second-story men and the abuse of transient *locataires*. Its only guardian was a peripatetic American widow with a penchant for real estate and too many books in her parlor. Worst of all, our apartment in Paris was empty, except for an already battle-scarred BHV couch, a couple of futon and a kitchenful of white goods from Samaritaine. It needed chairs and a table, at least. Culinary tools. A toilet paper dispenser. Some cushions. Towels already. A closet! A sconce for that light bulb in the kitchen.

Lights!

The place had no lights, except for a pathetic kitchen fixture and one lamp bought at Samaritaine so we could read at bedtime. Otherwise, at night, our *pied-à-terre* was a mineshaft with exposed beams.

(Yeah, big deal. Show me a mineshaft that doesn't have exposed beams.)

So

our next ordeal was furnishing Paris. Now, some people get a thrill at the prospect of interior decoration. They salivate over fabric swatches, fondle antique doorknobs and prowl flea markets like weasels in a prairie dog town. Not us. We wanted nice stuff, sure, but as little as possible. Our first seven years together had been spent in a forty-three square meter "mansion" in Tokyo. By Japanese standards, our apartment in Ebisu had been a spacious expanse. In America, it was akin to a linen closet. Our confinement in Tokyo, however, taught me to treasure openness, airiness. Space. In our Tokyo days, Junko and I would occasionally visit a major hotel just to stand in the lobby and spread our arms wide, giddy with the thrill of not scraping our knuckles on the walls. We resolved, in all our post-Ebisu dwellings, to minimize furniture, eschew clutter and populate our indoors with mostly books and music. This was our blueprint for Paris. Enacting it required another trip back to France, in winter, without Junko because, after all, she had a job. It meant Serge and Roberta, in a rented van, driving out to the Ikea store at Parc des Expositions, Paris' mecca of cheapo furniture.

It was a grey time, midwinter, and Paris is a grey city, the fortress color of metal and stone; a hard place that goes soft in a certain light. The light shifts, and with it the ambience. The sun may break through for no reason from a slit of unexpected heaven, a passing cloud will turn the gun-metal grey to pearl. A sense of elation might lie at the end of an obscure cul-de-sac, or, exploring a new quarter, my heart could shrink at the sudden onset of dark ...

Paris will show herself when she chooses. There is a dark curtain one afternoon or evening; the curtain becomes a veil, the veil is drawn for an instant (a bearded man lifts his hat to a homely woman on the omnibus—why?) when the dark comes down. Or the grey sky will close in, with clouds low enough to touch, then lift lightly as a pigeon wings its way across the Seine.—William Wiser, *Disappearances,* 1980

Languishing in Paris without my own true love could have been dreary save that Serge joined me within twenty-four hours. Time with Serge is an endless conversation. It passes quickly and volubly with violent leaps from snickering absurdity to resolute theology. Serge is the difference between European education—in which the habit of discourse and the art of debate are ingrained for life—and American education—which is mostly football and Bud Light. I go to Europe for many reasons, but one of its irresistible attractions is the renewal of my lifelong argument with Serge.

Besides talking, we had work to do. First, we had to pick

up this van from a rental garage on rue du Faubourg St.-Antoine, the "wrong" (eastern) end of the bustling and more fashionable rue de Rivoli. Guidebooks either disregard the rue du Faubourg St.-Antoine or subtly discourage the tourists from venturing there, especially after dark. It is an avenue not so much perilous as merely drab. For centuries, it has remained the closest residential suburb (now, of course, absorbed into the city proper) to the place de la Bastille, a place of riotous assembly and occasional warfare. This eastern tentacle is an enclave of the proletariat, the province during the Revolution of the sansculottes who reduced the Bastille to rubble. It harbors the furniture, carpentry and joining trades in a concentration of men with splinters in their fingers and chips on their shoulders, a volatile neighborhood where politics is colored slightly red—this hue derived as much from anger as from socialism.

The insurrection is very fierce in the rue Mouffetard and the Faubourg Saint-Antoine ... they are bristling with guns and barricaded like fortresses.—Ernest Renan, writing to his mother on 24 June 1848

Prosper Mérimée (who was a member of the National Guard or Conservative Militia) went on Sunday, 24th June, together with his friend Léon de Laborde, strolling down to the place de la Bastille, where they saw General Negrier shot dead and the head of his "Government" troops while entering the square. The rue Saint-Antoine was a battlefield. Crushed glass covered the streetway, all the shop-windows were staved in ...

Perhaps the most eminent victim of the "June days" was Mgr. Affre, the Archbishop of Paris. He was a man of powerful physique, and fine, imposing presence. The barricade barring the entrance to the Faubourg Saint-Antoine reached up to the second storey of the house we can still see jutting out between the street and the entrance to the rue de Charenton. The Archbishop was skirting the house to meet the insurgents and endeavor to prepare a mediation and thus to avoid the bombardment threatened by General Cavaignac. Just as he reached the barricade he was struck by a stray bullet, which seems, however, undoubtedly to have been fired by one of Cavaignac's men.—Alan Houghton Brodrick, ed., *The People's France: Paris,* 1950

The Métro got Serge and me safely to the place de la Bastille. No stray bullets stayed us from the grubby parking garage, where we muddled through the paperwork that granted us the use of a battered white van for the day. Suffering from jet lag, a temporary bout of double vision (relict of my onset, long since in remission, of myasthenia gravis), and a creeping terror of Parisian traffic, I turned the wheel over to Serge and refused to touch it all day.

Luckily, weaving our way west to Roberta, we didn't have to dodge any of the pigs that once lent a unique flavor to the streets east of the place de la Bastille on the rue du Faubourg St.-Antoine.

Until the 12th century, pigs were allowed to wander about at will in the streets of Paris, but during the reign of Louis the Fat, otherwise known as the "Wideawake" or the "Bruiser," the King's son was killed because one of the pigs had run under his steed's legs. Thereupon the monarch ordered all Parisians keep their pigs in styes. Excepted from this order were only the pigs belonging to the Royal Abbey of St. Anthony. The privileged swine could rout about all over the place, and wax fat among the offal denied to the porkers of the citizens. Much anti-clerical feeling was created by this invidious distinction between lay and ecclesiastical pigs.—Alan Houghton Brodrick, ed., *The People's France: Paris,* 1950

Roberta has spent the most active and formative quarter-century of her life dwelling in the heart of Paris, a city regarded even by many natives as the world capital of epicurean indolence. Roberta's American can-do style, however, has never been corrupted by the Parisian spirit of *demain*. Roberta gets up, goes out, finds it and does it. Mind, not all of Roberta's works in progress get finished as promptly as they are begun, especially if they require the services of a French workman. But Roberta always has several projects underway, with several more in the hopper. She's perpetually eager for a fresh challenge, always game for the next expedition, always ready to drop her knitting and motor out to Ikea—one of her shrines—to hunt cheap furniture and buy a new lamp. In France, one never has enough lamps. Lamps die like mayflies. The City of Light is a graveyard of dead bulbs, sparking sockets and blue smoke curling up from fuse boxes.

Roberta was ready when Serge and I heaved to on rue des Bourdonnais. Serge and Roberta, separated by two generations, regarded each other curiously and continued to do so forever after. Serge, with a mixture of affection and censure, sees Roberta as quintessentially American, pragmatic, impulsive and naturally amusing. Roberta's impression of Serge focused on his subtle air of intellectual superiority. This effect was muted somewhat by his charm but counterbalanced and aggravated by the resentful inferiority complex common to all Belgians the moment they cross the frontier into France. At heart, each Belgian is a put-upon Poirot, wearily reminding everyone he meets that, no, he's not French, dammit! Belgian!

Roberta and Serge spent the day studying each other clinically.

The English are boastful drunkards. The French are proud, soft, effeminate, the Germans aggressive and bad-tempered, the Normans vain and pompous, the Poitevins treacherous, the Burgundians brutal and stupid, the Bretons light and inconsistent, the Sicilians tyrants, the Lombards greedy and wicked, the Romans seditious.—Jacques de Vitry, *Historia Occidentalis,* 1596

Meanwhile, there were roads to negotiate, which Serge did admirably. We had Ikea to explore, where Roberta led the platoon. Ikea is a sort of particle-board Guggenheim. One works one's way upward in an elbowed spiral through several floors of indoor furnishings, most items simple, blond, solid, functional, Swedish and thankfully inexpensive. Each turning introduces a new variation on household goods—bedding, kitchen, office, lighting, *salle de bains*, etc. In each venue, one examines variations on the theme and collects chits bearing stock numbers. At the end, one follows posted arrows down to the warehouse where, after the cashier, a stockpicker piles one's new possessions onto a tumbril. Since, with the help of a catalog, Junko had specified virtually every item on our Ikea itinerary, I barreled through this ordeal, and a sea of weekend shoppers, in ninety minutes. In our gallop through Ikea, in one bold sweep, we had equipped our rue St.-Séverin hideout with all its fundamentals. We bought a table and chairs, floor lamps and end tables, bar stools and kitchen implements, cups, glasses, dishes and silverware, pots and pans, sheets and blankets. Serge and I probably would have broken an hour, left to our own devices, but Roberta was looking to buy a new lamp for her apartment ... and she was dispensing advice.

Roberta, for instance, had heard that the hot dogs at the Ikea snack bar, near the exit, were legendary. We tested the proposition. These cylindrical delectables might have been credible, indeed, if they had been christened something other than "hot dog," perhaps *"la tubesteacke royale"* or simply *"le chien chaud."* As this lunch fare was placed before us, however, we learned that the French have an idea about hot dogs.

This idea diverges dramatically from the original concept insofar as, once the French have honored the obligation that the thing ought to contain a) bread and b) osterized beef lips, surrealism—a Parisian innovation—applies. We three worked our way through three *tubesteackes royale* garnished with substances that bore a suspicious resemblance to aerosol Velveeta and Kraft Thousand Island salad dressing. Serge and I muttered faint praise like "Mm," and "Interesting," and "Well, ain't this somethin'?" after which we bolted our Cokes and hustled gaseously out into the February gloom to load the van.

In Paris, you can buy beer at McDonald's. Also, you know what they call a Quarter Pounder with Cheese in Paris? ... They call it a Royale with Cheese.—Vincent (John Travolta), in *Pulp Fiction*, 1994

The flavors of *le chien chaud avec la sauce des milles iles du Kraft* rebounded insistently on Serge and me throughout the drive back to Paris to drop off Roberta, deliver our cargo to rue St.-Séverin and even as we returned the van to its stall on rue du Faubourg St.-Antoine where, still, alas, no pigs roamed and no riots erupted. We spent our evening assembling chairs, testing light bulbs and then, to at least sublimate that stubborn Thousand Island upwelling, venturing out for victuals. The following morning, we argued over coffee, during which Serge thumbnailed his latest squeeze, a single mom named Pina, in whose eyes the light of marriage burned hot and steady. Having recently entered his third decade, Serge was feeling intimations of his mortality. He expressed the thought that, well, maybe he should make an honest gal of Pina and a solid citizen of himself. I said, "Well, okay, Serge. How bad do you love her, and how serious are you about attending parent-teacher conferences for the next twelve years to alibi the genetic, intellectual and temperamental deficiencies of another man's offspring?"

Serge went back to Brussels that evening. He broke up with Pina before the week was out. The timing notwithstanding, I demur credit for the rupture. It would have happened by and by. Serge is Seinfeldianly fussy about women. Junko and I, despite a checkered record of romantic and marital impulsiveness, are even more finicky about Serge's women. Under our gimlet scrutiny, they tumble like tenpins. Our objection, I guess, is that they're all, well, Belgian. Junko and I both want for our beloved son Serge the Parisian cupcake (*petit gâteau?*) neither of us can have for ourselves.

From the balcony of the Hotel Meurice, two men watched a young girl in a red dress ride her bicycle through the Tuileries, her blond hair flying in the breeze. "I like these pretty Parisiennes," General von Choltitz told the man beside him. "It would be a tragedy to have to kill them and destroy their city."—Larry Collins and Dominique Lapierre, *Is Paris Burning?*, 1965

Letter, from Benjie to Junko, 26 March '87: "French women ... so many of them have a particular look. They have small faces—or seem to have small faces ... these French women surround their faces with jet-black hair, shrinking them, and then they turn their eyes and mouths into little island fortresses in a pale expanse of face. The eyes are circled with an even line of black, intensely black, in stunning contrast to their skin and equally contrasted to the neon-red rosebud of lipstick below a nose that you don't notice. Now, eyeliner, mascara, bright red lip gloss—all that stuff is standard makeup procedure. But Parisian women somehow apply to it more intensity, and they create a uniquely arresting look, like Shirley MacLaine in

Irma La Douce or Édith Piaf in anything."

Of all the women in the world, the Parisian woman is the best to look at. When one knows her one discovers that she is not quite so different from other women as one would have supposed from the way that she does her hair. The discovery is something of a shock, but with it all, woman is the chief ornament of Paris as she is the chief industrial asset of France.—Sidney Dark, *Paris*, 1936

Benjie's Diary, 27 May '97, rue St.-Séverin: "On the way home from the Luxembourg [Garden], I stopped for five minutes (and was almost killed by a bus) taking photos of an arresting poster for Aubade lingerie. It was just a woman's hips and back, wearing only a taut lace thong, photographed in black and white. This poster is the sort of larger-than-life image that would stop people in their tracks in America, draw protest from militant Christians and feminist prudes and end up so defaced by graffiti artists that its casual, erotic intent would be overwhelmed by digressions. Paris is a city of *affiches*—grand, bold posters mounted on flagpoles, lining the great avenues, plastered on kiosks and soaring ten feet from pavement to roof on those beautiful onion-dome poster columns. Every trip to Paris, Junko and I find the most captivating of the latest poster cuties on the Paris scene, we name her Fifi and Junko takes my picture with her (as I pretend to read the *Herald Tribune*). [43] I was thinking that Fifi is just our little joke. But she's more. She's a synecdoche of Paris. Without its posters, its images, all larger, bolder and sexier than life—without the likes of Steinlen [44], Toulouse-Lautrec and Paul Colin [45]—this city would shrink into something more like San Francisco, picturesque but self-conscious, vibrant but orderly, sexy but embarrassed.

"Fifi eternally proclaims Paris' love affair with itself, its willingness to stand in the middle of the boulevard St.-Michel in nothing but a g-string and a smile."

Paris wears a Joseph's coat of advertising posters. She plasters

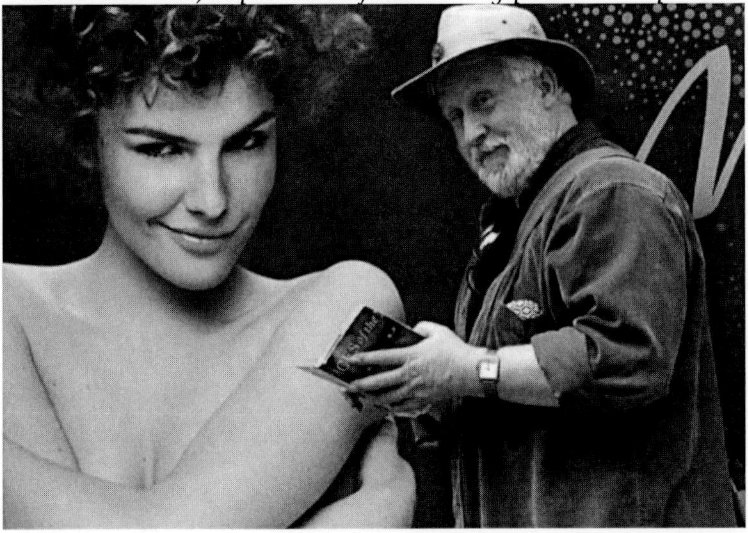

herself with posters. Posters give every artist who paints Parisian scenes the color spots that he wants. Paris covers the facades of her business buildings with huge signs and billboards, perches billboards on the edges of her roofs, turns every boarding around new construction into a billboard, uses dead walls of gardens and institutions as billboards, erects kiosks on her main thoroughfares for the display of posters, patches her post-offices inside and out with posters, lines the walls of her Métro stations with them.

—Robert Forrest Wilson, *Paris on Parade*, 1925

Serge is so picky that he harbors reservations even about *Parisian* women—who seem to him arrogant and self-congratulatory—although he enjoys window-shopping. So far, the only woman with whom he has not found fatal fault is

Junko. This dispensation doesn't solely derive from loyalty to me. Junko has powers to cloud men's minds. When first I met her, she was the dream lover of an entire fraternity of European journalists who knew her through her public relations career in Tokyo. These correspondents visited Japan regularly, partly to gather news of the Japanese consumer electronics industry but largely to hang out with Junko. From humble beginnings in Ikegami, Junko had absorbed the world like a poriferan and become the toast of three continents. She has the volubility of a UCLA cheerleader, tempered with a modest sophistication drawn from years of travel in Europe. Beyond her effervescence, her clinching charms are the almond eyes, the small lively form, the exotic allure of the Far East.

Benjie's Diary, 31 August, '93, Palais-Royal: "I just watched two Japanese tourists—girls—take each other's picture. I don't know if Junko can appreciate how attractive Japanese women are. The beautiful ones have features as simple as the face of a doll. And like a doll, they are toylike and portable. Unlike Western women, they are never 'curvy' or 'leggy' or 'zaftig' or formidable ... One only fears that they might be breakable, until one is assured that they are rather rubbery, as supple and stretchable as a bungee cord. They're beautiful, they're perfectly proportioned, they're smooth and rubbable, and they fit in your hand like a carved marble egg. And all these appealing qualities are evident by just looking at them. So, I'm glad I have one. And I'm glad she only *looks* Japanese. Junko has the mind of a Prussian general."

A month or so after I had bid adieu to Serge and Roberta and returned from the Ikea expedition, we had tenants in our barely furnished Paris apartment. A Frenchwoman in Santa Cruz, acting as our agent, had found for our first *locataires* a linguist and his fastidious wife, whom we soon took to calling Ike and Tina. Before the couple left for Paris, I talked to Ike several times, informing him that it was a new apartment (although in a *bâtiment ancien*) still only minimally equipped. As consolation, I gave Ike and Tina a generous reduction in rent. My candor, as events transpired, served mainly to alert Tina to potential discomforts, inconveniences and impositions. Through messages relayed via Roberta and by the helpful notes she left behind, Tina regaled us with our inadequacies as outfitters and landlords. We might love our place in Paris, we were informed, but the joint was hardly ready for the right sort of guests. Tina's month in Paris was a harrowing gauntlet of personal trials and minor indignities. For example, I had labored mightily to create, in our bedroom, the rudiments of a closet, by mounting a clothes bar long and sturdy enough to bear the full weight of Princess Di's spring wardrobe. Tina was unmoved by my contraption. Where, she wondered, was the chest of drawers? "You have no drawers," she wailed.

"There are no curtains," she whined.

And French washing machines? *Mon Dieu!*

Notes from Tina, 18 April '96: "Now—a few things we've discovered living here a few weeks:

"1) There is a definite problem re: The tracking of carpeting. The halls and foyer seem to retain dirt, and no amount of scraping the [illegible] seems to help. We finally resorted to removing our shoes upon entry.

"2) There is no electrical outlet in bath, so forget any notion of hair blowing or curling, etc.

[NB: Tina looked for four weeks and couldn't find the outlet in the bathroom. On our next visit to Paris, I found it immediately.]

"3) After discovering that there was only one fitted sheet and realizing we would need to use the washing machine after all, we'd like to suggest that you set the morning aside for this chore. We now appreciate the efficiency of our Maytag!

"4) We signed for the exterminator, who placed rat poison under the kitchen and bath sinks. He indicated they should be left—probably until eternity.

[NB: Itinerant "exterminators" in Paris are like Fuller Brush salesmen, hawking traps and rat poison door-to-door. Junko and I always turn them away. There are numerous problems in our loft, but rats are not among them. We're too far up for rats to climb. Even if one doughty rodent made it to *le cinquième étage*, he would have to deal with George, our *chat de gouttière*.]

"5) The bath curtain was only a temporary solution to the privacy issue ... Had I time and the proper equipment, I would have machine-sewed the hems, rather than stapling. The curtain rod holder has lost its stickiness and comes down every few days ...

[NB: The bathroom window, which fogs up within a minute of turning on the shower, faces a windowless air shaft and a picturesque but unpopulated cityscape of rooftops. There's nobody outside to look in. We removed Tina's makeshift curtain.]

"6) Our neighbors *en face* probably grew as disgusted looking at us as we did them. The 'café paper' would be much more attractive if I had calligraphy skills ...

[NB: Our *en face* neighbors across the courtyard have curtains but rarely close them, preferring to let in fresh air and catch the occasional glimpse of their neighbors (us). The male neighbor, young and fit, wanders shirtless from room to room, entertaining Junko obliviously. We haven't met him formally, so we simply call him l'Hunk.]

"7) Do not under any circumstances leave the toilet bowl cleaner standing on the sides of the bowl. When we arrived, the apartment had been cleaned and this solution left standing. We believe it etched the porcelain of the bowl."

[NB: Actually, this was a paint spill that occurred during

remodeling. Since the paint was water-based, the stain eventually eroded away.]

Our local victualers fared little better under Tina's withering scrutiny. We had mistakenly left behind a guide listing (according to the book) the better bistros of Paris. Ike and Tina trooped a few blocks to the closest one in the book—where Junko and I had never dined—and, afterward marked its entry with a critique. The comments were unsigned, but Tina's fine hand was recognizable.

Notes from Tina, 19 April '96: "Went to Allard ... the service was TERRIBLE—45 min between entree and plat. Further, the food was only so-so. For example, the frogs' legs were the worst we've had in Paris. M. Bouchard was not at all friendly and welcoming. We would urge you to save your francs."

From Benjie's "Instructions for Users: Restaurant Supplement": "Many of our favorite joints are listed in *Paris Bistros* by Robert and Barbara Hamburger, which you'll find in the bookcase ... it's a terrific book, and the choices are excellent ... Check the book, especially to note the specialty of the house. If you order the specialty, you can always expect the best food served there, plus an improvement in the quality of service." [46]

I have been in Paris for almost a week, and I have not heard anyone say calories, or cholesterol, or even arterial plaque. The French do not season their food with regret.—Mary-Lou Weisman

In the end, Ike and Tina did little harm, except for the nails they pounded into the bathroom wall to hold up the curtains that prevented prurient passengers on passing airliners from peering through the window and spying them in the nude. Our ensuing tenants were generally easier to please, among them Pa Yoshida, Junko's father—the true owner of the place—who joined us that summer after an exhausting flight from Tokyo.

Before he arrived, we worked feverishly to upgrade the premises and impress our benefactor. This work prolonged our Samaritaine Period. In three days, while both of us came down with a stomach virus that would linger for a week, we bought a stereo at Samaritaine—music, at last!—and we studied closet fixtures at BHV.

Benjie's Diary, 18 June '96, Parc Monceau: "We had lunch down the street from Samaritaine, at a brasserie near the Tour St.-Jacques, where the glacial pace of the waiter and Junko's apparent discomfort irritated me. We stayed mutually irritated all the way to St.-Michel, whereat Junko solved the crisis with the obligatory apology. She didn't really mean it, but a while later, as usual, we both meant it. Back home, there followed a brief sweaty period of screwing cleats onto beams, stringing a clothesline and hanging up wet sheets. The triumph of the day was a visit to Espace Loggia, where good old M. David remembered us and, after a call to Espace HQ, sold us a single futon for the kitchen mezzanine ... We are now equipped to sleep five. As soon as we buy more bedding—tomorrow if we're well."

By the time Pa Yoshida hit Paris, Junko and I had virtually kissed goodbye to the magical Paris that had made us desperate to own an apartment here. The cycle of bowel discomfort and endless shopping at Samaritaine and BHV, plus the pall of Tina's kvetching about bathroom curtains and bedroom bureaus, and the prospect of future tenants who might find similar fault with our charming Paris loft, had robbed us of perspective. The thrill was gone. We saw little of Paris now but our sorely laden trudge across the Pont Neuf to our neighborhood and the occasional café table where we could slump wearily, order a drop of joe and inspect the joint's W.C.

Despite a few tummy troubles of his own, as he adapted from Japanese to French cuisine, Pa Yoshida restored us. He looked around Paris with ravenous gaze.

Pa Yoshida had spent his life as a secret adventurer. His career as a chemical engineer in Tokyo, as a husband, father and tireless grandfather has been mostly SOP as old Japanese guys go. In his younger days, however, before the great Japanese tourist movement began, Pa Yoshida had the exceptional good fortune to be employed by an American company who wanted to send him on a tour of its U.S. operations. Pa Yoshida gave in to the idea without a moment's hesitation. He had no hard feelings about World War II or even the bombing of Hiroshima, which Ma Yoshida had witnessed and survived.

In America, Pa Yoshida saw Chicago and ate a steak the size of a Japanese bedroom. He gazed across Chesapeake Bay and ate softshell crabs. He spoke English (sort of) and got invited home by gracious American colleagues. He discovered Chivas Regal and saw New York. He returned to Ikegami a changed man, yearning for an entire life of such breadth and constant newness. He knew this dream was impossible for him, so—perhaps unconsciously—he plotted it for his second daughter. She became Pa Yoshida's surrogate globetrotter. Before she was twenty-two, Junko had lived in Connecticut, Germany and Italy. She spoke English like a West Hartford teenager, and after four years at one of Japan's most boring public universities, she landed a job in international p.r. that sent her gallivanting around the world, usually in the company of a hotel-collecting blowhard boss to whom she confidentially referred as The Owl. When Junko, already past the matrimony deadline for the right sort of Japanese girl, finally snagged her man, and he turned out to be a divorced American writer with no books in print and a spotty employment history, Ma Yoshida gasped and paled. But Pa Yoshida twinkled quietly. If Junko married this off-center *gaijin* rather than some corporate salaryman, the odds were good that she would not be stuck in Japan all her life. She would wander and explore. She would nourish her soul and feed her mind on the experiences her father had only, tantalizingly, tasted. So, later, when Junko and her American maniac undertook the folly of buying quarters in Paris, France, Pa Yoshida was hip to the possibilities and handy with cash. Here, at last, in the Fifth Arrondissement, was his little foothold in outer space.

And here he was, staying at the home of his daughter and son-in-law—not some economy hotel room overlooking the dumpster. Here, from this place, was a view—if you leaned a little perilously out the bedroom window—of the steeples of Notre Dame de Paris. Here he was, scanning the remarkable vistas of the Seine, reaping the reward of casting his child out into the world as far as he could fling her.

It was near dusk when we took Pa Yoshida walking. For the first time in his seventy-four years, he was loose in Europe with neither a deadline for dinner, an assigned roomie from Osaka, nor a tour guide waiting to herd him back onto the bus.

We went out for our first Parisian stroll, an indescribable experience for anyone. Wandering down to the Seine, we crossed the pont du Carrousel and found ourselves in the garden of the Kings of France. The Tuileries with a moon above. We stood there for a moment without saying a word, and then Riva burst into tears. Now, a woman's tears are as often as not a thing of mystery, but for once I understood. I felt that way myself.

"But, dear," I could only stammer foolishly, "what are you crying about? We're in Paris, dear!"

"I know," was her reply. "That's why I'm crying."

—Samuel Putnam, *Paris Was Our Mistress*, 1947

Our stroll with Pa Yoshida, over the Seine and around the Île de la Cité and then across the Pont Marie to the Île St.-Louis, was a voyage of rediscovery. Pa Yoshida walked slowly and wonderingly on stones where we had, that morning, rushed and tripped and cursed our burdens. He asked about places and events that had faded from our memory. He beheld views we had ceased to notice, much less enjoy. He reminded us why we were here.

At any season, and all year long, the view of the city from the bridges was always exquisitely pictorial. One's eyes became the eyes of a painter, because the sight itself approximated art, with the narrow, pallid facades of the buildings lining the river; with the tall tress growing down by the river's edge; with, behind them, the vast chiaroscuro of the Louvre, lightened by the luminous lemon color of the Paris sunset off toward the west; with the great square, pale stone silhouette of Notre-Dame to the east. The stance from which to see Paris was any one of its bridges at the close of the day. The Pont Neuf still looked as we had known it on the canvases of Sisley and Pissarro.—Janet Flanner, *Paris Was Yesterday: 1925–1939*, 1972

A final reminder. Whenever you are in Paris at twilight in the early summer, return to the Seine and watch the evening sky close slowly on the last strand of daylight fading quietly, like a sigh.—Kate Simon

Pa Yoshida's arrival coincided with an annual pagan rite in Paris. On the long white night of each summer solstice, Parisians throw a block party called the Fête de la Musique, an orgy of performance on every level of musical competence, from the orchestra of the Opéra de Paris to the inexplicable retiree who plays the musical saw every morning on the street corner at Sèvres–Babylone. During the Fête de la Musique, all the musicians—soloists, duos, trios, quartets, combos, bands, choruses, orchestras, brass fanfares, kazoo ensembles and unattached divas—play all at once, shoulder-to-shoulder, everywhere 'til dawn. This sprawling, ululating cacophony was Pa Yoshida's welcoming overture, and his lullaby.

Benjie's Diary, 22 June '96, rue St.-Séverin: "Our evening was a shamble along the quai with Pa Yoshida. We lapped Notre Dame, crossed from Île St.-Louis to the Left Bank on Pont de Sully, saw the La Tour d'Argent [47] and had kir on a chilly boat. Then, back to L'Ecluse, our nearby wine bar. We were the first to dine and were serenaded by the dregs of the Fête de la Musique, four loud French louts dedicated to besmirching the reputation of the Beatles, the Rolling Stones and the Who. My favorite numbers: 'Pernta Blanc,' sung to the bass line if not the tune of 'Paint It Black,' and 'Huhruh Skrrr,' the Buckwheat version of 'Helter Skelter.' We drank a nice simple red Bordeaux and ate some meat and fish with an excess of creamy sauce. But we escaped L'Ecluse for less than ninety dollars. We led Pa Yoshida to bed then through mobs who were working up to an aimless frenzy for the *fête*. We played gin and, about eleven, went out to study the mob, first pausing inside the church of St.-Séverin for some incongruously sublime organ music. Outside, it was wall-to-wall flaming youth. Bad rock bands everywhere, surrounded by swaying throngs swilling weak beer. Traffic jams and stalled buses."

All Paris is afoot. All Paris is in the streets. The murmurous Parisian night is a long hubbub of voices, and the cries of the singer and musician, of men and women, of fiddle and drum and trumpet, the splutter of the fireworks that soar in a long curve of light through the rose-colored night sky, the jests of festive revellers returning through the beribboned streets at dawn, the voice of conquest and disillusionment and hope undying, the voice of old Paris, unsilenced, unforgettable, making the night a brief historic carnival in a world without pity.—George Slocombe, *The Heart of France: Parisian, Provincial & Peasant,* 1934

By morning, serving as Pa Yoshida's guides, we saw our neighborhood clearly and happily once more, shining through its clutter of wine bottles and foraging tourists. We showed Pa Yoshida an ancient street marker etched into a building in the seventeenth century and altered in 1789 by anti-ecclesiastical revolutionaries. They had mortared over the "St.," changing our street for a while—'til Napoleon—to just the rue Séverin. We pointed out our local *clochards*, so familiar hereabouts that shopkeepers stop to philosophize in the square in front of the church with what Balzac called "these vagrants, these gypsies of Paris." Imagine New Yorkers pausing to bandy opinions with the homeless derelicts of 42nd Street.

There are various theories as to its [the word clochard*] etymology: that it comes from an argot term for "limping"; that it alludes to the bell announcing the official end of marketplace hours, when scavengers were free to collect unsold produce; that it evokes beggars who rang bells to accompany their pleas; that it summons a memory of when the post of bell ringer at various churches was given to the neediest member of the congregation. My favorite, though, is Jean-Paul Clébert's: that the* cloche *is the sky, and all* *who sleep under it are its children.*—Luc Santé, *The Other Paris*, 2015

We ran Pa Yoshida past the Roman baths on boulevard St.-Michel and sat him down for pink beer at a café *terrasse* on the boulevard St.-Germain, where the sidewalk parade mixed frazzled tourists with homeward-bound office workers and students from the Sorbonne and the Lycée Louis-le-Grand, where—among other French kids—Voltaire and Molière, Diderot, Géricault, Delacroix and Caillebotte, St. Francis de Sales, the Marquis de Sade and Jean-Paul Belmondo went to high school.

A long chain of cafés, each one with its little promontory of chairs and tables projecting into the sea of asphalt. These promontories are doubtless not exactly islands of the blessed, people though some of them may be with sirens addicted to beer, but they may help you pass a hot evening.—Henry James

Benjie's Diary, 7 November '95, rue St.-Séverin: "I finished reading Elliot Paul's *The Last Time I Saw Paris*, which chronicles the destruction of fellowship and community on the rue de la Huchette (one block away) in the buildup to World War II. Paul was despairing at the end, convinced that the magic of Paris had been lost, perhaps never to return. Of course, as shown by his postwar Paris writing, his pessimism was unnecessary. The spirit of Paris is eternally regenerative. But really, what a change in *this* neighborhood since the war. This was a rugged little working-class backwater, far from the tourist route—which stopped at Notre Dame and rarely crossed the Petit Pont. Now, this is barely a neighborhood at all. The ground floors are all tourist-trap restaurants, cheap gift shops, foreign exchange windows. Our building, I suspect, has few native Parisians in residence. We are a mix of expatriate yuppies, affluent singles, perhaps a few mistresses and probably a lot of absentee landlords renting to students, tourists or academics. A different neighborhood, but as lively, in its own way, as it was in the twenties."

Many Parisians ... have always been struggling against the essence of Paris, not realizing that what they saw as decline, as the growth of impersonality, as the increase of foreigners, as the sound of music that was not real music, was really their city's greatness, the thing that made it unique in the world.

—Richard Bernstein, *Fragile Glory: A Portrait of France and the French,* 1990

Inexplicably, having lived much of his life in the maze of Tokyo, where streets have no names and houses bear no numbers, Pa Yoshida struggled to decode the meticulously mapped streets of Paris. He walked around with a notebook, doggedly scribbling in *kanji*, recording street names in *romaji*, drawing block diagrams of intersections. Still, whenever we set him loose, he got lost for a while, turned corners at random and ended up finding his way back home by a mixture of migratory instinct, dead reckoning and drunkard's luck. Since his method was an unreliable science, we stuck close to him most of the time, lest he disappear into the labyrinth of Châtelet, never to be seen again. Fortunately, this oversight was not a twenty-four-hour responsibility. Junko's dad was accustomed to retiring early. We developed a habit of eating a light meal at dusk, then tucking Pa Yoshida into his futon and going out again for a second supper and a *pichet* of Côtes du Rhône. On the other hand, Pa Yoshida's early nights meant early mornings for all of us.

Benjie's Diary, 22 June '96, rue St.-Séverin:* "Today, we were up around eight, largely because Pa Yoshida got up at 6:30, and he was restless.

"He had set pretty hard restrictions on his sleeping arrangements. We had to close his windows, thus killing the cross-breeze downstairs. We had to hang a towel over some windows, killing the light that soft, through them yonder breaks—because it is a shibboleth of Japanese culture that people should sleep like vampires in tiny, hot, sealed, lightless, pitch-black suffocating coffin-like rooms. We humored him further by closing the upper window in the bedroom—the last breath of air. Of course, we also closed the door.

"After he was asleep and couldn't stop us, we opened our window and the door, thus preventing that buried-alive feeling so cherished among the fanged Yoshidas of Far East Transylvania. Junko is obviously the apostate daughter of the clan, sort of like that blonde among the Munsters."

Even though Pa Yoshida interrupted our cycle of shopping for domestic furnishings, we didn't entirely escape the grip of Paris' department stores. Like all Japanese travelers, Pa Yoshida was culturally obliged to go off questing for *omiyage*, beads and trinkets to hand out to everyone who didn't get to make the trip. Besides, he had his heart set on buying a sweater vest for himself. This pursuit turned out to be a test of skills I'd learned from observing Serge, on how to manipulate the territorial imperative of department store *vendeuses*.

Benjie's Diary, 22 June '96, rue St.-Séverin: "We also hit Ste.-Chapelle while we were on Cité, before heading over to Samaritaine. Pa Yoshida needed a new sweater vest. Easy to find, but he didn't like the available colors. 'Sorry,' said a fat, weasel-eyed sales clerk, 'do I look like I'm made of sweater vests?' (Well, you're stuffed with *something*, lardass.) Junko and Pa continued to ponder the colors while I slipped into the territory of a rival sales clerk. It was twelve feet away. Here, there were sweater vests in a veritable rainbow assortment. I summoned Junko and Pa Yoshida. The rival sales clerk shimmered to us in a trice. We found the perfect color. Pa tried it on. Like a glove. We bought it. The weasel, defeated, never looked at us again."

The French are tolerant to foreigners. They accept them—supreme flattery!—as similar to themselves and not merely wealthy phenomena to be flattered or exploited, or unfortunate immigrants to be exploited and despised. But they are not polite to them, any more than they are polite to each other."—George Slocombe, *The Heart of France: Parisian, Provincial & Peasant*, 1934

Pa Yoshida's Parisian interlude ended just as all our stomachs cleared up, and we could eat heartily once more. Never mind, we had a flight to catch. Junko sat beside Pa Yoshida on the eleven hours to San Francisco. But me?

A letter:

Mr. Mathieu C—

San Francisco

Dear Mr. C—:

You can probably picture my dread one morning last month as I occupied a seat on Air France flight 080 (Paris CDG to SFO) and saw, homing in ominously on the empty seat beside me, reinforced by two implacable French stewardesses, a parentless four-year-old boy, necklaced with a plastic dossier and richly laden with a bulging multihued backpack that appeared to be, at first glance, slightly smaller than Lichtenstein.

You can, I suspect, share the trepidation I felt when the boy plopped himself beside me, dismissed his escorts, said his name was something that sounded like "Gasbag" and proceeded to empty the backpack into our mutual laps, explaining what each item was and lamenting the fact that the largest—a radio-controlled four-wheel-drive miniature police car—was not fully operational due to an apparent shortage of 64-volt automotive batteries in central France. I mean, where's a Sears when you really need one?

As you probably would have done, I did my utmost to barricade my cul-de-sac window seat from the child beside me, piling up pillows and blankets and burying my face in a paperback ... then grunting reluctantly at his every explanatory utterance. However, a number of factors frustrated my intended disengagement. The first was that, this being the onset of the international family vacation madness, dozens of parents had decided to pack their children onto this particular Airbus, creating a sort of movable guerrilla bedlam that made it impossible for the flight crew to direct more than passing attention to this relatively harmless Gasbag creature. The second was that the boy—Gaspard, as it turned out—was exceedingly bright, surprisingly courteous and disarmingly charming.

Third, after five minutes of acquaintance with Gaspard, I discovered in him a character trait—deviousness—that won my loyalty. While he responded openly and agreeably to my desultory efforts to strap him in and prevent him running amok through Economy Class, he tugged cunningly at the heartstrings of each passing stewardess by playing the tragic role of the lonesome waif torn from his beloved sister and cast callously into the frightening blue yonder. When I told him to cut the act, he did so instantly, showing respect for an elder and superior cynic.

Thereafter, we calmed all crises of authority by simply invoking the slogan, "Up here, I am my own boss." Autonomy becomes Gaspard.

Another factor that lent Gaspard a somewhat exaggerated glow of maturity and self-restraint was the presence of a small and peripatetic excrescence named Jean-Carlos, a fellow four-year-old whose repeated visits to our section of the plane gave blessed relief to his parents—who had recklessly set out on an eleven-hour flight with three children under the age of five—but increased the danger of spontaneous Jean-Carlos abuse among every other adult passenger.

Jean-Carlos brought to mind vividly the feral boy in the film, The Road Warrior, *save that Jean-Carlos clearly lacked the feral boy's genteel forbearance and table manners. Jean-Carlos' territorial imperative was analogous to that of your typical foraging shrew, in that he regarded as his quarry anything within reach that was not welded to the bulkhead and ringed with razor wire. Interrupted in mid-burglary, Jean-Carlos had a tendency to clutch his booty and keen pathetically—after which, inevitably failing to elicit sympathy, he would resort to violence. Also, while Gaspard was demoralizingly (to me) bilingual, Jean-Carlos had the far more functional talent of apparently grasping no language at all. Thus, neither the French stewardesses, nor myself, nor even my multilingual Japanese wife were able to find words to convey to Jean-Carlos the simple sentiment: "Stop slugging Gaspard!"*

Eventually, Gaspard solved his Jean-Carlos problem by accepting my advice, which was, "Hit him back." Gaspard, to his credit, was bigger.

In all, Gaspard presented fewer headaches to the flight crew, and more pertinently to me, than any of the many children on flight 080. The only issues posed by your son involved a couple of near-collisions with food carts while he was sneaking up and down the aisle on his belly (in an admirable effort to elude Jean-Carlos) and the tendency of his toy police car to sound its siren for extended blasts, with no evident provocation. Otherwise, Gaspard was a gentleman whose patience and sense of humor, over a seemingly endless journey, exceeded that of most passengers ten times his age.

Three very small items of advice, however, if I may. First, I recommend, respectfully, that you teach Gaspard a slightly less limp handshake. Long ago, my grandfather enjoined me always to meet people with a firm grip and a steady gaze, on the theory that if you continue this practice throughout your life, you'll never lose hold of your self-respect and you'll retain—against all contrary indications—a certain stubborn reverence for the dignity of your fellow man.

Second, I encourage you to instill in Gaspard a greater appreciation for Greenland. From the air, the vast snowy wastes and snaking glaciers above the Arctic Circle are one of the rare thrills of the Paris-San Francisco route, especially when unobscured by darkness or clouds—as was true during our flight. Gaspard, however, was more fascinated by a video game provided by Air France. Gaspard did, however, redeem my opinion of his aesthetic sense by climbing onto my lap to gaze at the Pacific coast along Victoria Island.

Win some, lose some.

Third, although it worked on Jean-Carlos in a pinch, you might remind Gaspard that Benjamin was wrong and hitting is generally a lousy policy.

Finally, thank you. Besides being one of the most engaging seatmates in my experience, Gaspard rejuvenated my shaky belief in the heritability of civilization, even in an era when parenthood seems to be a paradox of cathode babysitting and leisure-time micro-coaching. Please tell Gaspard that Benjamin remembers him affectionately and wishes him well, forever.

Sincerely,

God would be perfectly happy in France because he would not be troubled by prayers, observances, blessings, and demands for the interpretation of difficult dietary questions. Surrounded by unbelievers, He, too, could relax toward evening, just as thousands of Parisians do at their favorite cafés. There are few things more pleasant, more civilized, than a tranquil terrasse *at dusk.*—Saul Bellow, "My Paris," 1983

RUE DE L'ÉCOLE POLYTECHNIQUE
LOTO
BAR BRASSERIE
L'X BISTROT VIN

8

"Chèque? Quel chèque?"

L*unch kills half of Paris, supper the other half.*—Montesquieu, *Variétés*

Benjie's Diary, 9 September, '93, rue des Francs Bourgeois & rue Vieille du Temple: "A Métro to Châtelet and we ducked into Chez Clovis for lunch. It was fascinating. Junko ordered the dependable old *entrecôte*, with beautiful Dauphinoise potatoes. The waiter, for some reason, pegged me as adventurous and pointed out the day's specialty. He said it was superb. Hey, I said, sure, I like that kind of stuff. He went away happy, and we proceeded to figure out what the hell I'd asked for, fearing it was probably snake entrails stuffed with locust brains. It was called *aile de raie*. We puzzled over this until Junko revealed that we actually had a food glossary in hand, in the back of our bistro guide. So I said, 'Gimme.' We quickly determined that an *aile* is a wing, so we breathed a sigh, knowing it wasn't guts but some sort of poultry. Chicken maybe? We found *raie*, and the book said, simply, 'skate.' Was this like 'punt'? No, I said, a skate is, let's see, a duck. Yeah. Like a teal. A kind of duck. Duck wings!

"We started eagerly anticipating my duck wings, while a voice in the back of my mind whispered, 'Dipshit! A skate is not a duck.'

"Oh yeah? So what is it?

"At this, until the waiter was encroaching with our plates, the voice was mute—and then, I remembered.

"'A fish!' I shouted. 'It's a fish. It's a ray! Like a Corvette.'"

The French do not let themselves be victimized into paying exorbitant prices for slices of certain fish which are shaped like steaks, when other tastier fish, shaped like fish, are available at reasonably fair prices.

—Elliot Paul, *Understanding the French,* 1955

Junko, being technically a pagan, has always been fetchingly inclined toward the occasional barbarous notion—sex on the riverbank, noshing on raw sea urchins like a sea otter or—in the case of December 1996—celebrating Saturnalia in Paris. I might have bridled at the suggestion—I might have pictured us snuggled 'neath a California tannenbaum, passing a jug of Freixenet and ripping open gaily wrapped packages—but we did have a little urgent business in France, and Junko had a handy week at the end of the year. Besides, we'd never seen Paris at the winter solstice.

See Paris in the winter when, at her sub-Arctic latitude, the sun at noon climbs no higher than halfway up the Eiffel Tower when seen from the Passy bank. It is the time of Seine floods, of rare snow that mantles the boulevards in strange beauty.—Robert Forrest Wilson, *Paris on Parade,* 1925

Paris in the winter is for connoisseurs of melancholy—lovers soon to be parted, merchants on the edge of bankruptcy, poets caught between rhymes and remittance, men caught between checks, horse owners whose steeds have come in last, playwrights who have just had a failure, women whose husbands have left them for younger, prettier, smarter, richer and all-around better *girls.*—Irwin Shaw, *Paris! Paris!*, 1976

Besides the allure of Paris in the snow, it was becoming urgent that I track down a check I'd written to Abbey National, our mortgage company. It was a big check and it had disappeared. Abbey National had never acknowledged receiving it. There had been a dramatic dip in our French bank balance but no word of a corresponding hike in Abbey National's assets. The check had been enlimboed somewhere between America and France since mid-October. No one had seen nary hide nor hair.

The check's history had begun with Pa Yoshida's visit to our garret. He was immensely pleased with Paris and disgusted with Japanese banks, who had reduced the interest rate on normal savings to negative returns. He was so deeply anxious that he might die any minute (despite admirable health) and lose his entire patrimony to the Japanese government's confiscatory death taxes that he liberated from Tokyo enough money to pay off the bulk of our Paris mortgage. Suddenly, one day in autumn, Pa Yoshida's latest bundle landed in our Paris account. My job was to move it upstate from Paris to Abbey National headquarters, a task I thought I could accomplish by writing a check on our Paris account. Two weeks before the anniversary of our closing on the apartment in Maitre Pedinielli's office, I sent the check by registered mail. Nothing came back. For a while, I wasn't worried. This was a brief while, made briefer by my already well-founded distrust of La Poste, France's devil-may-care postal service.

I enlisted Roberta. I asked her to call Abbey National. She talked to a Monsieur Bara at Abbey National. His reply: *"Chèque? Quel chèque?"*

A mysterious, disturbing response. The only proper solution was to return to France and ferret out the fate of the elusive remittance. In the meantime, I tried asking Citibank Beaubourg in Paris to stop the check. Citibank Beaubourg was spectrally silent. It was as though Citibank Beaubourg wasn't even there. Could our vanishing check be the microcosm of a greater cataclysm, the disappearance of an entire bank—lock, stock, barrel and the lovely, disdainful Sandrine? Were there sinkholes in the Marais? Had the Knights Templar asserted their eminent domain and absorbed all of Beaubourg into a sort of Masonic Vatican?

King Philippe le Bel, one of the most enigmatic and secret sovereigns who ever ruled France, had long desired to suppress the Order and confiscate its property, but before he dared to brave the Pope and take the audacious step of crushing the powerful Templars he called together at Chinon in Touraine a meeting of the States-General which, of course, voted in the King's sense. In May, 1310, fifty-four of the Templars were burned alive near the Abbey of Saint-Antoine, and on 11th March, 1314, Jacques de Molay, the Grand Master, together with the Commander of the Normandy Province of the Order, perished in flames on a little island that is now the western point of the Ile-de-la-Cité. They died protesting their innocence of "rebellion," "atheism," "high treason," "sorcery," "witchcraft" and the like, but they could not, in justice, declare themselves guiltless of their real crime. It was, indeed, a heinous one. The possession of vast riches. Legend says the men foretold that before the year was out, both the Pope, who, they thought, had abandoned them, and the King, who had ordered their execution, would appear before the Throne of God. And the two potentates did die within twelve months.—Alan Houghton Brodrick, ed., *The People's France: Paris*, 1950

Drawn by monetary mystery, we arrived in Paris the day before the dark solstice. Immediately, we ate, we drank wine copiously, we called Roberta—who was out somewhere (she is among the least housebound humans we've ever known)—and we tabled our worries. We went to see the Picasso portrait show at the Grand Palais. Certainly, finance is important, but the fugitive check had still shown no sign of appearing, and the weekend, when Paris banks reduce their functions to nothing beyond exchanging currency for foreign consumers, was upon us. The check wasn't going anywhere. Also, Serge was arriving the next morning. Besides, I had a strange case of face flu.

Benjie's Diary, 20 December '96, Sèvres–Babylone: "It started out a week ago, with a weird, itchy, swelling, pus-oozing condition that gradually engulfed the left side of my face, almost closing my eye. I compared it to an all-over cold sore, a fever blister of the kisser. However, on Monday ... Dr. Weiseman likened it to a hemorrhoid and promptly prescribed hydrocortisone cream—the moral equivalent of Preparation H. I've been smearing my face, my nose, my left ear, even my fingers with it for five days now. The doctor has no name for this affliction. He'd never seen it before and couldn't identify a cause. Luckily, his remedy was effective, although I live in fear of my virus generating a chemical antidote to Preparation H and mounting a face-devouring counterattack.

"Junko and I call it, variously, 'face flu,' 'hemorrhead,' and—because it makes my nose scaly, hard and reptilian—'gatornose.' [48] Meanwhile, the day before departure, I suffered a back spasm."

Our first morning after arrival, we avoided the quai. This was mainly to prevent Samaritaine from seeing us and sucking us in. But, like the House of Usher, it knew we had come back, and it wasn't through with us. Across the rippling Seine, it murmured to us its latest call to abominous Duty, Stern Daughter of the Voice of God. "Lights," it called out. "What about lights?"

I had postponed the job of putting up light fixtures on our last trip. Instead, we had gotten by, squinting at our kitchen range and bedtime reading beneath a few rickety lamps that Roberta had hastily installed for Ike and Tina. But procrastination was turning into crisis. Two French lamps had died on us in barely a year, and our apartment at night was starting to look like an *X-Files* episode. We needed a torch to find the toilet.

French houses, she discovered, also regarded electric light as something to be used briefly to prevent accidents and then switched off. It was not for squandering on reading in bed.—Henry Calvin, *It's Different Abroad,* 1963

My illumination schemes had always involved our beams. Our great slanted wall, our mezzanines and our ceilings were criss-crossed with dark oak beams older than the U.S. of A—gnarled, wormholed and half-petrified. No sooner had I surveyed our tracery of beams than I'd hatched the notion of attaching some sort of track lighting or spotlight system to them, running wires down to the numerous outlets the thoughtful M. Lafitte had installed along the baseboards. Alas, I'm no electrician. Terror of electrocution has haunted me ever since the day I touched the spark plug on my grandfather's lawn mower and turned my cowlick into a Jacob's ladder. I get shaky attaching speakers to my stereo set. The prospect of stripping insulation, twisting naked copper wires together, wrapping them with electrical tape and then plugging my makeshift blasting cap into *Électricité de France*, setting into motion an electromagnetic reaction that might very well reduce the Quartier Latin to a plain of ashes strewn with the corpses of children and poodles—well, this thought did not steel my DIY resolve. Still, I had to do something.

I seem to be the one person in the world thou art perpetually preaching at who or to who;

Whatever looks like fun, there are thou standing between me and it, calling yoo-hoo.

O Duty. Duty!—Ogden Nash, "Kind of an Ode to Duty," 1935

I decided to swallow my fear and face the job.

Right after breakfast.

Junko and I were still searching for an ideal breakfast place in our neighborhood. We began our experiments at the market street, rue de Buci, one of the Left Bank's liveliest crossroads.

On the Left Bank, running in a semicircle, just off the boulevard St.-Germain, is a little street called the rue de Buci, which I would recommend on a late Sunday morning. The outdoor market runs down the major part of the street, in front of the Hotel Louisane, a simple, inexpensive place where modest writers stay and during the fashion shows each year, some of the models—making the rue de Buci a good place to view striving intellectuals and young women who don't seem to have to strive at all. The market is one of the city's best, a cornerstone of fish and crustaceans, meats and fowl, game and inner organs, vegetables, fruits, wines and liquors, preserves, patés, cheeses, breads, pastries, chocolates, and other edibles for the refined Parisian palate. Many—but not all—of the French eat well, but the Parisians arguably eat better.—Richard Bernstein, *Fragile Glory: A Portrait of France and the French,* 1990

For Junko and me, finding a spot for breakfast, congenial and casual, with excellent croissants and large steaming bowls of *café crème*, was a mission from God. Our first jaunts to Paris had located us in the chic Sixteenth Arrondissement. From our borrowed flat on rue Dufrenoy, we would weave of an early morning toward place Tattegrain, an obscure junction on the avenue Victor Hugo. We sat always on the street, whatever the weather, and ordered our *deux cafés à la crème et deux croissants* (this was before my addiction to *pain au chocolat*) from the same waiter, who was only slightly more animated than a Buckingham Palace beefeater on guard. I would settle into that day's issue of the *Herald Tribune*, which I read more slowly than any other newspaper—partly because it was then the best-edited newspaper in the world, partly because it provided me in English each day's only dose of world events, and baseball [49]. Junko would read a little and then begin to sketch, fixing on a street or building in our view or caricaturing me, or—like Sem [50] or Daumier [51]—sneaking a portrait of the lady in tweed and hat with horn-rimmed glasses three tables away.

This morning ritual became for us the reality of Paris. The first whiff of *café crème,* the first bite of real croissant (not the Pillsbury facsimile sold at Dunkin Donuts) assured us that we were here, in the world of refined, indolent, elegant decadence, and we had nothing better to do than fritter an entire morning lolling in the sun in front of a red-awning temple of bourgeois sloth.

Yesterday's croissant is like an old girlfriend, not much to look at and worse to spend time with. The bloom is both fragile and brief.

The schedule of our mornings, therefore, is governed by the time at which the day's fresh croissants can be gotten warm from the baker's oven. It may be that all of Paris organizes itself around that moment, for hardly anyone goes to work before 9:30.—C.W. Gusewelle, *A Paris Notebook*, 1985

Starting out from our new apartment, it would have been nostalgic to renew this life-giving offertory at our old stand at place Tattegrain. That, however, would violate the first principle of the Parisian breakfast, which is that caffeine always precedes exertion. One must find one's first *pain* as close to home as possible, in the neighborhood, among faces, sights and sounds that populate one's quotidian routine. We needed someplace close, and rue de Buci—although a ten-minute walk—came first to mind because it was familiar and frenetic. It was, most days, where we bought groceries. And almost always, we could settle in for an hour to watch Paris' mortal parade.

Sand rose early the next morning and went out to get his breakfast. He went inland from the quai, up the rue St.-André-des-Arts, and turned off into the rue de Buci. There, from his table in a small café, he would observe the Buci market place and the faces of his new neighborhood. These were very different from the Right Bank faces, less obsequious and much less disagreeable, and there were representatives of every class on this noisy common ground. He had a comfortable feeling of being one of them, and, after his coffee, strolled up and down among the stalls.—Peter Matthiessen, *Partisans, 1955*

Given a number of choices, we breakfasted at L'Atlas, one of Buci's simplest cafés and an exemplar of *service continu*. Besides breakfast, L'Atlas served lunch and dinner, always featuring a cheap but commendable *plat du jour*. The *café crème* was adequate, the supply of croissants provided, crucially, by a *boulangerie* less than a block away. One morning, we ordered and watched as our waiter dashed off and around the corner. He returned a moment later bearing two croissants, which he then dropped onto a plate delivered to our table, still warm enough from the oven that I could tear it open and feel its breath on my face.

Benjie's Diary, 22 December '96, rue St.-Séverin: "Junko and I were having breakfast Friday at L'Atlas on rue de Buci, and I was noticing all the tacky collector cards of movie stars on the walls. I was saying, 'Ooh, Stewart Granger! ... They have Melina Mercouri! Tom Cruise! Al Pacino! Tyrone Power!'

"Junko interrupted: 'Ooh, they have Eddy Francmenu!'

"'Eddy who?'

"'Eddy Francmenu!'

"'Who the hell is Eddy Francmenu?'

"'Eighty. Franc. Menu.'

"'Oh.'"

The Left Bank is a place of lazy enjoyment and irritability; coffee, wine, garlic, bread, fruit, spices. The open-air market at rue de Buci lacks only Gene Kelly to tapdance his way past the cheeses and apples.—Herbert Gold, *On the Left Bank*

Sometime after breakfast, we turned our attention to the Métro, which took us swiftly, smoothly and with a blast of underground Russian music, to Gare du Nord to meet our weekend guest. Serge stormed into Paris this time by train. The terrorists had temporarily receded, and Serge's anxieties had calmed. Our first stop after Gare du Nord was an exhibition at Les Halles of the photos of Willy Ronis, whose images bespeak the timelessness of Paris' past. Robert Doisneau is the more famous of the great midcentury French street photographers, but Ronis is just a little less self-consciously romantic. Serge, a closet Marxist who knew nothing of Ronis, thanked us for the revelation.

Then, our artistic foray finished, with Duty's rodent teeth gnawing at my conscience, I posed the issue of electricity. "Serge," I said, "we need to install more lights in our apartment, but—"

Benjie's Diary, 22 December '96, rue St.-Séverin: "The highlight of the waning solstice afternoon was an expedition to Samaritaine in the throes of Christmas shopping, to figure out the mystery of overhead lighting in France. First, we examined the light fixtures, of which there are thousands. Serge looked at the bare wire leads extending from the fixtures and said, 'You need a *sucre* [sugar].'

"'A what?'

"'Downstairs,' said Serge, 'to *bricolage*.'

"In the electric department, we found first the long electric cords, ending in plugs, that lead to the light fixture. Then, in a nearby aisle, *les sucres*. A *sucre* is a little brass tunnel into which you stick wires, one from the cord, one from the fixture. Above the tunnel, two screws are mounted. Once the wires are tunneled, you turn the screws, blending the two wires and locking them into a conductive marriage. A single *sucre* consists of two tunnels in a plastic square that looks enough like a sugar cube to call it a *sucre*.

"Tomorrow, we can return to Samaritaine to shop for fixtures, cords, extensions, the works. We're ready for light!"

On the bank facing the bridge [Pont Neuf] there was originally a stone carving of Christ and the Good Samaritan, the memory of which was preserved in the nineteenth century when the Cognac-Jay family took the name of "La Samaritaine" for their department store.—Andrew Hussey, *Paris: The Secret History*, 2006

The surfeit of joy Junko and I milked from the discovery of the *sucre*—the device and the term, and its abundance at Samaritaine—was wildly out of proportion to its worldly significance. But it is through such tiny triumphs that one stakes one's claim on foreign soil. Our language struggle has been slow and arduous, marked by such word-by-word advances as the two meanings of *sucre*, especially for me. I've been three years in figuring out when I should use *qui* rather than *que*. I've recently ascertained that the subjunctive form of *"je fais"* is *"je fasse."* I just don't know why! And I know that nouns ending in "e" are usually feminine, except when you least suspect, at which point the French waiter in whose presence you've made the error in gender (these screw-ups always occur in the proximity of waiters) curls a lip and goes back to the kitchen to spit in your *gratinée*.

Junko has repeatedly explained to me the use of the invaluable interrogative *"q'est-ce que."* Over and over, she says I don't have to understand it literally to use it as a crutch for every question I'll ever ask a Frenchman. I bristle nonetheless at the illogic of the construction and grope for a grasp I will never attain.

Rosemary shook her head wearily.

"It's no use trying to talk to them in French," she said. "They don't speak the same French in France as you learned in school."—Henry Calvin, *It's Different Abroad*, 1963

Junko, you see, is something of a language savant. She learned colloquial English in one crash year among the Connecticutters of West Hartford. She learned passable German in less time. She can read the Korean alphabet. In every French class we've ever taken, she's the teacher's pet. On the other hand, I've determined that inside every smart guy there's a village idiot trying to get out. Mine always emerges, cockeyed and drooling, in foreign language courses. I lived almost seven years in Japan and wore out three different textbooks but never managed an intelligent conversation—or even two straight sentences—in Japanese. All I ever mastered was a sort of "stealth nihongo." I could gather the drift of two Japanese speakers—say, Junko and Hitomi—conversing past me. I would fake comprehension with an alert gaze, the occasional nod and the odd, knowing, *"So! Ne!"* or the old reliable, *"Naruhodo."* People would wonder, hm, how much does this *gaijin* really get?

Not much. I could figure out that someone was talking about my trousers, but I didn't know if the gist was "Nice pants" or "His fly is open." I'm still confused about the difference between a business appointment *(yakusoku)* and a prominent sumo wrestler of the eighties (Sakahoko). Speaking of sumo, I wrote a whole book about it without a clear notion of the distinction between, for example, a *yorikiri* and a *hiki-otoshi*. [52]

Adding to our language anxiety was the problem that the French vernacular required of novice Parisian householders is not the material drilled into students of your typical text, which tends to lean toward pencil identification, hotel reservations and hypothetical introductions to cute *chanteuses* at accident scenes.

"Ah! C'est dommage. C'est un accident! Je m'appelle Benjamin. Et vous, mon petit chou?"

Our questions dwelt more on the mundane and technical.

How does one say, for example, "Listen, pal, we know the heater problem is either the thermostat, the radiator adjustment or the relationship of the draft (*tirage!* I know this one) to the chimney. But how soon can you figure out which, when can you fix the sumbitch and how much is it gonna cost?"

Or: "What's up with the split-level bathtub?"

Or: "The leak seems to originate in the eavestrough and it's infiltrating the wall, melting the plaster and bubbling the paint and—Jesus Christ already!—what's the goddamn French word for 'mildew'?"

And that old standby: "Yo, Pierre! Is there a store around here that sells sanitary napkins?"

"Les serviettes hygiéniques?"

And *"hygiéne"*? Is it masculine or feminine?

When, on our own, we now and then blundered into ways to say some of these phrases, we would launch into a celebratory frenzy of high-fiving, hip-bumping and fist-pumping. This wasn't often. We're not sure it will ever be. We're realists. To articulate our domestic needs, we resort too often to Roberta. Or, we invite Serge for a weekend in gay Paree. He comes readily, tolerating recruitment for a little manual labor for blessed relief from Brussels' gray, clammy, windswept summers, winters, springs and falls, of which Serge eternally complains but cannot bring himself to leave.

With Roberta and Serge in reserve, our linguistic incompetence is a mixed hardship. It would be much nicer to know all the practical, nitty-gritty hardware terms and fix-it vocabulary compulsory to effortless habitation in the heart of France. On the other hand, our ignorance keeps our friends near and our minds ever curious and receptive.

And it does wonders for Serge's English.

Meanwhile, we'll never be quite as tongue-tied as we were when we were tourists. And (honest!) we've never been nearly as rude as the worst of them.

Benjie's Diary, 7 November '95, rue St.-Séverin: "Today then, at Mariage Frères, another American woman, in a cashmere coat. She, as usual, knew not a word of French ... You couldn't get a *s'il vous plait* out of her if you clipped electrodes to her genitals. She'd throw away the winning lotto ticket rather than skim a phrasebook. Anyway, I should talk.

"Anyway, so the clerk, an earnest young man who was using his limited English to its fullest in an effort to please this frozen fishstick (or just get rid of her), was trying to explain the tea list and suggest choices to her. She had no choices. Her deepest desires were revealed when she asked, with a hint of petulance at the man's sheer obtusity: 'Don't you have any PLAIN tea?'

"Behind this guy loomed a ten-foot wall of teas. The wall stretched fourteen feet to his right and thirty feet to his left. Canisters of tea were stacked two and three deep in several hundred cubicles on this vast barrier of tea. If ever there were a store that advertised—veritably screamed—its contempt for *plain* tea, here was the place. We were all gathered at Ground Zero of unplain tea. I remembered Mrs. Spratt, the pinched Puritan-American raisin woman at Chez René—a restaurant literally swimming in lamb chops, sausage, *foie gras, coq au vin* and *boeuf bourguignon*—ordering nothing but green beans—a vegetarian in Hell.

"Anyway, here was this anti-francophone American broad, demanding PLAIN tea. Appropriately, this did not register with the helpful clerk. She repeated the word 'plain' louder, rather cleverly assuming that the word 'tea' was not at issue. No light dawned. Since I had been hovering behind the scene for five minutes, I decided to help both parties and intercede. Over her shoulder, as gently as possible, I suggested, *'Thé ordinaire.'*

"He rushed away. He found it! Here. Ordinary as a dog turd. Perfect for the *Americaine!* You like it? Smell that! Nothing, right? Ordinary! Plain!

"During this, I realized that, though I had rescued the woman from shouting the word 'plain' ten or twenty more times into the poor kid's uncomprehending face, she never acknowledged my contribution, or my presence. She was not only rude to Frenchmen, she was rude to other Americans who pretended to speak French.

"Meanwhile, I was busy watching an equally poignant vignette. Two Japanese women—office ladies—deep in the throes of *omiyage* obligation. For them, the less plain the tea, the better. But the only tea they knew was green. So, they had to sniff every can and make their purchases separately, on separate budgets. Which meant their clerk, another patient, gracious young man who served them in an inventive pidgin of French, English and Jinglish had to endure every round of timid sniffing, whispered consultation and anguished indecision—twice. And *twice* he had to explain to them, somehow, to pay at the *caisse*, not him. He got through it all with a smile, but I sensed his exasperation when I stepped past the departing second OL and said, *'Cent grammes des Grands Augustins, s'il vous plait,'* and he beamed back, complimenting my French. Any port in a storm.

"Ironically, I think this is the same clerk who insulted my shitty French a year ago.

"Somebody should explain to him, someday, the concept of *omiyage*."

An Englishwoman at No. 25 (third floor) complained that the bread left at her door each morning was not wrapped, and therefore was dirty. Thereafter, the delivery girl carried inside her blouse, next to her rather clear skin, a sheet of newspaper, with which she wrapped Madame Spook's loaf before standing it against the door. Madame Spook's real name was Root, but the French could not seem to manage that."—Elliot Paul, *The Last Time I Saw Paris,* 1942

After scouting *bricolage* at Samaritaine and identifying the wires and *sucres* we would need, we put off queuing at the *caisse* and fled the Christmas rush. As the weekend unfolded, we noticed we were in the midst of the city's coldest Noël in years. The temperature hovered in the twenties Fahrenheit most of the time, dipping one night all the way to thirteen degrees. Foul weather inevitably launches Serge into rich and profane tirades of bilingual complaint. From his own oft-uttered words, we've ordered in advance the epitaph for Serge's gravestone, which will read: "It's fucking *cold* down here!"

We did our best to dodge the snowflakes and treat Serge to our favorite Latin Quarter haunts.

Benjie's Diary, 22 December '96, rue St.-Séverin: "On Saturday night with Serge at L'Échaudé St.-Germain, we were mildly disappointed It remains a really nice and cozy French restaurant, reasonably priced, except the ownership has changed ... with the change, dessert is no longer a sacrament at L'Échaudé. Junko had a great *agneau*. I had a fine duck *a l'orange*, which was supposed to have been *confit de canard*. Serge had fish. But the famous *tarte fine aux chaudes pommes* is gone. The two lovable old people who ran L'Échaudé got too old and took their *tarte aux pommes* out the door when they retired. Paris is impoverished. We took the tragedy in stride and made the best of dinner, but the thrill was gone.

"(By the way, my hemorrhead has receded steadily. My skin is dry and flaky, my gatornose still gatory, adorned with scabs. But I'm on my way to recovery.)"

A little south in the Rue St. Georges, the composer Auber [53] died. Auber never, if he could possibly help it, took off his hat. He composed with his hat on, he ate with his hat on, and if he went

Rue St. Etienne du Mont
Paris, Sept. 7, 2014

to the theatre he insisted on having a box in order that he need not take his hat off. Indeed, although he was not a Jew, he went to the Synagogue for the same reason, and would never go into a church.—Sidney Dark, *Paris,* 1936

Benjie's Diary, 24 December '96, square de la Trinité: "Sunday started with a trip to rue de Rivoli, ostensibly for Serge to change Belgian money into a whopping 160 francs. Afterward, however, we went to La Tartine and sat at the wrong pew. We tried to settle into a booth beside the bar. But, suddenly, boring down on us, like Methuselah unchained, an old guy [M. Bouscarel] roared from concealment and insisted that my bag, on the seat beside me, was an affront to future customers seeking that elite spot ... or something like that. In truth, that booth was Methuselah's *spot*. The ladies of La Tartine apologetically shooed us to safer environs. We went willingly, intrigued by Methuselah's indignation. As we watched his routine, we figured out what he was doing. He would sit a while at the bar, snorkle up a glass of wine, then shuffle across the floor to the back stairway, behind a door called 'PRIVE.' There he'd disappear for twenty minutes, probably to pee, nap and work up a thirst. Then it was back down to his spot, more wine, back to 'PRIVE,' et ad nauseam cetera.

"It's not much of a life, but it beats death 'cause he has wine and a warm place to piss. We ended up not begrudging him his spot, and we had a great lunch of red wine and rustic sandwiches."

La Tartine ... is the oldest wine bar in Paris, owned for 70 years by the family of M. Bouscarel, who selects the stock of more than 60 wines himself. He buys directly from Burgundy, Bordeaux, Rhône and Loire Valley producers, keeping the prices down and the quality up. The café is always filled with a vibrant mix of ages and personalities, happily sipping wine and munching.—Richard Saul Wurman, *Access Paris*, 1998

Benjie's Diary, 24 December '96, square de la Trinité: "We visited the new national library, near Bercy, which just opened. It's huge, with the biggest hardwood deck in the history of barbecue. I hope they use it for something like maybe the Polka Party to End All Polka Parties ...

"... went to Le Select Latin, where Serge bought us coffee and tarts, and we compared practical politics with family-values Socialist idealism for two hours. That gave us a little time to go home before we took Serge to the train. It was a great renewal, mostly talking. But with Serge, talk is life."

My personal law for survival on the Rive Gauche is to enjoy the monuments, parks, museums, churches and great public buildings, but pay attention first of all to the people. They are the distilled essence of France, essence of Paris—beautiful, ugly, surly, funny, greedy, generous, friendly, rude, seething with energetic complication. The best, useless and most fruitful occupation is to find a café terrace, buy a newspaper or guidebook or any book to prop against your cup or glass, and join the interlocking dramas of the street and the little stage on which you sit—the scholars, mumblers, the lovers, the brooders, the debaters, those looking deeply into their liquids or into each other's eyes. Now you're there. This was the place.—Herbert Gold, *On the Left Bank*

On our way to the train, we approached place St.-Michel via our historic little neighborhood alleyway, rue Xavier Privas, whose most loving description—by Elliot Paul, of course—was in the pre-commercial 1940s.

We turned right, from the pathway of the sun into the shadows. Victor Lefevrais was standing in the doorway of No. 3, and from across the street, not twelve feet away, the aroma of Strasbourg sausages steaming and sliced potatoes in deep fat crept out from the Petit Vatel. Squint-eyed old Prins was setting type, his nose four inches from his stick, his fingers picking letters from the cases with no need of light. A few men in caps and sweaters were at the six-footer bar in the coal and wine shop. One of the chambermaids from the Hotel de la Harpe was in the chair near the window of the beauty parlor, looking at the pictures in an old copy of La Vie Parisienne, *and looking like Medusa because of the permanent wave clamps attached by wires to her head.*

The herb doctor watched from the doorway of No. 9 as we, at the head of the column, turned into No. 10. Farther on, the courtyard was littered with crumpled sheets of torn newspaper in which vegetable and fruit peelings had been wrapped. A couple of fledgling birds had fallen from a nest in the roof gutter and lay dead on the stones. There were a few discarded bus tickets, some losing "tenths" from the recent drawing of the national lottery, and a torn en-tout-cas *(combination umbrella and sun shade) turned inside out. Puddles of slops and dishwater had run into the low spots where the flagstones had sagged, and dog turds reposed where the stones were upended.*—Elliot Paul, *Springtime in Paris,* 1949

From that picturesque and seedy condition in the time of Elliot Paul, rue Xavier Privas has devolved into a gauntlet of sightseer-snagging couscouseries. Each doorway frames a swarthy barker, done up in *Saturday Night Fever* duds, vaguely redolent of cumin, offering potential gastronomes the sole blandishment of luring the most spice-shy American tourist into the greasiest-spoon microbe hatchery in all of France: A menu in English.

Each barker leans panderously from his entry, murmuring sweet nothings *en anglais* to every passerby, praising his establishment's mundane grub beyond all credibility.

For anyone not yet aware of the ins and outs of couscous, I must explain that the name refers to two things: a basic grain-like cereal that might be compared to rice, and that cereal when it is served as a main course accompanied by a stew or ragout made of meat, poultry, or fish and whose principal flavor is that of ground cumin ...

"Couscous is like a fine-grained pasta that is made with ground semolina, a sort of white flour, and water. The flour and water are blended and rolled by hand or machine until tiny pellets are formed ...

"Larousse Gastronomique, *in its discourse on couscous, quotes an author named Léon Isnard in reference to its origin: 'It seems that the word couscous is a Gallic version of* rac keskes, *which means* crushed small.'—Craig Claiborne, *The New York Times Food Encyclopedia,* 1985

As we passed each couscous joint, each barker, in turn, assured us that his restaurant's semolina pellets were far more sublime and succulently seasoned than any of the other pellets available on rue Xavier Privas.

"Superb couscous, *m'sieur*! Melt in your mouth!"

"The best couscous you ever had. Beautiful! Like silk on your tongue. Our chef! A genius!"

"Couscous to make God cry! Truly! Come! Taste! A full course, only sixty-nine francs!"

"Oh, Madame, if you die without tasting our couscous, your heart will break. Your soul will wither!"

"Wondrous couscous! Sixty-seven francs!"

"Miraculous couscous! Sixty-five francs!"

"Sixty-four!"

"Sixty!"

And so the hue and cry rang out, all down the narrow, curving street, unavoidable. Rue Xavier Privas is so tight that it's impossible to steer a wide berth around a dead fledgling, much less a full-grown Persian in a Pancho Villa mustache and a neon-green blazer. One can only straddle the rain gutter in the middle of the alley, smile and mutter over and over, "No ... no, thanks ... no ... *merci,* no ... sorry ... no, already ate, thanks ... no, sorry ... no ... hey! Hands off!"

At last, the final barker hove into view. He leaned into the pedestrian passway, all blue jaws and seductive smirking. He had overheard every preceding pitch and price, up and down rue Xavier Privas. He knew every purveyor and *plat* from rue St.-Séverin to rue de la Huchette and knew we had dodged each of them. What more could he add?

His voice went soft, soothing, sympathetic, his demeanor somehow philosophic.

"Same stuff," was all he said.

We collapsed into laughter and staggered onto rue de la Huchette on drizzle-slippery cobblestones.

I love Paris in the winter, when it drizzles."—Cole Porter

The drizzle lingered. Serge was gone, which meant our respite from financial responsibilities was finished. We finally had no excuse not to follow the cold trail of the personal check, made out to Abbey National, that had seemingly slipped into the Sartrean void, despite registered mail and the efficiency of the two greatest postal services in Western civilization. The next day, we headed to the Agence Beaubourg of Citibank, in the history-haunted heart of the Templars' realm. The building still stood, its Citibank logos blue and bright. But there was no Citibank within. It was gone. Madame de la Salle, Monsieur Decaillon, even the sultry Sandrine—

lock, stock and ATM—they had all up and taken a powder. What was this? Had Templar ghosts infiltrated the block and silently garroted every rival capitalist? Or worse, had some swindle left the gullible branch bankers of the Agence Beaubourg penniless and on the lam? Had throngs of panic-stricken depositors stormed the teller windows and emptied this Citibank's coffers down to the last *sou*, devouring our nest egg and blighting our Parisian future?

All the population of Paris hastened to the bank to get coin for their small notes; and silver becoming scarce, they were paid in copper. Very few complained that this was too heavy, although poor fellows might be seen toiling and sweating along the streets, laden with more than they could comfortably carry, in the shapes of change for fifty livres. *The crowds around the bank were so great that hardly a day passed that someone was not pressed to death.*—Charles MacKay, "The Mississippi Scheme," in *Extraordinary Popular Delusions and the Madness of Crowds,* 1841

There was a note on the bank's door. Citibank Beaubourg had moved—to 30, Champs-Élysées. Okay, so no Mississippi Bubble and no amazing resurrection of the Knights Templar—yet. We took a few steps toward the Champs-Élysées but then realized we needed a stiff espresso and a little shelter from the freezing rain. Neither Junko nor I like to do financial stuff, although we had been doing an awful lot of it ever since we launched our harebrained apartment-in-Paris *bagatelle*. We were fiscally exhausted ... and wet.

The eave troughs of Paris, on an inclement day, drip tears of bitter memory. London, when the weather closes down, can be ponderous in shades of gray and black. But Paris is never sad or sullen in a rain.

A charming painter's sky rolls up behind the old turrets and spires, giving artistic importance to the moment. The first drops tap against awning or window glass. Umbrellas unfold like a thousand bravely-colored rain flowers, and the gaiety goes on. For every sidewalk café that fronts upon the wetness there will be three others, somewhere, facing cozily away. The people rearrange themselves. The exposed tables empty, the dry ones fill.—C.W. Gusewelle, *A Paris Notebook*, 1985

After coffee, we summoned the aid of Roberta, who had done some preliminary research and had discovered somewhere in Europe, deep in the entrails of Citibank, a functionary with the apparent power to stop our renegade check and heal our French account. This savior's name was Madame Pellegrini.

Benjie's Diary, 24 December '96, Le Relais Paris Opéra [54]: "I wrote the wandering check on 21 October ... I addressed it to Abbey National's new HQ in Lille and wrote it to the attention of M. Desbonnet. Meanwhile, I faxed M. Decaillon at Citibank Agence Beaubourg to cancel our automatic debit (*prélevement*) to Abbey National. Neither missive hit its mark. The fax to M. Decaillon was swallowed by Agence Beaubourg's sudden stealthy move to 30 Champs-Élysées. It is evidently a French tradition, when moving from one office to a new office, to heave all office machinery and client files into the streets (preferably from a sixth-floor window), douse them with gasoline and set them afire, all the while chanting that 'the *ancien régime* is dead. History begins today!'

"This is as good an explanation as any for the disappearance of every fax I've sent to Citibank France, plus a letter or two.

"Nonetheless, I talked with M. Citiphone in Brussels, who

said that Mme. Pellegrini, the woman cited to Roberta as the key figure in Citibank HQ, was out to *déjeuner*.

"So … we all went to lunch at Le Robe et la Palais, a wine bar/restaurant near Samaritaine that Roberta has listed in Fodor's *Affordable Paris*. She's a contributor, the mistress of Paris nightlife.

"Our lunch was swell. I had veal and splashed sauce all over my shirt.

"At Roberta's, we recommenced the Personal Check That Wouldn't Die saga. Roberta began by calling our *notaire*, Nicole Pedinielli, who said the next time I try to pay, I should send the check to her.

"This, however, had no effect on the mortality of the lost check. It was still out there, its profligate heart throbbing treacherously, questing after a devious endorser. Roberta handed me the phone. I hate it when people do that. I dialed Citibank. I got Mme. Pellegrini. She immediately demanded, 'How did you get my name?'

"I did not say, 'I didn't get it. I have one of my own.'

"Instead, I said, simply, 'Roberta.'

"'Roberta who?'

"'Beardsley. She's right here.'

"I explained who Roberta was but only got far enough for the punctilious Mme. Pellegrini to recognize that Roberta doesn't work for Citibank.

"'Who,' Pellegrini interrupted, 'told *her* to contact *me*?'

"'Actually, I don't know,' I said.

"This really irritated her—having her name known to someone out there in the consumer universe. I suspect it's what decided her to keep alive the Personal Check That Wouldn't Die.

"'You're not supposed to know my name,' she said.

"'Well, I do, don't I?'

"Mme. Pellegrini ground her teeth, audibly."

The overengrossed departmentalist is one who suffers parochialism, localism, mental and emotional hardening of the arteries. He is so attached to his office and to his formally defined function that he is is *that office and function. He is conservative, intransigent, ritualistic.*—F.W. Howton, *Functionaries,* 1969

Benjie's Diary, 24 December '96, Le Relais Paris Opéra: "She said she couldn't really continue our conversation unless I told her my Citiphone secret code, which is not the same as my Citibank ATM secret code. We have three Citibank accounts in two countries and three different ATM cards, and a Citibank MasterCard which has a secret code of its own, but if we didn't have a Citiphone secret code—which was a new wrinkle on me—we were no better in the eyes of Citibank and Mme. Pellegrini than a couple of *clochards* cadging francs at the post-office entrance.

"'You must get a letter from the beneficiary, testifying that he won't cash the check,' said Mme. Pellegrini.

"'Say what?' I said over the static emanating from my disbelieving ears.

"Mme. Pellegrini repeated this howler: 'You must get a letter from the beneficiary, testifying that he won't cash the check.'

"This seemed a pretty counterintuitive check-stopping policy, especially for a modern outfit like Citibank. What if the 'beneficiary' were a swindler or an extortionist? But by this time Mme. Pellegrini was so immovable that any effort at argument was futile. I hung up, told Roberta that we needed a letter from Abbey National disavowing the delinquent check. Incredibly, M. Bara at Abbey said he'd do it right away, although he, too, thought the idea a trifle odd.

"So ... later that day, Junko and I went to Citibank for cash and found that our balance was intact. In two months, no one had cashed or—apparently—even *found* our check.

"Next day ... back to Citibank at ten o'clock, opening time, where we found a coherent woman at the info desk named Samara—no Mme. Pellegrini. She, too, thought it weird that our check could not be stopped instantly, and even weirder that the recipient had control over whether it oughta be stopped.

"Samara said she would leave word with our account guy, M. Decaillon, to stop the check. This might not work, we understood, because two previous messages to M. Decaillon had vanished into Fax Limbo. However, we'd never before had a personal employee of Citibank—Samara—on our side before.

"On the other hand, this might not have lasted. Samara said she was gonna call Mme. Pellegrini. If she seduces Samara to her way of thinking, we're back to Square One, and our check will continue to walk the earth, pale, restless, moaning for a quietus that will not come."

For the past two hundred years France has been governed by people who know how to pass exams.—Shusha Guppy, *A Girl in Paris,* 1991

It has occurred to me that the proper text for understanding the bureaucratic mind is not one of the obvious classics of this genre, such as William Whyte's *The Organization Man*, Sloan Wilson's the *Man in the Gray Flannel Suit*, or even C. Northcote Parkinson's ironic masterpiece, *Parkinson's Law*. These guys are helpful but dated and insufficiently radiological. Real perspective on functionaries like Mme. Pellegrini comes, most vividly, from the mental ramblings of cubicle-dwelling species below the human level, written by their most sympathetic and insightful chronicler.

I have completed the construction of my burrow, and it seems to be successful ... it is secured as safely as anything in this world can be secured, yet someone could step on the moss or break through it, and then my burrow would be open, and anybody who liked—please note, however, that quite uncommon abilities would be required—could make his way in and utterly destroy everything. I know that very well, and even now, when I am better off than ever before, I can scarcely pass an hour in complete tranquility; at one point in the dark moss, I am vulnerable, and in my dreams, I often see a greedy muzzle sniffing round it persistently.—Franz Kafka, *The Burrow*, 1931

Christmas came to Paris. Junko and I ferried into the countryside to a village called Nogent-le-Rotrou for dinner among the family of an old Tokyo friend, Virginia Kouyoumdjian, who had made her fortune in financial consultancy during the Japanese bubble and bought her dream house in rural France. It's an ill wind that blows good to no one worthy. Over *fois gras* and roast goose, we shared the mystery of the vanishing personal check and the pathology of Mme. Pellegrini. On the day after Christmas, the social whirl continued. With most all of Paris sealed and reverent, we accepted an invitation to Asnières-sur-Seine, to the new abode of Patricia and Eric, niece and nephew-in-law of Jean and Margaret. We had met Patricia and Eric during one of our sojourns at rue Dufrenoy. They were young and unselfconsciously attractive and about to have their first daughter, Léa. Since our first meeting, Patricia and Eric have changed and grown. The charming and ladylike Léa was augmented by a second, more circumspect daughter, Lucile. We dine with them on almost every return to Paris, enjoying their passages, testing our French, teasing their children and eating their provender. It's always best with Patricia and Eric when we see them separate from Jean and Margaret. We love both couples, but Eric is a teacher's union Socialist still too young to curb his tongue. Jean and Margaret, dismayed by the social unrest in France since the end of its colonial empire and the vast diaspora of North Africans into the northern *arrondissements* and *banlieues* of Paris, have shifted their electoral allegiance to the right-wing National Front of Jean-Marie Le Pen. We forgive them. Eric does not.

I wrote once about Jean and Margaret but changed their names to Gustave and Gabrielle and their reaction to Paris' racial makeover. Painstakingly, I tried to justify my tolerance of their xenophobia.

From Benjie's column, Lost in Babylon, Mainichi Daily News, 11 October '95:

PARIS—So ... if your friends are racist, does that make you a racist by association? Worse ... if you find out they're racist, must you forsake their friendship?

I faced this little social dilemma with my oldest French friends recently—let's call them Gustave and Gabrielle—when they cheerily announced that they are devout followers of France's foremost nativist, Jean-Marie Le Pen.

"Of course, we vote for Le Pen," said Gustave. "He makes sense!"

Gabrielle added proudly, "Racist? Yes, we're racist." They leavened this naked assertion, however, by noting that, after a fashion, "Everyone is racist, if he's honest about it."

Where've we heard that alibi before?

The charm of my racial discourse with Gustave and Gabrielle was that they're prone to more candor than their hero. Le Pen, a skilled hatemonger, never couches his bigotry so bluntly. Instead, he attacks "immigration" as an economic burden on the native French.

Le Pen's evasion ceased to be available to Gustave and Gabrielle last year, however, when their beloved and charmingly irresponsible nephew, Pierre, took up with a lovely Portuguese woman—let's call her Salaambo—with whom he soon became a father. As great-aunt and great-uncle of an adorable half-immigrant little girl, Gustave and Gabrielle had to reconsider their all-embracing bias against the huddled masses. Conceding that the occasional Lisbonite or Lett might be charitably melted into France's ethnic pot, they've focused their xenophobia on the real enemy.

Gustave and Gabrielle have realized it is only the dusky and the inky among the interlopers—the Arab and the Algerian—who exploit native tolerance beyond all endurance, who lounge and lurk around the *banlieues*, fomenting unrest, glutting the welfare rolls, ballooning the crime rate and mongrelizing the pristine culture of Montaigne and Monet, Voltaire and Baudelaire, James Baldwin and Josephine Baker.

"Yes," Gustave and Gabrielle said flatly, "the Arabs and the blacks are inferior people ... Yes. Inferior!"

Yikes.

I've met my share of middle-class racists, but few so open and ingenuous. Maybe such frankness is a French thing. Maybe Gustave and Gabrielle trust me, an old friend, with their deepest secrets. Perhaps they're weary of concealing their animus behind euphemism and politesse?

History—one of Gustave's passions—tells us that the poor have always been seen as genetically disposed toward indolence and failure. Before France had dark-skinned minorities, it had sunburnt peasants, also dismissed as slightly less than human—else they would not be so deservingly poor. If Marie Antoinette were alive today, she'd be urging Algerians to eat baklava.

I pressed the issue impolitely. "Okay, let's say Arabs and blacks are inferior. Let's admit they're incapable of enriching, attaining—or even appreciating—the civilization created by Greek philosophers, white Frenchmen, educated Jews and Francophile WASPs. Only one issue remains then:

"What should we do with them?"

My implication was inescapable. Having found ragheads and darkies impervious to evolution, the only alternative is to dispose of them. Gustave and Gabrielle hesitated at this because of history. The twentieth century has seen more people slaughtered for their race than any other era in human existence. This is the century of the pogrom, the epoch of the lynch mob, the heyday of the Holocaust.

And the pogroms rage on, against gypsies [lately euphemized as "Roma"] in Eastern Europe, against Muslims in Bosnia, against Tutsi and Hutu and Tutsi again in Africa, against Shiites in Iraq, Tamils in Sri Lanka, Indians [also euphemized as "Indigenous"] in the Amazon, Negroes in South Central Los Angeles.

I had offended Gustave and Gabrielle. I had crossed the line and taken their convictions to a length they refused to tread. I'd pushed their abhorrence of the swarthy underclasses to its logical extreme.

Call it the Satirist's Conundrum: "What should we do with them?"

It's the practical—direct—question too ugly to answer. It's the wet blanket that ruins the gracious pleasure of racist parlor talk.

But in the twentieth century, beyond the parlor, we have dared to answer this question, and we've answered it too often to count. We have thoroughly and physically explored racism's logical extreme. We have killed, on an industrial scale, every race and tribe that has suffered the misfortune of scratching at the bottom of the social ladder. We've speared ten million babies on our righteous bayonets. Afterward, though, we hesitate to brag about our accomplishments. In veiled language, we continue to indulge in racist complaint but, like Gustave and Gabrielle, we recoil at the consequences of our words.

For my friends in Paris, as with my closet-bigot acquaintances in California, Boston, Tokyo, racism has become a sort of conversational ellipsis. We deplore it tersely and, quickly, change the subject. We declare society "color-blind" and wash our hands of poverty. We identify, we isolate, we incarcerate. We etch fresh red lines around the ghetto and pretend that "they" like living there.

Gustave and Gabrielle are condemned to being typical, full of racist talk but alarmed at any hint of racist action, frightened of their own hostility. Recreational racism is their hobby, the comfort of their old age.

Of course, I'll not forsake them. To do so, in the face of their utter harmlessness, would be sanctimonious. Besides, when they grow tedious, as they often do, it's easy to tweak their shame and change the subject, or—better yet—scandalize them with unseemly disposal proposals. Sterilization? Concentration camps? I'm certain that, as long as they live, they'll do nothing worse in response to their racial fears than stand passive in evil's presence—should evil, of the sort they both witnessed in France from 1940 to 1945, once again rear its head.

A terrible prospect? Probably so, but after all, to be a spectator at the pogrom is not evil, exactly—as long as you don't applaud.

The problems of the future are becoming a haunting reality. Rallies show the rise of intolerance and the arrogance that comes with it, which makes even more disarming the visible satisfaction of the Arab and Black African workers who enjoy such things that we overlook, such as the running of the trains on time. Even the garbage collectors feel proud to be part of a well-functioning machinery, with the medical-looking gloves they have to wear. In no cities of the world can the workers be as beautiful, coordinated, urbane, as they are in Paris. I hear them chat under my windows. There is no place that foreign workers would like to go more than Paris, with its beat, its legend, its traditions of labor unions and admiration for the travailleurs. So fanaticism looks out of place here, although it's becoming a part of daily life.—Etel Adnan, *Paris, When It's Naked*, 1993

Our evening with Patricia and Eric went off without politics. We talked affectionately, as we should, of Jean and Margaret—their age and illnesses, their frequent trips to Cannes to escape the lung-riddling chill and pollution of Paris, and their deep great-aunt/great-uncle love for Léa and Lucile. We talked about Junko's journalism and my eternal struggle with the fortresses of publishing. Patricia talked about balancing motherhood with her job as an office manager at a company nearby at La Défense. She praised Eric for his devotion to caring for the girls and for cooking meals when Patricia had to work overtime. Eric talked about golf, his latest athletic passion, as though it were the perfect metaphor for every challenge in life. Meanwhile, slowly, he assembled, melted and stirred a fondue.

Benjie's Diary, 27 December '96, Le Mandarin, blvd. St.-Germain: "We all hung around the kitchen for an hour or so, drinking Alsatian wine made by their upstairs neighbor's brother, and melting cheese. To make fondue properly, per Eric's method, you rub the pot with *l'ail* and pour in a glass of good white wine for each person. You add a cup of kirsch and pile the pot full of Comté, Emmental and Gruyère. Then you stand around melting and stirring this together forever over low heat. You talk, you drink, you nibble, you brag, argue, find out about who's sick in the family and who's well. You get a fix on how things are at work and who went where for vacation and where everybody will go next year. You continue the process at the dinner table after the cheese is all melted and all the stale bread in Asnières is broken into dunkable chunks. Eventually, the fondue is down to a slimy yellow puddle and you switch to salad and *gateau* and Calvados and, hey, it's one in the morning. And Patricia and Eric have relatives piling into the house at nine the same day."

The good Parisian drinks all, devours all, swallows all.—Louis-Sébastien Mercier, *Tableau de Paris,* 1782

Benjie's Diary, 27 December '96, rue St.-Séverin: "The good news is that Samara at Citibank Paris got through to the elusive M. Decaillon, who has issued absolute assurances, after covering his ass three different ways, that our check has been stopped as thoroughly as it is possible to stop a check in France. We're still suspicious whether the Personal Check That Wouldn't Die is truly dead. But we're pretty sure the son of a bitch is in the ICU."

Our last evening with Roberta was an extemporaneous booze-up at a pub called the Mayflower somewhere in the vicinity of Panthéon. I had stumbled across it a day or two before and knew the general direction. We ended up returning there by circling and fanning, which was time-consuming and, in the blustering cold, exceedingly uncomfortable. Finally plunging into the warm pub, we chose not to move again for hours, cuddling by a heater and surviving on John Courage beer and French snacks. I meant to ask the proprietress where we were, but the issue lost its relevance after an hour or so. It might have been place de la Contrescarpe, perhaps place de l'Estrapade—or neither.

Other forms of punishment [for heresy] included the strappado, *an Italian device which stretched the victim's limbs to breaking point and dislocation as he was lowered slowly above a fire. The place de l'Estrapade, now a gentle and green crossroads in the heart of the Latin Quarter, was named after this device.*—Andrew Hussey, *Paris: The Secret History*, 2006

We emerged woozy and affectionate from the Mayflower into a Paris night that crackled with frost. A starless sky sent down dry white flakes. A wandering mistral blew uphill toward Saint-Étienne-du-Mont—or whatever church it was that we passed on the way home. After hugging Roberta and shoving her optimistically toward the Seine, we tightened our mufflers and scouted our neighborhood for a café and a last espresso before giving up the evening and going to bed. But we were too late. The holidays were too much upon the city. It is a rare night in Paris when one cannot find caffeine and the companionship of strangers.

As I came out it began to snow. A wind like a carving knife cut through the streets—and everybody began to run—so did I into a café and there I sat and drank a cup of black coffee. Then for the first time I felt in Paris. It was a little café and hideous—with a black marble top to the counter garni with lozenges of white and orange. Chauffeurs and their wives & fat men with immense photographic apparatus sat in it—and a white fox terrier bitch—thin and eager ran among the tables. Against the window beat a dirty French flag, fraying out in the wind and then flapping on the glass. Does black coffee make you drunk—do you think? O feel quite envirée (Oh Jack I won't *do this. It's like George Moore. Don't be cross), and I could have sat there three years, smoking & sipping and thinking and watching the flakes of snow.*—Katherine Mansfield, a letter to John Middleton Murry, 1915

Benjie's Diary, 28 December '96, UA flight 961: "It was one of those nights in a bar when all the talk is friendly and inconsequential, and time flies and you never want to leave. Junko showed off her drawings, and Roberta revealed that Alexandra, whom I met last February, had a little crush on me and didn't like me talking so much about Junko. All I remember of Alexandra is that she was a New York-style sharkette who had good legs. Or at least she made a point of convincing me she had good legs."

Paris at night is a street show of a hundred moments you might have lived.

—Courtney Maum

Place Maubert
May 7, 1998

9
Paris Veterans

W*hat cannot be learned in Paris is not worth knowing.*—Prince Saionji

In 1989, in the Marais, Junko and I had come across an odd little store called Callisto, aimed at the tourist trade. Its eclectic stock-in-trade included scarves, ties and clothes, jewelry and art. The only unifying theme seemed to exist entirely in the fancy of its proprietress, a frail and elegant lady, always dressed as though she was just leaving for an embassy reception, whose name we never learned. She carried an amusing—playful—line of jewelry, polished disks and stylized animals, cats and dogs and bears. These delighted Junko. We returned often enough in following years that the gracious lady would remember us. Each time, Junko bought a pin or pair of earrings. Each time, our hostess would ask to see Junko's watercolors and say, "You must exhibit these. If you sometime stay long enough in Paris, I have space here."

Benjie's Diary, 19 May '97, rue St-Séverin: "Our biggest disappointment was dropping by Callisto, the shop near the Picasso Museum where Junko got her favorite earrings. We found it closed, with a notice that the lovely woman who had operated the shop, only fifty-three years old, had died in January. She had always been so gracious and thoughtful. We have no idea what happened."

When I woke up, it was one of those dim afternoons when Parisians turn on their electric lights just after lunch. A whitish sky was covering us all and some of the whiteness was running over the buildings. It was a good moment to think of death.—Etel Adnan, *Paris, When It's Naked*, 1993

After we learned of the death of our kindly *vendeuse*, Junko and I changed our strolling habits in the Marais, no longer drawn to the corner of rue des Quatres Fils and rue Vieille du Temple. On our way to Callisto, we had often stopped for lunch at the popular and congenial corner restaurant, Le Sévigné. When last I referenced that place online, it carried an epitaph that read, simply, "Closed permanently." These two losses of outposts familiar and cherished are part of a pattern in Paris life, and in the life of any great city. Change is constant but rarely welcome. In my readings on Paris, I regularly encounter the lament that Paris ain't what it used to be in some bygone good old day, that it's been ruined by the ravages of time, or immigration, by tourists, by modernity or the erection of that unsightly steel tower.

Wiser heads, perhaps mine among them, observe that the greatness of Paris is its power to absorb change without losing its vibrance. Paris is a living organism that sheds its dead cells and grows new ones, without altering its form or sinking into senescence. Junko and I miss Callisto but we've found a little shop on rue Racine and another on rue St.-Paul, each with a similar stock-in-trade with friendly *vendeuses* who wait on us hospitably. In place of Le Sévigné, we've found warmth and refuge at Le Petit St.-Paul, La Pie Noir, Le Roi du Pot au Feu and dozens of other small, bustling bistros. I keep a list, adding and deleting as they come and go, their menus and actual existence as changeable as the living city.

The whole of Paris is a vast university of Art, Literature, and Music ... it is worth anyone's while to dally here for years. Paris is a seminar, a post-graduate course in everything.—James Thurber

The word Junko and I eventually evoke when we return to Paris is "rhythm." Every city has its rhythm—San Francisco languid, New York jazzy and lurid, Tokyo staccato. The rhythm of Paris is an aimless stroll and a song by Yves Montand, hummed while a cat mewls from a doorway and pots clatter in a kitchen two floors up with the window open. Dance to this if you can. It takes time to synch one's feet to the beat. We know it will come to us by and by. It always does. We're Paris veterans. But until the rhythm slows our pace, soothes our nerves and creeps heartward, we've been known to turn testy and prone to outbursts. Sometimes harmony comes to us after a night's recovery from twelve hours in transit. Sometimes it's days away.

Wait for it.

And noise—the greatest lover of Paris can not deny her noisiness. Big American cities thunder; Paris rasps and blares and screams.—Robert Forrest Wilson, *Paris on Parade,* 1925

Benjie's Diary, 8 June '97, Bar Brasserie Le Castiglione, rue St-Honoré: "Junko's mood was ominous. I tried to encourage her to drop all her packages and go back out. She had more than an hour to work on her picture of place St.-Michel that George had commissioned. She balked, insisting that she wasn't going to draw just because I put pressure on her to draw. No sir! Then, finally agreeing that she sort of wanted to go out into the blazing sun and draw place St.-Michel, she pinched her hand as she was closing the hall closet door (*really* painful) and had a conniption. 'I hate Paris! I hate drawing! I hate everything!'

"Into the toilet, for some reason.

"Back out, whining and crying.

"I hugged her, which was kind of like hugging Muggsy Bogues after the first quarter, like hugging a warm, wet dish sponge.

"But she quieted down. We went out and, in jig time, she'd done her best painting of the trip. She came home glowing. Art had conquered again.

"This morning, she went back out, did another one facing the other way (toward the fountain), even better.

"She's hitting her rhythm."

Following the river in the general direction of Notre Dame until one came out in the place Saint-Michel, one found himself in the Quarter of the Schools, a quarter which for some seven centuries had been riotous with intellectual life. I do not believe I ever went down the Boul' Mich' without thinking of that vagabond, thief, cut-throat, pimp and poet, François Villon, who once swaggered along this same thoroughfare.—Samuel Putnam, *Paris Was Our Mistress,* 1947

Paris is the city of joy where the naive are taken by the neck and blackened on the scaffold, and where villains hold all sway. Get out of the thick city walls as quickly as you can! Purse-cutters and knifemen lurk in the dark.—François Villon, *Ballades en jargon*, 1460

Back in Paris in late spring 1997, we made a resolution. "Benjamin," said Junko, "from now on, we're going to have days when we don't do anything practical. No trips to Samaritaine or Habitat. No necessities.

"Yes, Junko."

She was right. If, on a non-Samaritaine day, we needed a light bulb or a toaster, a soap dish or a box of detergent, we postponed the purchase. Instead, we sketched and painted, we wrote and read, we dined and drank. We wandered. Paris is a paradise for wanderers. We began to see the city again of our original infatuation, its mighty vistas and its secret glimpses.

The Parisians have been very good at creating visual delights. They have managed it partly by cunningly enhancing what was there already—the river especially—but partly by the most brilliant and inventive creation. One of their fertile techniques has been to use or if necessary invent forms that are not merely striking in themselves but have a double role: for example, things that can be seen through—the Arc de Triomphe or the Carrousel or the Ports Saint-Denis or the transparent Pei Pyramid—or seen around—the Vendôme column, the Concorde obelisk—or seen between—the long lines of clipped trees in the Palais Royal, or the Jardin des Plantes or the Luxembourg Gardens—or seen underneath—the pretty bridges, the great arch of the Eiffel Tower or the new Défense arch. I have seen no other city where such devices have been so widely and so skillfully deployed. It is this combination of imagination and ruthlessness that gives Paris its unique character.—David Gentleman, *David Gentleman's Paris*, 1992

Benjie's Diary, 7 May '98, place Maubert: "We had followed the advice of a writer ... and ventured to the place St.-Georges in the Ninth. At first, we were a little disappointed. It was so small and unimposing. But there was a café, and as we sat in the window with glasses of sauvignon blanc, the place emerged. The buildings are a graceful sweep. The statue in the middle of the fountain (of Gavarni the designer) is elegant and wry. Junko made a small, lively painting as we felt the rhythm of Paris renew itself with us."

An ever-increasing light seems to make objects increasingly sparkle. Aroused flowers burn with the desire to outdo the sky's azure by the energy of their colors, and the heat, turning scents visible, seems to make them rise to the stars like smoke.—Charles Baudelaire, *The Parisian Prowler: Le Spleen de Paris*, 1857

Once we had made our anti-Samaritaine resolution and rationed our house-furnishing obligations, we not only got back to the random, endearing Paris of our old days. We also began to enjoy once more the creative labor of building our Latin Quarter loft from a naked shell of petrified beams and white paint. Often, when Junko was scampering around Europe interviewing sources in the consumer electronics industry, I was able to while away my solitude by working alone on the dwelling I've come to call Chez Hypotenuse. When Junko was in Milan, for example, buttonholing ST Micro muckymucks, I was downstairs at Samaritaine in search of a bilingual hardware clerk. I needed to hang pictures, mount a range hood, install lights. I could do nothing without the basic tool of every Parisian *bricolageur*—the indispensable *perceuse*.

Benjie's Diary, 28 May '97, rue St.-Séverin: "I was a veritable whirlwind today, performing all sorts of manual chores, flawlessly! Sometimes it occurs to me that I missed my calling as a lowly guildsman, hammering out wagon tongues or fitting terra-cotta pipes in dark tunnels. I proceed into assembly projects and the misty Realm of Tools with great trepidation, but I'm usually saved by my plebeian roots and a certain talent for puzzle-solving.

"I had to dispatch Junko to Milan this morning ... and then I had time to kill with my *Herald* and coffee. Samaritaine didn't open until 9:30.

"Here was my challenge: to buy a drill—*perceuse* (your basic common everyday French word)—capable of penetrating our rock (or rocklike) walls, so I could hang our *tableaux* on our *murs*. I had to do this in French and add to this chore the right bits and screws, and those plastic thingies you pound into the holes in the wall to screw the screws into them.

"I did it.

"I obviously seemed confused, and the sales guy I cornered spoke no English. Zilch. So my French was the only resort.

"Did I say I did it?

"Yeah, well, this guy had a drill he wanted to unload—a Peugeot. I thought they made cars. But he marked it down to 279f, making it the cheapest drill in Samaritaine, and I said, 'You betcha, Alphonse! Standard or automatic?'

"He also had a handy-dandy package of about twenty drill bits for *bois, béton, métaux, pierre dure,* you name it ... the bits came with a lifetime supply of those little plastic thingies."

[Later]

"I had seven prints to hang. I unwrapped my new *perceuse* and studied it. Looked like any other drill. Heck, I used to ream I-beams at Addison Steel with a drill the size of a bear cub.

"Nonetheless, I tried two practice holes, one in the hallway, which was messy, and one in the gas closet, neat as a pin.

"After that, it was all downhill. My holes were all neat, my pictures all hung square and I was finished hours before the Habitat deliverymen brought up my next test of manhood."

[Later]

"The interesting feature of Habitat furniture (*meubles*), once it came, was that the directions, although printed in four or five languages, presumed a prior knowledge of some fairly esoteric fastening devices. I had never, for example, built a drawer. I had to build three drawers. After staring for a while at an oddly shaped screw and its strange circular female counterpart, I intuited their relationship. The bizarre thing is that I just sat there staring at them, for ten minutes, 'til they somehow made sense."

[Later]

"For the butcher block I had to figure out that a screwlike device is actually a sort of nut, while a corresponding screwlike device is more of a bolt, and that a little cuplike doo-hickey is a collar for the bolt.

"None of this was apparent. It wasn't even suggested. If you hadn't ever worked before with this screw-nut screw-bolt bolt-cup arrangement before, well, screw you.

"I stared for a half-hour. I fussed. I fitted things together. It came to me. It worked.

"The butcher block is in the kitchen. Snugly nestled between sink and range. Junko will be ecstatic. I'm ecstatic. These pieces of our puzzle fit our *pied-à-terre* This apartment is as homey and livable as our house in San Carlos—moreso because it's ours.

"Of course, we haven't figured out a way to live here yet."

Once upon a time, to be in Paris—if you were a foreigner; certainly, if you were an American—was in itself a kind of victory. But it seemed presumptuous, if you weren't French, to go on living in Paris.—Susan Sontag, foreword to *A Place in the World Called Paris,* Steven Barclay, ed., 1994

Eventually, among the new features of our apartment, thanks to the *perceuse*, I was able to frame and hang three of Junko's paintings and attach bookshelves to the walls beneath the great slant of the ceiling. Junko was amazed at my bookcase, mainly because my building something like that was like that proverbial dog walking on its hind legs. It's not that he did it well ...

Meanwhile, we began to suffer the normal vicissitudes of home ownership, irritations aggravated by our customary distance of 5,583 miles. While absent from Paris—and sometimes when we were present—we depended on Roberta to stick her nimble finger into various dikes and summon the appropriate *service de dépannage*.

Sometime in 1997, the rain gutter outside our middle dormer popped a leak, and water infiltrated our living room wall, damaging the paint and plaster, coating the historic BHV sofa with a furry, surrealist relief in mildew. Roberta eventually brought in Mme. Carnet, the administrator of the *syndic*—the building cooperative—to view the damage and order *gouttière* repairs. Roberta also hooked up with our insurance guy, M. Hulot (fresh from vacation), and even made inquiries about a painter to fix the devastated wall. Someday our painter will come ...

Twice, in '97 and '98, our winter renters couldn't get the heater to work. First time, Roberta was in Paris to help out the tenants. Next time, Roberta was in California, and we were in Osaka. We got a call at our Osaka hotel from a woman in our Paris apartment who said her children were freezing. I didn't tell her that it's stupid to bring children to Paris any time of the year but particularly in the winter when Euro Disney—the only reason to bring an American kid to France—is closed. Instead, I gave her advice about getting the heater to kick back in. Apparently, my advice failed, but the Massachusetts booking agency that had placed the woman and her delicate offspring in our apartment eventually tracked down a *chaudier* repairman. Meanwhile, we later learned the woman kept her little ones warm by opening the oven door and turning the temperature up to "broil."

On a happier note, we began to entertain our friends and loved ones in Paris.

Jill came often.

Chez Hypotenuse Guest Book, 27 September '97: "This trip was one long meditation. I am grateful for the silence yielded by no TV, radio, stereo; for the exercise of the stairs; for the gentle sound of a curious pigeon on the eaves. This is a place for reflection and celebration—and your joy in being here permeates this place."—Jill Ramsfield

It was Jill who spotted the naked girl one night. She was framed in a dormer opposite our own, in one of the smaller garrets on the *5éme étage*. Almost instinctively, I named her Grisette, after the charming and willing street girls of Parisian legend, described by—of all possible poets—Oliver Wendell Holmes, "the gay grisette, whose fingers touch love's thousand chords so well."

He comprehended that I wanted to see a grisette. Then he showed me dozens of them. They were like nearly all the Frenchwomen I ever saw—homely. They had large hands, large feet, large mouths; they had pug noses as a general thing, and moustaches that not even good breeding could overlook; they combed their hair straight back without parting; they were ill-shaped, they were not winning, they were not graceful; I knew by their looks that they ate garlic and onions; and lastly and finally, to my thinking it would be base flattery to call them immoral.—Mark Twain, *The Innocents Abroad*, 1869

Our neighbor Grisette had fine, generous, erect breasts that bounced merrily as she cooked and served dinner to an unseen guest. Junko and Jill gaped. I glanced, then looked away. I feigned disinterest, partly because I think spying on neighbors is an activity properly pursued in solitude, partly because our lights were on and Grisette could easily see us leering at her chest, and mostly because it's embarrassing to men when women try to act like guys. Junko grunted like a middle linebacker.

"Whoa!" said Jill in a fratboy woof. "Nice tits on her."

I covered my face.

The girlish vulgarities of Jill and Junko notwithstanding, one of the pleasures of any historic city, but especially in Paris, is its intimacy with the Joneses. Paris was built without reverence for personal space. The founders strove to fit as many Parisians into as small a Paris as possible. Once, indeed, the city's bridges were lined with huts and lean-tos. We are thankful for this spatial economy. The buildings that have survived the bulldozers of Baron Haussmann, including ours, are ancient and big-windowed. They face one another across narrow shafts and postage-stamp courtyards. Air conditioning is expensive and uncommon. People open their curtains and windows casually and unselfconsciously—naked grisettes and couples dining on small convertible tables or lounging on the zinc-plated roof, housewives tending window-box geraniums, children bouncing on beds and lovers coupling boisterously. Paris is a round-the-clock screening of *Rear Window*.

I opened the window and was captivated. The famed Paris skyline really truly exists! Jumbled roofs, chimneys with tiny balconies. Church spires here and there, television aerials, wires, a splash of washing, pots flowering on sills, now and again a flat roof, an old man having a sly kip, children skipping to some chant. Beautiful.—Jonathan Gash, *Paid and Loving Eyes*, 1993

And when you get tired of too much modern "philosophy" and too many paradoxes, you have only to look across the way, up the rue de Rennes, so reassuringly bourgeois, and see, perhaps, a winter sky all crimson and cobalt close down upon a city still autumnal, while just one lighted window high up makes a luminous, blurred outline for a fat man in his shirt-sleeves and smoking his pipe.
—Alan Houghton Brodrick, ed., *The People's France: Paris*, 1950

Benjie's Diary, 25 May '97, rue Galande: "I woke up at about three, listening to a woman on Casanova's balcony, screaming orgasmically but without an orgasm. She was just a ditz without consideration for the neighbors. I was awake two hours."

Ninotchka, it's midnight. One half of Paris is making love to the other half.—Melvyn Douglas, *Ninotchka*, 1939

My sister Peg has joined us once in Paris. We traveled with her down the Loire and then finished her visit with several languid autumn days in Paris—where her backpack was stolen in the place des Vosges. Nothing irreplaceable was lost, however, and our encounter with the Paris police taught us that cops everywhere are equally blasé and fatalistic when it comes to petty theft. "Are you insured?" is always their first question.

As consolation, we took Peg next morning to one of her Paris objectives: Les Deux Magots.

We went to the Left Bank, and he showed me where F. Scott Fitzgerald and Hemingway did some flamboyant talking and serious drinking. The bareness of the bar surprised me. I expected a more luxurious room with swatches of velvet, deep and comfortable chairs and at least a doorman. The café's wide windows were bare of curtains and the floor uncarpeted. It could have been a coffee shop in San Francisco's North Beach. High up over the façade hung a canvas awning on which was stenciled the romantic name DEUX-MAGOTS.—Maya Angelou, *Singin' and Swingin' and Gettin' Merry Like Christmas*, 1976

Benjie's Diary, 14 September '97, place des Vosges: "We had an interesting breakfast among the swells and overdressed tourists, in perfect sunshine, at Les Deux Magots. Our issue was the croissant deadline. We didn't straggle in until 11:45, whereupon we tried to get a croissant for Peg. No dice, said our waiter. It's too late, he said, for croissants. The pantry is bare. All we have left for layabouts who don't breakfast 'til mid-day are *tartines au buerre*. Okay, we conceded, three of them. Soon, they arrived—long, crunchy and smeary. Meanwhile, all around us, croissants were swirling and cascading among patrons, delivered by our very waiter, other waiters, every waiter. Why do these people qualify for croissants, but not us? Did they arrive just before last call? Did they order the full tourist-ripoff Deux Magots Continental Breakfast with a rich variety of fine breads, fruit compotes and coffee beans ground personally by Juan Valdez? We never asked, partly because our *français* is *mauvais*, mostly because we knew our waiter would have a) an airtight alibi and b) an air of insulted pride. Not worth the aggravation."

The Deux-Magots is now rather vieux jeu, *out of date, and its clients not in the Saint-Germain "swim." It is, however, not a bad place to begin one's explorations. The* Magots *may be seen adorning one of the columns inside the place. They are grotesque "Chinese" figures, for* magot *is, in French, one of those blessed words of many meanings among which are "hoard of money" (do not confound with* mégot, *a cigarette end), "a Barbary ape," "an ugly mug or a scarecrow," and "a grotesque Chinese figure." When one has made up one's mind in which of these four categories the* magots *of the "Two Magots" really belong, it is time to move on.*—Alan Houghton Brodrick, ed., *The People's France: Paris*, 1950

By our second year as neophyte Parisians, Junko and I had become adept at the quick-strike Paris foray. Paris should be unfolded slowly and lingeringly, a rule not consistently observed. We developed the technique of the alternate mini-tour for friends passing through too hurriedly to slip into the city's rhythm. Our strategy was to select a few sights to see—perhaps the Rodin Museum and the allée des Cygnes with a surprise at its tip—usually without regard to our guest's wishes, and to punctuate these tourist treats with languorous interludes at scenic cafés, ending each excursion with a mighty feast at a boisterous bistro. One of our favorite visitors was Patrick Pollino, my former boss and a lifelong friend worthy of the title *mensch*, whom we treated to a carnivorous repast at Chez René (in the non-tourist section). It turned out to be—to quote Irwin Shaw about another Paris feast—"a ceremony, an act of devotion, a celebration of the mystic nature of food, a reverent wallowing in gluttony that erased for two hours all memory of the drugstore sandwiches and hasty milkshakes of your native land."

Benjie's Diary, 25 May '97, rue Galande: "Junko and I had both concluded that Patrick was a fool for *charcuterie*.

"On the menu, we saw nothing as obvious as an *assiette de charcuterie*, but we had seen huge plates of assorted sliced sausage (*saucisson coupé*) served before at Chez René. So, I deduced that the assortment of *cochonailles* was the ticket. We ordered that for two (me and Patrick) while Junko got a nice pot of *rillettes*. The *cochonailles* began disconcertingly with the arrival of a slab of cold smoked pig ribs. I maintained my composure. An adjacent American woman (let's call her Phyllis) squealed significantly at the sight of the monstrous rack.

"I grabbed a knife, sawed off a rib and ate *cochon*. It was great. Patrick followed suit. We began reducing the ribs noticeably.

"Suddenly, the plot thickened. We had no idea that the *cochonailles* came in chapters. Chapter Two was an immense plate of *saucisson sec*, unsliced, hard as rock, in at least seven permutations. They covered most of our table. 'Oh my God, Benjamin,' said Patrick. Phyllis burst into hilarity. Mr. Phyllis chuckled. The French people looked away tastefully.

"All this theater notwithstanding, and despite the fact that several of the *saucisson* were so *sec* that cutting them was like slicing a mop handle with a butter knife, the meat was yummy. And Patrick, sawing doggedly through one leathery sausage after another, did the pig proud. He went through seventy francs' worth like a Norwegian farmer at a smorgasbord in Waukesha. His eyes bulged. His chair creaked.

"Then came the *boeuf bourguignon*."

Paris is a place for encounters. Everything converges to it, and that's why its cafés hold such magic: the world comes to them while you're sitting, human life meets its destiny.—Etel Adnan, *Paris, When It's Naked,* 1993

By Christmas 1997, when our guests were my insouciant daughter, Ellisa, and her beautiful sidekick, Shelley Clarkson of Knoxville, Junko and I had fully restored our romance with the streets of Paris. We felt almost at home. Most of the time, when Junko wasn't traveling on business, we knocked randomly about town with our eyes alert for pictures—to shoot or to paint, preferably from the *terrasse* of a congenial café. We began to believe, at long last, that we had not been that foolish to sink a root into a Paris where we had yet to find a means to reside permanently. It came to us that we had been so persistent in our pursuit of our *pied-à-terre* because of "encounters."

Encounters happen in Paris. They happen everywhere, of course, but in Paris they are Parisian. Paris is a paradox. It is perhaps the most visited, most admired city on earth, and yet it's an unwelcoming place. Paris doesn't send out brochures or pitch itself on television as a vacation mecca. Paris awaits, but Paris does not beckon. One ventures into Paris vigilantly, alert to snubs, slights, sneers, aware that the natives are aloof and inscrutable. The wonders are myriad and breathtaking but cool to the touch. To be touched in return by Paris, to feel the warmth beneath its surface requires philosophical patience and an openness to being surprised—sometimes pleasantly, but sometimes ...

On our first visit to Père-Lachaise, Paris' magnificent cemetery—where LSD-nostalgic pilgrims cluster at Jim Morrison's graffiti-smeared headstone, but where Molière lies beside La Fontaine, Yves Montand beside Simone Signoret and Oscar Wilde reposes beneath an angel-airplane made of granite—Junko and I packed a picnic. We found a bench on a sunny cobbled promenade and spread our repast between us.

Suddenly, *plop*! Squeezing into eight-odd inches beside Junko, a Paris *oban*, dressed for perpetual mourning, sat herself down, wriggled until Junko surrendered two more slats of bench and stared implacably into the distance—

immobile, inscrutable. I looked around. It was a quiet day in Père-Lachaise. The walkway was punctuated with benches like ours, each one empty, except ours. Our bench was a traffic jam. Junko and I looked at each other, checked out the *oban*. She was a sphinx.

We accepted her challenge. Leisurely and volubly, holding our turf against the *oban's* occasional territorial butt-shift, we devoured our cheese, gnawed our baguette and drank our cheap red wine 'til we were tipsy. When we were finished in our own sweet time, we left the bench to the *oban* and shuffled hand-in-hand toward the mortal remains of Corot and Delacroix. We looked back. The *oban* passed a decent interval *in situ*, perhaps three minutes, then also stood and headed elsewhere. She had made her point, that Père-Lachaise is for the beloved departed, not for hayseeds from Milwaukee to snarf their lunch and guzzle plonk. We later spotted her on the graveyard's highest hill, resting on what was probably her regular bench, gazing proprietarily over the serpentine rows of mouldering mausolea.

Being French to the core, and warped by experience and education, Christophe thought of foreigners in Biblical or classical terms, as if they should be nomads from Galilee, senators in togas from ancient Rome, slim potentates of Egypt with the morality of eels, or animated Greek statues dressed by Fantin-Latour [55].— Elliot Paul, *Springtime in Paris*, 1949

Junko's encounters as a painter in Paris tend to shatter the preconception of the standoffish Parisian. Tourists, especially the American ones, will creep up behind her cautiously and peek over her shoulder to check her work. They never speak, apparently frightened that she'll spot them and start quoting prices. Junko has sold her work rarely, however, even in the face of exorbitant offers, which always come from the French. Once, painting at a crossroads in Château-l'Évêque, she was accosted by the owner of the house on whose stoop she was perched. She apologized. He said, *"No, no, c'est beau. C'est très beau!"* He offered her first a pillow to sit on and, second, to buy the painting. Junko accepted the pillow but, gently, demurred the sale. Somewhere among my diaries, I have a copy of the man's address, to which I promised to mail a color copy of Junko's painting, but never did. Guilt gnaws at my vitals.

Once, while Junko sat on a curb on rue de Vieux-Colombier laboring at a difficult portrait of the unmatched towers of the church of St.-Sulpice, a Frenchwoman interrupted her with a series of sympathetic questions. Was Junko a student? Perhaps an art student? Junko said she just painted when she had time, usually just in Paris. The woman asked if Junko had a place to stay. If not, there was an extra bed in her apartment. Junko smiled and insisted she was fine. The woman lingered, watching Junko paint, praising and encouraging her. She moved on reluctantly. Junko sighed, her whole day, because of this brief encounter, a triumph.

Artists are rarely pestered by passing citizens or by loafers; a few loungers may look on, but comments are few, and for the most part, the painters are left alone to paint. And painting is one of the recognised occupations calling for indulgence, understanding and sympathetic treatment. One will rarely be refused a corner in which to set up an easel. Indeed, without the painters painting in the streets, the Paris scene would lose much of its intimate charm.

For despite the bustle and scurrying in many thoroughfares and in some parts of the town, the general impression is that men make use of the city's streets as though they were for all to do as they will. Men are at ease in their Paris, and free to run if they like or saunter, to sit for hours or to keep moving. Paris offers each man what he would like to find.—Alan Houghton Brodrick, ed., *The People's France: Paris*, 1950

Recently, in our neighborhood, we discovered a pub cheap and cheerful enough to draw us frequently to Happy Hour. It's called Corcoran's on rue St.-André des Arts, and it's a hotbed of encounters. One night, Serge struck up a conversation with a severe-looking Irish girl named Anne. It turned out she was looking severe merely to scare off, among potential suitors, the timorous and inarticulate. Serge is neither. By the time Junko and I left Serge to pursue his courtship, Anne had transformed into a bonny lass unfolding her life story to our ladykilling Belge. When Serge finally got back to Chez Hypotenuse, he had arranged with Anne a rendezvous in Brussels. *Bien sur*.

The same night at Corcoran's, a rumpled and mildly inebriated Frenchman tapped my arm and asked if I spoke French. I replied, *"Un petit peu."*

Graciously, he switched to English to ask me where I had acquired my jacket. It was a Green Bay Packers team jacket in the classic leather-sleeve style worn ostentatiously by high-school athletes. Peg had it made to order for me around 1989, when the floundering Packers were an embarrassment to Wisconsin, and there was no demand anywhere in North America for Packers merchandise. A patch on the shoulder commemorates only the first two (numbers I and II) of Green Bay's Super Bowl appearances. I briefly explained the garment's origin to the Frenchman and said, "They don't make these anymore. It's sort of a collector's item."

"Well," said my companion, who probably didn't know who the Packers are or where Green Bay might be, "it's one of the most beautiful things I've ever seen."

This from a man who lives in the city of the Louvre, the Luxembourg Garden, the Champs-Élysées and the view from Montmartre.

But he was on his fourth pint of Guinness.

For the people of Paris are so foolish by nature that a juggler, a pardon-peddler, a mule with bells, or a fiddler in the middle of a public square will gather a bigger crowd than a good evangelic preacher ever could.—François Rabelais

Encounters in restaurants are unavoidable. Parisian restaurants, especially the cheap, rustic bistros that Junko and I prefer, tend to squeeze their patrons. Often a dozen small square tables will be lined up and jammed together along a wall that would accommodate no more than four tables in the equivalent American floor space. Placing someone on the inside chair or banquette requires the waiter to briskly pull the whole table forward and angle it, creating a narrow gap into which the patron may squeeze, while diners on either side shield their plates and clutch their wineglasses to prevent disaster from a swinging handbag or unruly overcoat. It is customary for the woman in a male-female couple to occupy the seat against the wall, but in such a restaurant, the wiser course is to consign this place to whoever has the best bladder control.

In such close quarters, one eventually learns to cultivate the Parisian art of creating privacy where no privacy seems possible. One leans close to one's partner across the table. The couple finger their wineglasses and speak in tones not so much of secrecy but of breathy intimacy. To Junko, I speak softly but clearly, and around us grows a cone of gracious exclusion, open to the waiter, open even to a polite inquiry to a neighbor about a menu item or, perhaps, a misplaced glove. But, through the miracle of body language and muted discourse, actual engagement—from neighbors on either side—is *très gauche*. One adapts to this elbow-to-elbow style of dining. One comes even to enjoy it. As the evening transpires, Junko and I fill the gaps in our muted conversation with a surreptitious interlude of eavesdropping, during which we count the Americans in our midst or try to decipher the dialog between the French couple to our left. When we suspect we're being overheard, we defend our privacy by lapsing into pidgin Japanese.

Sometimes, however, the joint is so small that even our cleverest defenses fail. This happened once at a tiny bistro on rue Lobineau called Le Petit Vatel, where we met Ed and Sara-Page, a couple from Media, Pennsylvania, whose main focus in Paris—and everywhere else they go—was its gardens. People who love gardens are among the least objectionable casual acquaintances on earth. How can you not like someone, with dirt beneath her fingernails, who has a crush on zinnias? On the night we met Ed and Sara-Page they had just come from a fairly well-kept Parisian secret called the Promenade Plantée—which appears on almost no map of the city (the exception being the map given out free by the Printemps department store).

The Promenade Plantée René-Dumont, where Junko and I later spent a leisurely Sunday afternoon, is an abandoned elevated railroad line formerly connecting Paris to the town of Verneuil-l'Étang in the northeast. Now, it leads eastward from the place de la Bastille. It looks down on the polyglot Socialist neighborhoods of the hardscrabble Twelfth Arrondissement along boulevard Daumesnil, tapering to street level around boulevard Poniatowski [56]. Atop the massive arched viaduct where trains once ran, the rails were ripped up in 1969. They were replaced by a walkway, benches, a forest of shrubs, flowers and blossoming trees, and a thousand vistas of Paris. The promenade runs right through apartment blocks along the way so that one is almost within touching distance of the local balconies, rear windows and laundry lines. One modern edifice has been built around the promenade. Fellow strollers tend to be families, airing out their children or recovering from a week on the job. The benches seem to be the province of loners, their faces in a book or their chins in their hands.

Vauvenargues says that public gardens have pathways haunted mainly by disappointed ambition, unfortunate inventors, thwarted fame, shattered hearts, by all those tumultuous and secretive souls in whom a storm's final sighs still rumble, and who retreat far from the insolent gaze of the joyous and the idle. These shady refuges are meeting places for those maimed by life.—Charles Baudelaire, *The Parisian Prowler: Le Spleen de Paris,*1857

Often, we have learned, Parisian encounters involve no actual contact. Ideally, one merely sits back at a sunny table on a *terrasse* or a bridge parapet as the drama of the city unfolds.

Benjie's Diary, 27 May '97, rue St.-Séverin: "Junko finished with an economical landscape of the Seine, from the Pont Neuf, while I watched a crew of photographers/stylists doing a photo shoot with a frizzy blonde in black clothes. She had to run up and down a stone wall, waving a shawl about 250 times while two illegal aliens without shirts took pictures of her with a telephoto lens from the Cité side of the river. Meanwhile, her directress flapped and waved and gesticulated and straddled the wall, egging the languid blonde into a semblance of elfin whimsy. Mainly, the model looked scared shitless of pitching off the wall and dashing her brains (well, the contents of her skull) on the cobblestones below.

"When this performance finally ground to a halt, a stylist led the blonde across the *pont* to the Cité side, where she changed into a black tank top and black toreador pants. Eventually, with the model's hair re-frizzed and her ass-crack peeping cunningly over the rim of her elastic waist, the illegal aliens took her behind a tree and had her clutch a huge iron ring attached to the stone wall, while they immortalized her in a prolonged series of sadomasochistic *tableaux*. They were still shooting when we left.

"Ah, Paris!"

Shopping around the Galeries Lafayette for a New York lady who needed a rose-paneled garter belt, some black silk hose, and a whip, I ran into Bootsie Flowers, an American girl on the staff of Vogue *I used to date in London. We fell into each other's arms.*

"Bootsie, whatever are you doing here out of season?" I queried, mystified. "Everybody but simply everybody is in Biarritz or Sardinia."

"I know—isn't it horrid?" She made a moué. "Work, my dear. I'm researching an article on the bateaux mouches*—you know, those sightseeing boats that ply up and down the Seine."*

"What fun, darling," I said. "Are you still living with that greenish hophead, Eric what's-his-name?"

"No, with a dwarf, a Touareg from the Atlas Mountains."—S.J. Perelman, "Paris on Five Dolors a Day," in *Eastward Ha!*, 1977

In November 1998, Junko was invited to dinner by a professional colleague, Jean-Jacques Maleval, whose cluttered and evocative apartment was nestled among the poor and drug-infested precincts of the Eighteenth. During a gentle evening of food and drink, Serge—who was with us—bonded with Jean-Jacques' jolly wife, Isabel. It turned out that Isabel was an antiquarian, an occupation somewhat endemic to history-soaked nations like France. Her stock-in-trade was antique tools—hammer and tongs, vise and auger, wine press and bungstarter, plane, chisel, pincer and hickory nutcracker—which she sold from a stand in the labyrinthine flea market that stretches every which way among alleys, galleries, *shotengai* and culs de sac at Porte de Clignancourt on Paris far northern Périphérique. The address of Isabel's nook, elegantly titled "Présents Passé: Art Populaire," was equally evocative: "Les Puces (fleas) de Saint-Ouen, Marché Dauphine, Boutique 23." When we went to visit Isabel at work, Serge and I cleverly left behind her name card. So we simply wandered, asking the occasional flea-marketeer if he or she knew where the lady with the old tools hung out. After Serge had spent a half-hour, in sub-freezing cold, negotiating the price of a three-dollar penknife with a junk dealer, we navigated circuitously into Marché Dauphine, whose name we had forgotten but where we suspected Isabel's presence. Marché Dauphine proved to be a soaring, glass-roofed arcade, with shops at both street level and on a wrought-iron mezzanine. We climbed up and asked about Isabel. Someone pointed to our right and said she might be thataway. We were crossing a steel bridge to the next mezzanine when we looked down to the bright cavern of winding shopfronts to see Isabel. She was bundled against the winter in a brilliant red parka and woolly bear scarf that made her look like a first-grader bundled off to school in January. She waved her arms semaphorically and we could see her smile, even from fifty yards away and fifteen feet in the air.

Afterward, we talked and enthused over the beautifully crafted, hand-smoothed tools that crowded and spilled from her little cubbyhole in the *marché aux puces*. But I remember best the moment we spotted Isabel, glowing and bouncing at the sight of Serge and me and how this merry apparition defied the reputed aloofness of the native Parisian.

The national genius of the French people is more expressed in this city than in any other manifestation of itself. The tenacity of the peasant, the quick wit and adaptiveness of the townsman, the suspicious independence of the provincial—something untamable yet gentle, something reckless yet wise—all have their part in the fiery composition of the Parisian. He is of all metropolitans the one in whose blood, as in that of Paul of Tarsus, runs most vividly the proud sensation of being born the freeman of no mean city.—George Slocombe, *The Heart of France: Parisian, Provincial & Peasant*, 1934

As Junko and I restored our Paris rhythm throughout 1997, we came to regard our apartment as a sort of "encounter insurance." As long as we had our tendrils tangled among the roots of the plane trees of boulevard St.-Michel, we could always anticipate the prospect of some strange, unsettling or charming happenstance among the people whose city we love above all others. As our French improved (if ever), there would be more encounters, deeper immersion into the city's daily life, insights into the ordinary and pleasures as common as the discovery of a good butcher or a perfect breakfast nook.

And so it happened. Despite its charms, by April of 1998, we had deemed rue de Buci too far to walk for coffee at the crack of dawn. As we sought a closer venue, we discovered just around the corner, in the back room of our neighborhood *boulangerie*, a breakfast sublime. That spring, we were attending French classes at the Alliance Française on boulevard Raspail, for which we had to rise by seven o'clock. One morning, hopefully, we stuck our heads into the *boulangerie* and weaved our way past glass cases filled with flaky delectables, past the bar, into the salon. There, the baker himself, a Buddha of a man as wide as he was high, spilled over the edges of his straining wicker chair, finishing off his daily half bottle of shift-end rosé. Under the indulgent gaze of our roly-poly baker, we had a perfect Parisian breakfast, reasonably priced and sympathetically served. Within three days, the bartender was greeting us familiarly and delivering our *café crème*, Junko's croissant and my *pain au chocolat* without bothering to ask. And M. Buddha was smiling and waving us to our customary table beside our new friends, artist George Ball and Jason, his golden retriever. We were home, almost every morning, at Aux Gourmets de Cluny.

From the Weekly Screed, 11 October '24: "Once, coming home from our fish restaurant [Le Bistrot du Dôme], we were in need of a bottle of wine for the next day, but it was late. Most wine shops had closed. But as we passed Le Quin Cave on rue Bréa, the door was open. Hesitantly, we entered. The owner, large, florid and friendly, descended on us. We asked about a nice drinkable *vin rouge* and he took us on a voluble tour of his racks and cubbyholes. While we were considering our choice, another couple came in. The owner quietly asked us to wait while he disposed of them, and after they'd left, he closed and locked the door. His name, he told us, was Frédéric, and he liked to have a little bubbly after closing up. But he hated to drink alone.

"So, a little after midnight, at the oak bar in the back of Le Quin Cave, we shared a bottle of pinkish champagne with our new friend, Frédéric, who had looked us over and recognized that we were, somehow, despite our language barrier and disparate roots—in Wisconsin, in Tokyo, in Languedoc—'one of us.'"

The usual district market in Paris is an extensive affair. You move down a tarpaulin-covered quarter-mile of stands in a double file stretching along the central promenade of some boulevard. A few strange things greet your eyes—sea snails and repulsive rays on the fish counters, green nuts in their shucks, heaps of cheap and luxuriant artichokes, and a certain unfamiliar abundance of slaughtered and bled rabbits.—Robert Forrest Wilson, *Paris on Parade,* 1925

Not long ago, in America, every market-town main street featured a row of storefronts that provided all the comestibles necessary to cook breakfast, pack school lunches and put dinner on the table. As the millennium turned, Sam Walton's big-box invasion gutted those retail blocks and hollowed the hearts of ten thousand hamlets. The pleasure of hopping from shop to shop slipped into the realm of fond memories and nostalgic novels. In Paris, however, there remain thriving oases where victualers, each purveying a discrete category of provender, cordially serve customers who move from vendor to vendor with string bags and wheeled carts.

When Junko and I bought our apartment in Paris, it came with the market at place Maubert, a historic locale where we quickly became regulars at the *marché*—the farmers' market—that fills the square with sellers of fruits and vegetables, meat, fish, cheeses, goose liver and duck *rillettes*, nuts and olives and steaming *choucroute*, clothes and hats and flea market odds and ends every Tuesday, Thursday and Saturday (as opposed to the *marché* at place Monge that operates on Wednesday, Friday, Sunday). But even when the transient vendors are present and shouting at place Maubert, the storefronts are filled and busy with neighborhood folks who know them well and trust their quality. When first we encountered the storefronts of place Maubert, we beheld, clustered close along the square's façade, from left—at rue de la Montagne Ste.-Geneviève—to the right, a horse butcher, a delicatessen, the greengrocer's corner, the fishmonger, a vast and bustling butcher shop beside a vendor of *charcuterie*, then the storied Laurent Dubois *fromagerie* (including eggs and milk) next to the wine shop, beside a *boulangerie* that became so famous for its croissants that queues sometimes curled around the next-door café, Le Village Ronsard, which anchors the corner of place Maubert and the rue des Carmes.

The most picturesque feature of the "Place Maub" was certainly the notorious cabaret, Pére Lunette, founded about 1857 by a certain Lefèvre who graced his nose with a pair of spectacles—hence the name of the establishment. The front of the cabaret was crowned by two enormous goggles surmounted by the invitation: "Come along to Old Lunette's!" everybody gathered there: apaches, pimps, drunkards, strumpets, a select crowd.—Jean Émile-Bayard, *The Latin Quarter Past and Present,* 1921

After filling our market basket, we often sat at the café listening to the nearest greengrocer sing the day's specialty—*fraises des bois, clémentines* or wild asparagus—to the throngs of scowling housewives who perused his produce and grilled him about its provenance. We had learned the first rule of the *marché* the hard way, as do all foreigners, by getting yelled at for touching the tomatoes.

The fruit and vegetable man is young and handsome and an incorrigible skirt-chaser. If an attractive woman comes to his stall he tells his downtrodden assistant, "I'll take this one." Of course, it would be sacrilege to palpate or even touch any of his produce; he's always shouting at Americans who can't read the warning sign—naturally, since it's written in French.—Edmund White, *Our Paris: Sketches from Memory*, 1994

Benjie's Diary, 5 June '97, rue de Buci: "Next rule: You have to wait in line—even if you can't figure out where the line is. Elsewise, they'll ignore you, pointedly, 'til the cows come home and the *flics* flush you out of the plaza.

"Generally, the market is a positive experience. It makes you feel Parisian. The vendors are friendly because they're in business, and the market is very competitive. I even got a smile from the *oban*, who scolded me for fondling her *poivron*.

"'Hands off my *poivron, paysan!*'

"Where have I heard that before?

"I did get nudged by a fellow customer. I think she was a customer. She was next in line behind me at the booth, where I got another *poivron*, plus mushrooms and tomatoes. I felt her looming, like a large, unstable land mass—Hawaii or Japan. She shuffled, grunted, nudged, mumbled at the injustice of waiting for action from the dilettante in front of her.

"After I got my veggies and was arranging my change, I looked back. Turns out it wasn't another *oban*. It was a hippo in a print dress and white wig, speaking French."

Anyone who has shopped for daily necessities, making the rounds of bakers, butchers, dry cleaners, fromageries, charcuteries, crèmeries, *opticians, tailors,* traiteurs, *and other small merchants, cannot possibly think that the French, as a whole, are less polite than any other people. The problem for the short-term visitors to France is that they do not come in contact with this aspect of life.*

—Richard Bernstein, *Fragile Glory: A Portrait of France and the French*, 1990

Benjie's Diary, 18 November '98, Le Saulnier, blvd. de Strasbourg: "At the supermarket yesterday, to pick up last night's repast: chicken and carrots, *haricots verts* and new potatoes. Buying produce in a French supermarket is roughly similar to mud-wrestling but not as gentlemanly or sanitary. The heart of the struggle is the automated scales. One places one's produce (if one can elbow through a throng of myrmidon-*obans*) on the platform of the scale and then pushes one of about fifty '*touches,*' each of which bears the name in French and a tiny picture of the veggie in question. The problem is that most of the housewives in the store regard this one square meter and the three scales as their personal fief for as long as they occupy the produce department. Your Parisian produce department is about one-eighth the size of a similar space in an American supermarket but with more produce. Open turf is as rare as Carolina parakeets. Each housewife is armed with a little cart designed to strike, when thrust forward, at testicle level. A favorite tactic is to park one's empty cart at the scales—nothing in it—and leave it there. The *oban t*hen goes to the leek section, selects her leek and returns to the scales, where her cart has been blocking access and tripping people. She leans over her cart, weighs her leek, gets her little price sticker, drops the leek into cart, *leaves the cart* exactly where it is and heads for the *pommes*. She gets her *pommes*, repeats the procedure, goes off for *tomates, haricots verts, artichauts*, etc.—always leaving the cart to hold her place and frustrate her rivals. It isn't unusual to see four carts jammed into a 1.5-cart area, at the scales, while four female sluggers do their marketing.

"I was fighting my way through this gridlock yesterday, with a bag of new potatoes, when I saw an older lady—who had foolishly entered ground zero without a cart—wedged between two parked carts and helpless to find the right '*touche*' on the scale. Like me, she had spuds. But her eyesight was obviously weak, and she was feeling the pressure of the crowd and the two carts sandwiching her. She was like Luke Skywalker in the belly of the Death Star as the walls of the garbage room slowly closed in on her.

"I leaned across the cart-jam, saw her '*touche*' and said, '*Quatre-vingt dix.*'

"'*Quatre-vingt dix?*'

"'*Oui.*'

"'*Oh. Merci, m'sieur.*'

"'Eh.'

"No one helped her. Everyone looked away disgustedly. I had violated survival-of-the-fittest and allowed the wounded deer to live one more day in the Paris jungle.

"But, as the old lady wormed out of the trap, she left an opening, which I exploited to weigh my own potatoes.

"The little things."

Little things lent Junko and me the occasional illusion that we had arrived, not perhaps as Parisians but at least as veterans of the city. The barkers who manned the entrance to each Greek or North African restaurant on our street ceased to blandish us as we passed, recognizing us as denizens rather than as easy pickings—or pickings at all. At Knossos, the restaurant beside our doorway, the cheerful host who stood loquacious vigil there, in rain or shine, sweltering heat or crippling cold, welcomed us home whenever we approached and never thought to impose on us his plate of shrimp or his dubious promise of culinary ecstasy for a measly sixty-nine francs. We had earned exemption from such overtures. We began to recognize the neighborhood bums, who shifted operation among three or four posts, most often along the fence outside the *église* St.-Séverin, or in the doorway of Le Saint, our local disco *caveau*. One resident *clochard* had a hangdog but dignified spaniel who once informed Junko that she was standing too close (reading a concert poster) by silently, briefly, instructively (no hard feelings, lady) biting her finger.

We occasionally paused, apropos to nothing in particular, to spontaneously rejoice in the blessed folly of buying our little refuge in Paris.

Benjie's Diary, 30 May '97, L'Atlas, rue de Buci: "Walking toward our door from rue St.-Jacques, I look up. The early sun reflects off the modest steeple of St.-Séverin, illuminating the eight-hundred-year-old stone and spreading sharp-edged shadows among the buttresses, roof peaks and gargoyles. The gargoyles jut out over the street, blind and gape-mouthed, stained, wind-scored and eternal against a jagged lapis sky. *Seeing* this street is a humbling stroll through time and art. It's a miracle of history that has survived the depredations of countless generations of demolition-mankind. *Living* on this street is a stroke of remarkable fortune.

"I started out on Pearl Street in Tomah, Wisconsin, pop. 4,500. Now, my address is rue St.-Séverin, Paris. This might be the greatest impossibility since Tiny Tim had a Top Forty hit."

Paris is not a city of heights. Its architects, out of respect for man, have made certain that man is not dwarfed by his works here. It is a city built to human scale, so that no man should feel pygmied here. Parisians are devoted to their sky.

—Irwin Shaw, *Paris! Paris!*, 1976

We've always thought it's bad form to be smug about owning an apartment in Paris, even while visiting the owners of trophy houses and McMansions in Palo Alto and Marin County. But now and then our humility gives way to gloating.

Benjie's Diary, 30 May '97, L'Atlas, rue de Buci: "There's hardly a better smugness than the moment we click open the door to our building and step out onto rue St.-Séverin. At that hour, the Knossos next-door has set tables out in a row across its frontage. One table nudges into our doorway. Ideally, two yokels from Dayton are sitting there, plucking the anchovies off their *salade Niçoise* and hiding them in a napkin. They look up, surprised for a moment, then complacent—as though people are always coming out of a doorway into their evening meal. But we've delivered our message. We live here, you alien excrescences. This is our house you're munching in front of. You're just passin' through, paleface.

"We have our hooks into Paris, and nothing quite affirms that feeling like emerging from the secret sanctum behind our green door into a throng of transient, evanescent, gawking tourists. It's our daily victory dance."

Chez Hypotenuse Guest Book, January '98: "What's fun ... is that you have your own *door* right in the heart of St.-Michel, to open sort of grinning over to other bunches of tourists staying at hotels, saying, 'Well, mine is *un appartement!*' And then you disappear behind the door!"—Mari Sugiyama Shimamura

There was a first-class row going on between the higher Paris clergy and the St.-Séverin priests. Relatives of a former Vichy official named Henriot, who had been tried and shot as a collaborator and traitor, had applied to the head abbot at St.-Séverin for a memorial mass on the anniversary of the execution. St.-Séverin, the church with the workers' congregation, had refused to stage masses for convicted and executed Collabos. Eventually, after much discussion, the mass was celebrated at Notre Dame, where proletarian worshippers are seldom seen and never heard. The prevailing theory was that any sinner, whose relatives had the price, was entitled to a memorial mass, whatever his politics.—Elliot Paul, *Springtime in Paris,* 1949

Perhaps my most shocking welcome to the neighborhood was my unexpected, although reserved, acceptance by George

Whitman, proprietor of Shakespeare & Co. Mr. Whitman and I had independently developed a shared disdain for most of the patrons of his famous bookstore. They are a hodgepodge of literary arrivistes who come to linger in the musty stacks absorbing dead glories and yearning for a kind glance from the adamantly unkind proprietor, who sits slumped at a cluttered desk reading, answering queries with monosyllables and gloomily collecting exorbitant payment for cherished volumes that would go back to America with the coveted stamp of Shakespeare & Co. on the frontispiece, where most would languish dusty and unread on a bookshelf underneath the TV.

Her business self Miss Sylvia Beach chooses to call "Shakespeare and Company," and a portrait of the bald bard appears on the shop sign hanging on front of No. 12m Rue de l'Odéon. It says something for Miss Beach's own personality that she has never succeeded in giving her trade name much currency. People in Paris know the place as Sylvia Beach's bookshop and not as "Shakespeare and Company."—Robert Forrest Wilson, *Paris on Parade*, 1925

Charles Winzer, a Polish-English friend of Adrienne's, made a signboard, a portrait of Shakespeare, to be hung outside. Adrienne [Monnier] didn't approve of this idea, but I wanted it anyway. The signboard hung from a bar above the door. I took it down at night. Once, I forgot it, and it was stolen. Winzer made another, which also disappeared. Adrienne's sister made a third one, a rather French-looking Shakespeare, which I still have.—Sylvia Beach, *Shakespeare and Company*, 1959

Having, on numerous occasions, sensed George Whitman's disdain for his customers and his reluctance to gratify their hunger to bask in the shop's history, I ignored him as coldly as he disregarded me. I restricted my browsing to the cheap paperbacks displayed on the terrace and often forwent the rubber stamp impression that identified the source of my purchase. I had read of Whitman's genuine prominence in Paris' English-speaking literary circles and his occasional kindness toward itinerant poets. He was known to adopt the odd literary waif and give him lodgings upstairs above his shop. But I saw none of this solicitude in his day-to-day bookselling, and I was too proud to grovel for a grudging smile. I assumed our standoff was permanent. I was certainly not the one likely to relent.

The famous Shakespeare and Company of George Whitman, who used to hint that he was descended from Walt Whitman. His shop on the rue de la Bûcherie, a few steps from the Seine, has been a hangout for poets and college kids since it was called Le Mistral many years ago, before George adopted the name of Sylvia Beach's bookstore-publishing company, which first printed James Joyce. He keeps open late at night and has frequent mass Sunday teas for visiting geniuses. He is, as e.e. cummings once said about someone else, a delectable mountain, albeit a skinny and irascible one.— Herbert Gold, *On the Left Bank*

Benjie's Diary, 8 June '97, Bar Brasserie le Castiglione, rue St.-Honoré: "With less enthusiasm, I went over to Shakespeare next, where the dyspeptic old fart (Whitman) sat at his desk, eating, making gross throat noises and growling at the clientele. He was in the background while I explored the Paris-lit section, which—this being Shakespeare & Co.—was heavily picked over. This turned out to be a blessing. The remaining volumes were the most idiosyncratic. One was an ancient lyric about Paris and other parts of France, *The Heart of France*, by George Slocombe. It's not dated, but I'll figure that out as I read. The passages describing sites and emotions in Paris are wonderfully florid and overwrought. The other book is the opposite: *The People's France: Paris* by a caustic Brit named Alan Houghton Brodrick, published as a veritable encyclopedia of Paris in 1950. It's a highly opinionated encyclopedia. It overflows with minute detail, historical surprises, gossip and private digression. When I presented it to Whitman to buy, at 150f, he said, in his grumpy voice, 'Ah, you're buying *this*?' His tone suggested that he thought he would never unload this white elephant. I said (but got no answer): 'Shouldn't I?' But then, he unexpectedly boiled over with curiosity and broached a question.

"'Are you a journalist?' he asked.

"I said, 'After a fashion.'

"'Ah. Freelance.'

"'Well, I'm a writer. But I've been a journalist. I used to run a newspaper in Massachusetts. A weekly.'

"He smiled.

"Honest to God.

"The old gargoyle cracked a smile.

"He told me he used to write a column for the *Town Crier* in Newton [Mass.]. He described it. I mentioned Mansfield. I praised the *Town Crier* as one of the jewels of weekly New England journalism. He lovingly stamped both my books—an impressive performance because his stamping directly reflects his opinion of the customer.

"For scum, he doesn't even stamp the book.

"For normal peasants, he barely inks the rubber stamp and then applies it lightly, indifferently and smearily.

"This was my experience.

"Now, something new.

"He spread the cover gently, he sat the rubber stamp fastidiously on the middle of the inkpad and leaned on it. Ink bubbled at the edges. Then, delicately, he set the inked stamp in the center of each book's frontispiece, pressed down and lifted surgically. The stamp, each book, was dark, vivid, readable.

"Here was respect.

"Of course, the most satisfying feature here was that I had never given Whitman an inch ... I had disdained him as a grouch and a snob. When, finally, my higher qualities became apparent to him through my bizarre taste in books, it was Whitman who made the overture.

"He smiled at me. Not I at him.

"He ended by inviting me to the open house today at four. But Junko wanted to paint, and I was ambivalent about cozying with the local literary gang. If it's as easy as it seems, that will come—along with all the concomitant jealousy, duplicity and backbiting."

"Writing in Paris is one of the oldest American customs," asserts Van Wyck Brooks in a book on Washington Irving. "It all but antedates, with Franklin, the founding of the republic." For two hundred years—from Benjamin Franklin to James Baldwin—writers have sought Paris, walked the same streets, stayed often in the same hotels. Paris—crossroads of the West—is the place away from home where Americans talk and write best.—Noel Riley Fitch, *Sylvia Beach and the Lost Generation: A History of Literary Paris in the Twenties and Thirties*, 1983

Even during our Samaritaine Period, one Paris habit that did not wane was our annual return to the Crazy Horse. For several years after the death of Alain Bernardin, this was a mildly dispiriting exercise. The club suffered a steady exodus of its best soloists, including Akky Masterpiece, who had taken her Paris pedigree and her endless legs to America. Afterward, in Las Vegas, she became one of Sin City's most flagrantly promoted showgirls, which included an elegant photo spread in *The New Yorker*. We saw her several times during our annual visits to the Consumer Electronics Show, one of Junko's reportorial obligations. Eventually, the Stardust was reduced to earthly dust by the march of development and we lost touch with Akky.

To a first-time patron of the post-Bernardin, post-Akky Crazy Horse, the show probably seemed as ebullient and offbeat, as sexy and irreverent as any bunch of dancing naked ladies could ever be. But they didn't synchronize quite as crisply, bump as thumpingly or grind quite so lubriciously. The biggest loss was that their eyes lacked the unnerving glimmer of irony.

My measure of the Crazy show had always been the grand finale, a jungle-drum ensemble in which the girls strut the stage in spangles and spike heels, singing to the audience the brazen lyrics of a song titled "You Turn Me On." Under the direction of Bernardin, this number was a daunting enticement. Each girl—breasts erect, legs scissoring, pubis winking furrily—would fix her gaze on a chosen male in the audience and roar her desire for his sexual might. From the orchestra section, the viewer's temptation—as this stunning nude woman stared into his eyes—was to look away or, preferably, lower his chin and ogle privately her honeyed flesh. But if you harbored any self-respect, you could not—dared not—look away. To give in was like losing a flinch contest in the fourth grade. Unless you met her piercing gaze and held tight—Akky always chose me—she was the alpha, and you were the slave. If you matched her flirt for flirt and scored a stalemate, there was a certain penance. You had proved your mettle but missed out on all that close-up tits and ass. "You Turn Me On" was the apotheosis of Bernardin's devious showmanship. He knew that sexual power flows from the eyes, in the flash of enticement and the unspoken dialog. He knew that whoever starts that wordless exchange, the one who makes first eye contact and holds it toyingly, is boss. Nothing happens unless she decides. This tension was the essence of Bernardin's finale.

After Bernardin's death, the subtly altered "You Turn Me On" epitomized the Crazy Horse's loss of vitality. The girls were either not told, nor willing, to look fiercely into the eyes of their voyeurs. They withdrew, stared into space, became as detached and objective as their audience.

Over the years, I did my best to stay in touch with Polly Harper. She stuck loyally with the Crazy Horse through the transition from Alain Bernardin to Bernardin's far less flamboyant and imaginative children. I spoke and wrote to Polly about the fading of the girls' stage presence. She evaded my efforts to elicit her feelings about the club's changes, doing her duty to corporate reticence. By the fall of 1998, the financial decline that had begun under Bernardin had finally been arrested. The Crazy had opened a branch show in Monte Carlo and summer stock in resort cities like Montreux. A public relations office popped up, tasked with enhancing the Crazy Horse's image and conducting "outreach" to the annual flood of tourists in Paris. The turnover in dancers had ceased to be so dizzyingly fast, and the staff had stabilized. Bernardin's selfish suicide had taken from Polly a father figure and, from Paris, a unique impresario. Polly's loving bond with Bernardin, her patience with his madness and her understanding of his vision set her apart from her new bosses and from the girls who succeeded her—and Akky, Friday, Sofia Palladium, Betty Buttocks, Nouka Bazooka, the Blackwits—on the Crazy's tiny, kinetic dance floor.

Polly worked to keep alive the Crazy Horse not because it's as beautiful and disturbing as Bernardin had crafted it. It can't be. But from the time she was little more than a girl, wide-eyed, black and beautiful, the Crazy was Polly's family, which means that any Crazy Horse de Paris—even the homogenized post-Bernardin version, where "dead" girls now parade nude in a glimmering storm of inoffensive triangles (rather than the crucifixes that Bernardin had streamed across their flesh)—is better than no Crazy Horse at all.

Benjie's Diary, 18 Nov. '98, Le Saulnier: "Polly, more directly and candidly than ever before, admitted that much of this electric force has gone from the Crazy. The girls are shy, and they don't look at you at all.

"They stare into the distance. They are—truly, nakedly—vulnerable...

"This explains, I think, Polly's new sense of devil-may-care. Though she has secured herself at the Crazy, she knows what has been lost and that it will never be restored. Bernardin's spirit—his fanaticism and his signature—passed when he died. The business remains ... The show memorializes him, but it no longer embodies Alain Bernardin."

One must take Bernardin seriously when he calls himself a painter on the living body, when he stretches surrealism into a total performance. With him, the act of becoming naked, the nude itself is the portal to the dimension of art. Thus, he has become immortal in the same way the Beatles are immortal in rock, Raymond Loewy in design, Saint-Laurent in high fashion.—Brice Couturier, *Lui,* May 1991

Each parting from Paris reminds us that we really haven't made it here. Once, a friend said to me, "It must kill you not to be there all the time." In fact, we enjoy the cycle of trips to Paris and the variety this lends to life. At worst, our absences from Paris are a collection of nagging frustrations, largely generated by tenants who devise ever more ingenious forms of petty landlord abuse.

From "Instructions for Users: Chez Hypotenuse": "Here are a few new rules we've developed in response to the behavior of tenants who certainly ought to know better. Use these either as guidelines or as commentary on the human condition.

"a) Please don't hang anything on the wires around the mezzanine.

"b) Please don't steal the five-centime coin on top of the refrigerator. We need it to turn the refrigerator on and off. It's worth less than a penny, for Pete's sake!

"c) Please restrict all bodily discharge to the sinks or toilet. Specifically, don't pee on the beds. Or couch.

"d) Please don't use the utility table in the kitchen as a cutting board. There are three (3) real cutting boards.

"e) Please eat at the kitchen counter or at the table. Don't eat on the couch. If you insist on eating on the couch, give us a break, and don't grind your spilled potato chips into the rug with the heels of your hiking boots.

"f) If possible, please don't wear your shoes past the entry. Think of this as a Japanese apartment.

"g) Please don't steal the *arrondissement* map book or the menu master. People need these more than anything else.

"h) Please don't use the oven to heat the apartment. This is inefficient and expensive (for us, not you) and dangerous. Besides, would you do this in your own home?

"i) We have anticipated the occasional breakage. If you break something, for God's sake, own up to it. Leave a note. Apologize. We probably won't ask you to pay for it. What you shouldn't do is throw away the wreckage and hope we won't notice it's missing. This is kid stuff."

I love it tenderly, with all its warts and stains. I am indeed only French through this great city.—Michel de Montaigne

Sometimes, we feel that these might be the very best of times for us in Paris. We have to—*we must*—visit Paris two or three times a year. We have no choice. There are repairs to make, toilet paper and cleaning supplies to buy, bills to pay, workmen to meet, friends and relatives to guide through the streets of the Marais and past the ghosts of the Revolution, the Commune and the riots of '68. There is Roberta. There are Jean and Margaret, Eric and Patricia, Léa and Lucile.

Everybody has stuff they gotta do. They have to get up and go to work every day. They have to work late and humor the boss. They have to drop the kids off and pick the kids up. They have to go to the dentist. They have to lose weight, exercise more, take their vitamins and eat their greens. They have to get the oil changed and the tires rotated. They have to return every year to Sioux Falls or Cranston to spend the holidays with the family.

Us? We have to go to Paris.

We have to stroll past Notre Dame every few days to check out the state of the scaffolding and smile at the Quasimodo Follies. We have to feast on *coq au vin* at Chez René and drink Brouilly at Au Chai de l'Abbaye at least once every trip. We have to make sure our favorite greengrocer is still the Pavarotti of place Maubert. We have to paint watercolors, we have to stop for espresso or kir at several dozen *terrasses*, we have to feel each other up on the Pont des Arts in the moonlight, and we have to take a long walk hand-in-hand from place St.-Michel all the way to the place de l'Opéra, where the human parade passing the Café de la Paix is the most captivating on earth.

I know of no pleasanter way of spending an hour on a summer's day than in sitting outside the Café de la Paix, opposite the Opera and at the very centre of Paris, and just watching the people—people from all sorts of countries and in all sorts of clothes, the foreigners, varying from schoolmarms from the Middle West to strange Armenians, carrying over their arms the carpets that they never seem to sell—who on earth ever bought a carpet outside a café?—and far outnumbering the native-born Parisians.—Sidney Dark, *Paris,* 1936

We have to go to Paris. But because we also have to go back to America every time, the pleasures of Paris, in absentia, regain their freshness. It might be possible for Paris to become mundane—it almost happened to us during our Samaritaine Period—but this tragedy is inconceivable while we continue shuttling hither and back from season to season. Every return is a safari. We face an embarrassment of choices—whether to linger in the city or venture south to Burgundy, north to Champagne, west to Brussels and Bruges and our Belge friend Serge, east to Munich and Bavaria and our German friends Klaus and Marlene ...

Gauche ou droit?

Graveyards or gardens?

Museums or flea markets?

Cafés or cabarets?

Croissant or *pain au chocolat*?

Meursault or Juliénas?

The choices are tortuous and unnecessary. Eventually, we can do both, do all.

In Paris, we have habits, haunts and an undefinable rhythm. But we have yet to establish anything like a routine. It seems slightly blasphemous to associate the term "routine" with Paris at all. If our belief in Paris' infinite capacity to please and surprise is a romantic illusion, all the better. This we can handle. Junko and I have perpetuated our own romance by ignoring a lot of scary realities. We are artists of self-delusion. The reality of living, working, shopping, falling ill, growing old, climbing the stairs all the time in Paris while striving to sustain our romance with the city might turn out, in the long run, to be impossible. We suspect the nurture of our *joie de vivre à Paris* will be merely difficult, and mostly fun. If the thrill begins to wane, well, we'll take a picnic to that bridge when we come to it.

Meanwhile, Paris is a champagne interlude that comes along regularly, just about when we need it.

Of all the Seine bridges, the Pont des Arts is the pleasantest to sir or walk on; it is reserved for pedestrians, and it is really a promenade between the sky and water for students, nursemaids, children, old gentlemen and for painters having another go at the classical view of the Pont Neuf and the Ile de la Cité, picking out the light on the Tour St.-Jacques, struggling to get that flaking-gray shade of the river buildings.—V.S. Pritchett, *Down the Seine,* 1963

The Seine. I have painted it all my life, at all hours of the day, at all times of the year, from Paris to the sea.—Claude Monet

Benjie's Diary, 9 June '97, place du Châtelet: "Last night was picnic night on the Pont des Arts—and not just for Junko and me. It apparently occurred to everybody. We got in from painting at about eight and quickly packed a picnic bag of wine, bread, *rillettes*, cheese, tomatoes and olives. It was cloudy and a little blustery, so we took extra clothes and headed for the bridge in hopes that the clouds would drift off and the sunset would glow.

"In fact, all that worked out.

"We set up our little high tea on a bench in the middle of the bridge and watched the clouds slip away from the sun, over the Louvre and off to the west. We also watched as two guys parked at the railing near us, blocking our view of the sunset. In a moment, they were joined by another guy and a woman, who were followed by a woman, a man, a woman—all grad-student age. They began to break out beer (Corona), gin, potato chips and munchies. They spread a tablecloth and covered it with booze. One guy set up a radio and started playing—no kidding—cha-cha music.

(Jazz is supposed to be a Parisian passion, but you never hear it on the Paris streets. Cha-cha, yes. Miles Davis, *non!*)"

All the splendid pageant of old Paris is seen from the Pont des Arts, that footbridge between the Louvre and the Institut de France, which is the most important possession of the inspired idler in Paris, all the white domes and towers, the pillars of the stone bridges reflected in the green water, and the spire and towers of Notre Dame still, as if suspended, in the pearly air. There is an animated beauty in these works of the dead generations which tears at the heart.—George Slocombe, *The Heart of France: Parisian, Provincial & Peasant*, 1934

Benjie's Diary, 9 June '97, place du Châtelet: "By the time Junko and I were nibbling the last olive, a full-scale cocktail party had developed all around us. Up and down the bridge, but not quite as intensely as our little corner, picnics were busting out. The weather was warmer, the sun hung gloriously on the Seine and lovers kissed and groped against the rail. In the midst of this ruckus, which we seem to have incited, several women were fully decked out in slit-leg windblown silk cocktail dresses. Our favorite was a Rubens brunette who circulated among 'our' party, posing evocatively against the setting sun.

"The cocktail gang finally drove us off the bridge. We walked, contentedly, into the Left Bank and ended up at St.-Sulpice for café and *chocolat chaud*. We got home after eleven, Junko set out her clothes for the trip to Lausanne, and we fell asleep almost instantly."

March 4, 2018
Le Square
Trousseau

Epilogue

All cities, with the possible exception of Venice, have the right to change, and for good or ill, Paris has chosen to alter her face and figure in a thousand different ways.—Irwin Shaw, *Paris! Paris!*, 1976

I would not have undertaken this manuscript if Junko and Roberta had not nagged me to do so. When I finally gave in and tried to open the "Apt. in Paris" file on my Mac, the computer balked. The word-processing program I had used to write this book, on a previous Mac, was obsolete.

However, after a moment of dismay, it came to me that this blank slate posed no great hardship. The task of transcribing these 90,000-odd words presented an opportunity to reconsider, revise, edit and embellish a story I'd written some twenty-five years before. Besides, I had fun adding a new element, an appendix of endnotes (see below) that elaborate some of the more obscure references dropped along the way—like the strange death of Henry II and the secret grave in Montmartre of Théophile Steinlen.

As I've revisited this manuscript, I've been a little annoyed by the know-it-all pose struck by the author. But I left this "tone" largely intact. After all, I've been a know-it-all since high school, and my attitude—especially in reference to Paris—hasn't really mellowed over the years.

Indeed, if anything has changed in Junko and me since we undertook to acquire our spot in the Fifth, it is a) how much more we've learned about Paris and b) our awareness of how little we actually know. One of the city's daunting virtues is that it prevents anyone from becoming an authority. It holds too much history and hides too many mysteries.

Since Junko and I moved in, I've taken the Métro to the terminus of every line and walked back toward our garret at Kilometer Zero, flaneuring along the great boulevards and damp alleyways, barging into every church and roaming every park and garden, dropping into the handy café when I needed a rest, stuffing albums with photos and filling my Travel Diary with notes that will never be read.

Although it retains its original contours, Chez Hypotenuse has undergone many changes. The couch that Serge negotiated away from the "Vulture" at BHV has been replaced—twice. We are now laundering our clothes in our second *lave-linge*, cooking on our second range and keeping our leftovers in our second refrigerator. We've had our *chaudier* replaced twice and we hold our breath every time we return to Paris, twist the dial and pray for heat.

At long last, after the turn of the millennium, Léa found for us a stalwart workman named Girard who plastered and repainted the water-damaged section of wall beneath the gutter. With Léa by his side, Girard also ripped up our cruddy one-ply carpet and installed a paneled floor in both our rooms.

Several years ago, the condo board fired our building management company and hired a new one. The new *syndic* discovered a pattern of mismanagement by its predecessor that verged on criminality. The new team assessed each unit owner a substantial amount to undertake the *ravalement* (renovation) of our building's exterior—required every ten years by the city government—including a new roof. The latter improvement was especially welcome for Junko and me because we live directly under the roof, which has leaked on a regular basis ever since we bought the joint. Miraculously, however, the old roof survived the millennium cyclone, with hundred-mile-an-hour winds, that hit Paris between Christmas and New Year's in 1999.

Junko and I were able to reside full-time in our Paris apartment from 2002 to 2007 because Junko was promoted to the position of European bureau chief for her publication, *EE Times*. We moved to New York thereafter when Junko moved up again to editor-in-chief at *EET*. Meanwhile, I applied myself to writing books, mostly fiction, under the watchful eye of a gentlemanly literary agent in New York, Jack Scovil.

Pa Yoshida, the benefactor of our apartment in Paris, suffered a series of small strokes and succumbed in 2005. I wrote a brief description of his offbeat funeral and cremation in Chigasaki.

From the Weekly Screed, "A Japanese Funeral," 25 October '05: "I think I spotted the moment when Pa Yoshida passed from this life to whatever comes next. While we were strewing him with orchids and lilies, Ma Yoshida made an ironic remark. Junko—expressing the legacy of a father who conveyed to her an irrepressible *joie de vivre*—laughed. No one looked up. No one was shocked. Ma Yoshida was laughing, too. Mirth, at this intimate and easygoing funeral with everybody gently handling Pa Yoshida's mortal remains, didn't seem incongruous. More than that, it seemed necessary.

"If ever there was a perfect exit cue for Pa Yoshida, it was Junko, laughing."

Despite being thoroughly irradiated in the nuclear devastation of Hiroshima on 6 August 1945, Ma Yoshida lingered into her ninety-second year, losing her mobility and powers of speech along the way. But as long as Ma Yoshida was among the living, Junko made three or four journeys every year to spend time with her mother. Her every visit infused Ma Yoshida with a joy that was obvious, although she struggled to articulate it. She even seemed happy to see me, mostly because, as the only *gaijin* within a ten-block radius, I was so easy to recognize.

While she was still able, Ma Yoshida made two trips to Paris, once on her own with Junko's Uncle Matsuda and once when we were able to take her to some of our favorite haunts.

From the Weekly Screed, "The atomic mother-in-law," 15 April '22: "I remember a night in Paris. It was cold enough to keep even most Parisians home. Braving the chill, we took Ma Yoshida to a little Italian restaurant on the Île St. Louis called Castefiore (it's gone now). The bistro was almost empty when we arrived. The proprietor, a British chef whom Junko and I had known for years, had sent his staff home. He waited on us personally. After we had finished, with no other customers in the place, the chef (tall and handsome) brought us dessert and sat with us.

"He proceeded to charm Ma Yoshida, asking questions that Junko translated. He hoped she had enjoyed his cuisine. He scoffed in disbelief when she admitted her age. He praised her excellent taste in fashion. I sat back and watched with quiet pleasure as Ma Yoshida's years melted away, exposing in her blushes and smiles, that inner schoolgirl, that hint of playful vanity that life's troubles—a war, a bomb, a radioactive nightmare, a daughter lost, her husband gone—had fought so hard to crush.

"When she was not exactly 'sweet' sixteen, Ma Yoshida—pretty little Kiyoko—had encountered, smack-dab in the center of his atomic inferno, the Grim Reaper. But after a moment, after trembling at the slaughter he had wreaked, she kicked him in the shin and walked away—a bounce in her step and a twinkle in her eye."

Chastened by the aggravation of dealing with *locataires*, we stopped renting our place to tourists in 2002 and left it empty when we were not in Paris.

But it wasn't really empty. Léa grew up, earned a place at one of France's elite universities and studied the twin disciplines of architecture and engineering. While in school in Paris, she frequented our apartment and resided there for more than a year. Léa has become one of the most respected young architects/engineers in Paris, editor of a book on the subject and the founding president of an association of young people practicing their dual professions.

Léa, of course, besides being brilliant, is beautiful and blonde. Her similarly beautiful sister, Lucile, who had always been shy and reticent with Junko and me, had a transformative experience during a trip to New York. She was taken under the tender mercies of poet Steve Bluestone and his wife Mary Jo. She saw the sights of the Big Apple, grew confident with her English and exposed to us, when next we saw her, a vivacious personality. She now works outside Paris in the company that makes Laughing Cow cheese (which Lucile calls "easy cheese").

Léa's mother, Patricia, has segued into retirement and taken up golf, among her other activities. Her husband Eric is busy with golf also, giving lessons and competing in tournaments appropriate to his age. Lately, because we love the family, we avoid discussing politics. Patricia and Eric have gravitated from their youthful socialism toward a kinder, gentler version of Margaret's Napoleonic nativism. Margaret, after Jean's death, sank into a seclusion that kept Junko and me away and troubled her family. We missed her funeral because we were in America.

I'll always try to remember Margaret a little tipsy from good wine, and laughing like a teenager.

Unlike Margaret, Roberta seems immortal. She might be a vampire. She resides still, shouldering daily through a movable hobo encampment, on rue des Bourdonnais. She continues to entertain throngs of friends, as well as her children and grandchildren. Both she and Junko have survived breast cancer, shrugging it off like a moth-eaten afghan. We've celebrated Thanksgivings and Christmases with Roberta. She has invited me twice to discuss my novels with her reading group. She's been active for decades with Democrats Abroad and fights to protect the rights of American citizens who live overseas, a Sisyphean struggle. A conversation with Roberta is, as always, an exhilarating trip through a hall of mirrors.

After a dalliance with a girl whom we called Meatloaf—but forgot why—Serge discovered Valerie, his true love. Although refusing the conventionalism of marriage, Serge and Val nonetheless settled down into a conventional family life in a little house in Rixensart, just outside Brussels. They have two sons, Benjamin and Martin, for whom Junko and I serve (uselessly) as godparents. Despite Serge's atheism and iconoclasm, Benjamin and Martin both attended parochial schools and joined the Boy Scouts. Whenever we meet again, Serge still attacks me—and Junko—with a lung-crushing hug.

In the last few years, we have acquired a *chat de gouttier,* George the cat, whose owner is one floor below and whom we've never met—nor do we wish to. George prowls the eavestrough outside our windows in hopes that one might be open. After he squeezes inside and carries out his usual inspection, he likes to interrupt my work and sit on my lap. He has been known to break the occasional vase.

We haven't returned to the Crazy Horse—which continues to thrive on the tourist trade—in at least ten years. The last we heard of Polly Harper, she had been dispatched to Las Vegas to organize a Crazy Horse franchise there. Although Junko and I made annual trips to Vegas for the Consumer Electronics Show, we've never thought of looking up the local facsimile of the Crazy Horse, nor have we harbored any hope of finding Polly.

On several occasions, however, we met with Akky. She both performed and helped to manage the floor show at the Stardust. But that was years ago. The Stardust, of course, is gone and Akky, as far as we know, has receded into the suburbs of Las Vegas. We think she's married now, perhaps with kids—who must be gorgeous—and we hope she's finally making use of the law degree she earned at the University of Nevada.

George Ball, the gentle artist with whom we often had breakfast at the *boulangerie* on boulevard St.-Germain, passed away, partly from heartbreak, after the death of his dog, Jason. We learned of George's demise from Brian Spence, who continues to operate the Abbey Bookshop on rue de la Parcheminerie. Brian provided a model for one of the protagonists in my novel, *Skulduggery in the Latin Quarter.*

Among the haunts mentioned in this memoir, we visit Chez René less often. The menu has altered, including the tragic deletion of the bistro's peerless *coq au vin*. The management is a little less congenial than once they were. Now, we dine more often at the Bistrot du Dôme and at a new discovery, La Pie Noir on rue de la Montagne Ste.-Geneviève. Our next-door Greek restaurant, Knossos, has become a sort of French bistro called Flagrant Delice, where—of course—we never eat. We used to faithfully patronize Au Chai de l'Abbaye on rue de Buci as our first stop when returning to Paris. But it was taken over after the pandemic by a corporation. Suddenly, a neighborhood wine bar was turned into a tourist trap and—like L'Échaudé St.-Germain—we had to kiss it *au revoir*. Our replacement jet-lag hangout is a café called L'Annexe de la Petite Périgourdine on rue des Écoles. The head waitress knows us there. In a city as big and daunting as Paris, it's a comfort to be recognized as you come through the door.

Speaking of rue des Écoles, our morning coffee for years was a *boulangerie* there. We were welcomed daily by Stephan the manager and sometimes hugged by Patrick, a burly merchant mariner who worked there whenever he wasn't at sea. But Stephan moved on a few years ago, the place was redecorated and changed its name. The woman in charge, who had secretly chafed under Stephan's leadership, asserted her dominion. She installed a self-service cashier machine and did her best to regiment her patrons. We bid the joint a regretful adieu and moved our morning routine to the ancient and drafty Pâtisserie Viennoise on the rue de l'École-de-Médecine. There, we're greeted warmly by Séverine, plump and charming, who knows our order and who, when one of us is alone, asks after the other.

On weekends, when the *patisserie* is closed, we splurge at the elegant Les Éditeurs, on the carrefour de l'Odéon, which has the loveliest croissants of any café we know. We still shop for basics at place Maubert. Our regular vendors at the *marché* greet us familiarly.

And we still know where to find the best bowl of soup in all of Paris.

But Paris, as it must, has changed. Among the changes over this quarter-century was the closing of our furnishings store, Samaritaine, and then—when all hope seemed lost—its reopening with a new coat of paint. Meanwhile, inexplicably, Paris lost its two most luxurious food stores, Fauchon and Hédiard—where we loved to shop—in the place de la Madeleine. I can't explain that. Notre Dame burned, but President Emmanuel Macron rallied the nation—and an army of craftsmen—to rebuild it exactly as it had looked before the fire. Meanwhile, of course, the French people sustained their tradition of despising their president regardless of his noble deeds and good intentions.

All told, Junko and I have changed more than Paris. In the time we've owned our apartment on rue St.-Séverin, I've dragged Junko to several of my high-school class reunions, which are a sort of laboratory for the ravages of time. We depend on name tags to recognize the grownups who were once teenagers together at Robert M. La Follette High. Otherwise, I might mistake a guy named Steve, whom I used to greet in the hall, for a different guy named Bill, who was in my gym class for four years. Without name tags, I couldn't tell Shirley, who flirted with me once, from Linda, on whom I had a brief ninth-grade crush.

Paris, on the other hand, despite the passage of centuries, the trampling of invaders and the erection of that ugly tower in Montparnasse, will never need a name tag, a signpost or a chyron on the bottom of the screen.

Paris will never be mistaken for Cleveland.

Endnotes

This is not a comprehensive listing of every reference to Paris, to France or to other obscure items in this story. I've taken the liberty of limiting these explanatory notes to only the more interesting names dropped and terms mentioned. I believe, for example, that everyone should know who Steinlen was—and where he's buried.

CHAPTER 1

1. Georges Brassens (1921–1981) is one of France's most beloved singer/songwriters, also regarded as one of the nation's great twentieth-century poets. His most popular songs, including "Le Gorille," about an escaped gorilla with a huge penis, are humorous, satirical and risqué.

2. Monique Andrée Serf (1930–1997) chose the stage name Barbara in honor of her Ukrainian grandmother, Varvara Brodsky. A Jewish girl born in Paris, she was hidden with her family during the Holocaust by conductor Jean-Paul Penin. During her singing career, she was close to Jacques Brel and Georges Brassens. She struggled for years but scored a hit with her own songs at the Théâtre des Capucines in Paris in 1964. After that, she signed a contract with Philips Records and became one of France's most popular *chanteuses*.

3. Lili St. Cyr (1917–1999), arguably the most renowned striptease artist in American showbiz—and unquestionably its most creative—was a Minnesota girl, born Marie Frances Van Schaack in Minneapolis. Her stage name, used first in her Las Vegas act, is a patronymic of the child-saint Saint Quiricus (Cyriacus). The highlight of her long career was at the Gayety Theatre in Montreal from 1944 to 1951, where she was dubbed "Montreal's *femme fatale.*" The city's Catholic clergy condemned her act, and she was charged but later acquitted for behavior that was "immoral, obscene and indecent." Among her innovations was the "flying G," the climax of her dance, when a stagehand pulled a fishing line attached to her g-string, which flew into the balcony as the stage went dark.

4. This is probably a reference to César Baldaccini (1921–1998), a sculptor who created ironic and transgressive works by welding and soldering metal, often using pieces of scrap. He designed the César Awards trophy, the French equivalent to the Academy Awards' Oscar.

5. André Gustave Fernand Raynaud (1926–1973) was a popular French stand-up comic star, actor and singer.

6. Raymond Devos (1922–2006) was a French humorist, stand-up comedian and clown, known especially for sophisticated puns and surreal humor.

7. In 1922, after a series of Hollywood scandals, the film industry under the leadership of Will H. Hays, a politically active lawyer, created the Hays Office, which initiated a blacklist, inserted morals clauses into actors' contracts, and in 1930 developed a Production Code that detailed what was morally acceptable on the screen.

8. Kiki de Montparnasse (1901–1953) was a French cabaret performer, painter, and artists' muse, a sensual fixture in Parisian bohemian circles who modeled for many artists, including Soutine, Modigliani, Cocteau, Foujita and Alexander Calder. She had a long and torrid affair with Man

Ray, whose most famous photo, *Le Violon d'Ingres* shows Kiki's bare back with f-holes painted in black onto the print to suggest her body as a musical instrument.

9. The next time we saw Akky was her image on a Las Vegas billboard dressed mostly in sequins and feathers. Proclaimed as "The Showgirl of the 21st Century," Akky was the headliner of the floor show at the Stardust.

CHAPTER 2

10. In her prime, Agustina del Carmen Otero Iglesias "La Belle Otero" (1868–1965), a Spanish actress and courtesan, was the most sought-after woman in Europe and the star of the Folies Bergère.

11. The Organisation for Economic Co-operation and Development (OECD)was founded in 1961. Its fifty member nations strive to coordinate economic policy on a global scale and to mediate disputes among both its members and non-member nations, among them Brazil, India, Indonesia and China.

12. Alice "Spot" Twombly, formerly an English teacher in Madison, Wisconsin, where Benjamin was one of her pupils, is a lifelong friend. Her sister, Verandah Porche, was consort to Ray Mungo, founder of the Liberation News Service. Ray and Verandah eventually forsook politics and went up-country to a patch of land called Total Loss Farm, where Verandah continues to live.

13. The Abbey Bookshop, at 29 rue de la Parcheminerie, was founded in 1989 by Brian Spence, a handsome Canadian. Its overflowing inventory of new and used, mostly English language, books is a calming literary refuge from the tourist-packed Shakespeare & Co. nearby. If you drop in to browse, Brian is likely to offer you a cup of coffee with a drop of maple syrup. A watercolor of the façade, painted by Junko, appears as the cover image of my novel, *Skulduggery in the Latin Quarter* (Last Kid Books, 2019).

14. The popular title for the executioner who dropped the blade of the guillotine was Monsieur de Paris.

15. Jean Anthelme Brillat-Savarin (1755–1826) was the original foodie. Although a lawyer, politician, judge and deputy of the Estates-General, he claimed a place in history in 1825 with a compendium on the pleasures of the table, *The Physiology of Taste: Or Meditations on Transcendental Gastronomy: A Work Theoretical, Historical, and Programmed.*

16. Jeeves, valet and butler to Bertie Wooster in novels by P.G. Wodehouse, is one of the great comic creations in fiction. It was Wodehouse, describing the liquefaction of Jeeves' ambulation, who devised a new meaning for the verb "to shimmer."

CHAPTER 3

17. Scottish philosopher and essayist David Hume (1711–1776), whose experience of Paris preceded the French Revolution, is little cited today, but his skepticism, eclecticism and eloquence inspired Charles Dickens. Hume influenced economists Adam Smith and Jeremy Bentham and foreshadowed Darwin's theory of evolution.

18. Our first communal carrying case for vital travel documents was a black leather zippered wallet with numerous pockets for tickets, passports, luggage claim tags, etc., about nine by four inches. After the original black thing wore out, we replaced it with a similar wallet. This one is red, but we still call it the "black thing."

19. Until their numbers were decimated by conscription in World War I, gangsters called *apaches* ruled criminal Paris. In *Paris: The Secret History*, Andrew Hussey wrote that "*Apaches* [the name was inspired by the appearance of Buffalo Bill at the 1900 exhibition] were soon the stuff of legend, known for the red scarves they wore around their necks, the knives [*zarin*] they carried in their pockets, their capacity for drink and a tendency to knock their women about apparent in the

Apache dance that lingers forlornly in a heavily diluted form in the present-day."

Street thugs, as suggested by Elliot Paul, continued to carry the appellation.

(An *apache* hangout in Montmartre and its denizens is one of the locales in my novel, *Bistro Nights*.)

20. La Friterie, a tiny shop on rue Galande forced into a lopsided trapezoidal shape by the impingement of two larger buildings, across from the renowned cabaret Aux Trois Mailletz, was a rare purveyor of *frites*, a Belgian delicacy known in America as French fries. Seemingly simple, *frites* are almost never prepared as artfully as Henri did while he was in business. Alas, Henri retired, depriving Paris of a dish difficult to reproduce. Since then, the locale has been renamed "Odette" and redecorated preciously with an emphasis on plastic flowers and a menu of cloying sweets and confections, rendering it a tourist magnet and one of the Left Bank's most iPhotographed attractions.

21. Dating back to the era of the post-World War I "Lost Generation" crowd (Gertrude Stein, Man Ray, James Joyce, Kiki, Ernest Hemingway, Tsuguharu Foujita, George Antheil, Elliot Paul, Sylvia Beach, etc.), the joints that have been deemed the four great "literary cafés" of Paris—where all these intellectuals hung out—are La Coupole, Le Dome, La Rotonde and Le Select.

22. Alfred Perlès (1897–1990) was an Austrian writer less known for his handful of nostalgic books than for his associations with more famous authors, namely Henry Miller, Lawrence Durrell, and Anaïs Nin.

CHAPTER 4

23. The "wards" of Paris are *arrondissements*, numbering twenty in total, arranged in a snail-like pattern from the First (*1er*) in the heart of Paris to the Twentieth (*20ème*) on the eastern perimeter. If you've been to Paris, you already knew

this.

24. It seems silly to compose a reminder so soon after his departure from the international stage, but the public memory grows ever shorter. François Maurice Adrien Marie Mitterrand (1916–1996) was France's longest serving president, from 1981 to 1995. Although his political career began in the Vichy government that collaborated with the Third Reich in World War II, he bailed on that regime, joined the Resistance and emerged eventually as an opponent of Charles de Gaulle and leader of the Socialist opposition. One of our favorite aspects of Mitterand's presence in Paris was the regular blockade—by the national police—of the little rue de Bièvre, because one of the buildings on the block was the residence of the president's mistress. When he was visiting her, the street was off-limits.

25. Anthony Martignetti was the star of a classic TV commercial, filmed in Boston, for Prince spaghetti. You can still view the ad online using the key words "Prince spaghetti" and "Anthony."

26. The Moral Rearmament movement, founded in 1922 by American minister Frank Buchman, has a fascinating and checkered history. Based at first at Princeton University, Buchman preached the "Four Absolutes": absolute honesty, absolute purity, absolute unselfishness and absolute love. Controversies moved MRA from Princeton to Oxford in England, where the movement drew an international following and, when World War II began, praise from Harry Truman, chairman of the U.S. Senate's Truman Committee investigating war contracts. Buchman lost some credibility by uttering pro-Nazi statements like: "I thank heaven for a man like Adolf Hitler, who built a front-line of defense against the anti-Christ of Communism." Nevertheless, MRA's postwar efforts, centered at Mountain House in Caux, were deemed instrumental in reconciling leaders of nations at war. By the late twentieth century, MRA had lost most of its followers and

all its cachet. In 2001, the MRA movement changed its name to Initiatives of Change.

27. A leader of the Gallic Aulerci tribe and one of the earliest rulers of Paris, when it was called Lutetia, Camulogène burned the town down as a tactic against the Roman invaders. This wasn't a good idea. The Romans killed him in the Battle of Lutetia in 52 B.C.

28. Junko's periodical, *Electronic Engineering Times*, was for many years the Bible of the electronics industry. She wrote for *EE Times* for thirty years, in Tokyo, Europe, Silicon Valley and New York, eventually serving as its editor-in-chief and earning several awards for excellence in journalism.

29. A *rente viagère* is a curious French financial instrument that allows the owner of a property to sell it without moving out. The buyer secures ownership but agrees to regular payments while waiting for the aged owner to die. There are incidences of the occupant surviving well into her nineties and outliving a "buyer" who—in a death watch of twenty years or more—never got to move in.

CHAPTER 5

30. Among the literary celebrities in Paris' "Lost Generation" American expatriate community, most are out of print and forgotten, except by a handful of Master of Fine Arts aspirants. Harold Stearns might serve as their archetype. Although deemed, at first, a prolific essayist and critic, his output shrank drastically as he hobnobbed with his fellow "Montparnassos," gambling, begging loans from friends and drinking himself eventually to death. Ernest Hemingway used Stearns as a model for the indigent Harvey Stone in *The Sun Also Rises*.

31. I've changed Monsieur Lafitte's name because this chronicle includes a few personal details about the building owner.

32. Among the Lost Generation writers who chronicled the

goings-on among Paris.' expatriate artists' colony, Malcolm Cowley had perhaps the longest and most productive career. In his memoir, *Exile's Return: A Literary Odyssey of the 1920s* in 1934, he etched the epitaph of his Paris days. He wrote that "our whole training was involuntarily directed toward destroying whatever roots we had in the soil, toward eradicating our local and regional peculiarities, toward making us homeless citizens of the world." He became editor of *The New Republic* and took part in the creation of the leftist League of American Writers. During World War II, Cowley was forced from his job as an analyst for the War Department's Office of Facts and Figures by the House Un-American Activities Committee (HUAC). He spent the bulk of his career as an editor at the Viking Press, nurturing a new generation of American literature.

33. The Cimetière du Père-Lachaise, founded by Napoleon in 1804, is one of our favorite haunts. Located in the Twentieth Arrondissement, it's Paris' largest and most prestigious graveyard. Among its residents are Yves Montand side by side with Simone Signoret, Colette, Frédéric Chopin, Édith Piaf, Marcel Proust, Marcel Marceau, Olivia de Havilland, Sarah Bernhardt, Oscar Wilde, Georges Bizet, Jim Morrison, and Sir Richard Wallace. The cemetery is named for the confessor to Louis XIV, Père François de la Chaise (1624–1709).

34. Judge Joseph Force Crater, a justice on the New York Supreme Court, disappeared, never to be seen again, on August 6, 1930, just as the state was beginning an investigation into corruption in New York City. A national dragnet and an almost unprecedented wave of publicity, speculation and conspiracy theories followed after his disappearance. Judge Crater was declared dead in 1939, and his case was closed forty years after his disappearance.

CHAPTER 6

35. In the span of three years, Charlton Heston twice experienced earth after the Apocalypse, first in *Planet of the*

Apes (1968) and then in *The Omega Man* (1971). The latter was directed by Boris Sagal and starred Heston as the very lonely survivor of a pandemic. The film evoked a predecessor, Vincent Price in *The Last Man on Earth* (1964), and foreshadowed an entire genre of post-Apocalyptic downers, from *Soylent Green* (again with Heston) to the Mad Max franchise and beyond.

36. Ernest Cognacq (1839–1928) was a salesman and entrepreneur originally from the Charente-Maritime region of southwest France who failed several times in business before hitting the jackpot in Paris with the development of La Samaritaine. His Belgian architect, Frantz Jourdain (1847–1935), pioneered Art Nouveau and iron-frame architecture in France. In later additions to Cognacq's department store, Jourdain transitioned to the Art Deco style, although Parisian regulators forced Jourdain to hide his original metal frame beneath a stone façade. Note that historian Norval White spells Cognacq's name without the terminal "q."

37. On 30 June 1559, King Henry II of France insisted on one last joust in a tournament. The lance of his opponent, Gabriel de Lorges, Count of Montgomery, Lord of Lorges and Ducey, a French nobleman of Scottish extraction, pierced the king's helmet, sending a shard into Henry II's eye that entered his brain, killing him. Montgomery was forgiven for the king's accidental death, but he later converted to Protestantism, becoming an enemy of the state. In 1573, he was captured while attempting an insurrection in Normandy. He was beheaded in Paris on 26 June 1574.

38. François Ravaillac (1578–1610) was a religious zealot who believed he was on a mission from God to convince France's most beloved king, Henry IV, to convert the Protestant Huguenots to Catholicism. When the king decided to invade the Netherlands, Ravaillac thought Henry IV was launching a war against the Pope. Determined to kill the king, Ravaillac stalked him and seized his moment when Henry's carriage was blocked by wagons carrying wine and hay on a Paris

street. Ravaillac plunged into the king's coach and stabbed him to death. On May 27, 1610, Ravaillac was taken to the place de Grève and was tortured one last time before being pulled apart by four horses, a method of execution reserved for regicides. Historian Alistair Horne wrote: "Before being drawn and quartered ... he was scalded with burning sulphur, molten lead and boiling oil and resin, his flesh then being torn by pincers."

39. *Bricolage* is the elegant French term for all the tools, materials and sundries that go into a do-it-yourself project.

40. "W.C." Years after I originally wrote this passage, I began to see a few posted notices in cafés and restaurants restricting the use of toilets to patrons. Once, on rue des Archives, I was actually halted and turned around on route to a toilet. However, the standing convention is that, in a typical joint, the waiters are too busy serving customers to bother standing guard at the door to the john.

41. Félix François Faure was an undistinguished president of the Third Republic (1895–1899), in office during the Dreyfus Affair—the antisemitic imprisonment of a Jewish military officer—which he tried to shrug off as a *fait accompli.* While France's automobile industry led the world at the time, he was heard saying to his nation's carmakers, "Your cars are very ugly, and they smell very bad."

42. Raymond Nicolas Landry Poincaré was president of France (1913–1920) throughout World War I. During that time he was gradually overshadowed by his arch-rival Georges Clemenceau, who seized from Poincaré control over the negotiations for the armistice.

CHAPTER 7

43. Since our first trip to Paris in 1990, it has been my habit to buy the morning American newspaper, published in Paris, to read with coffee and *pain au chocolat* in a favored *boulangerie.* For years, this paper was the storied *International Herald*

Tribune, which evolved from two U.S. newspapers that long sent correspondents to live in Paris and report on its doings, the *New York Herald* and the *Chicago Tribune*. In recent years, with the acquisition of this landmark daily by the *New York Times*, the historic masthead has been expunged. It is now *The New York Times International Edition*. Typically, I still read it in "hard copy" while Junko pores through the *Financial Times* on her mobile phone.

44. Théophile Alexandre Steinlen (1859–1923) created some of the most recognized and beloved poster art in Parisian history, including the ubiquitous black cat promoting *La tournée du Chat Noir*. One of our most pleasing discoveries was Steinlen's grave, a modest memorial tucked into a leafy corner of the small, charming Cimetière Saint-Vincent on the back slope of Montmartre.

45. Paul Colin (1892–1985) was one of the most prolific illustrators in twentieth-century Paris, his designs bridging the movements of Art Deco, Cubism and Surrealism, his figures angular, geometric and "jazzy." He designed posters for artists and theaters such as the Folies Bergère, the Moulin Rouge and the Théâtre des Champs-Élysées, as well as for movies and advertising. Today, originals of his work sell at auction for six figures.

46. If ever there were a movable feast, it would be the bistros and restaurants of Paris. Some, like Le Procope, have existed for a century or more. Others come and go in a matter of months. Junko and I have long maintained a list of places—far less comprehensive than the Hamburgers' guide—where we have dined and found everything more than satisfactory. We revise regularly, adding new discoveries and deleting when necessary, and share our list with friends traveling to Paris.

47. One of Paris' most famous, prestigious, expensive restaurants, La Tour d'Argent on the quai de la Tournelle is best known for its duck dinner and its view. The cannier

tourist, dumbstruck by the price of a meal upstairs, can resort to its sister restaurant on street level. La Rôtisserie d'Argent is a genial bistro where the duck is pretty much the same, and the street-level view is interesting in its own right. Once, as we dined at a window table, I saw a breathtaking woman passenger on a motorcycle, her hair in the breeze, her legs bare to the hip, her skirt floating in the wake of the bike. Before I could point her out to Junko, she was gone.

CHAPTER 8

48. "Face flu."

After searching our memories for a possible cause of the crusty rash on my face, we remembered a weekend excursion to Edgewood Park in Redwood City, California. We found out too late that this park is rampant with poison oak. In our research, we learned that the symptoms of contact with poison oak, especially the onset of face flu and gatornose, were consistent with mine.

49. Although I still read the successor of the *International Herald Tribune*, *The New York Times International Edition* in Paris, I no longer regard this English-language lifeline with the same reverence. Over the years, the head office in New York has seen fit to expunge, without explanation or apology, numerous features vital to the wandering American. These include the weather report, the daily baseball and weekly football scores and, most tragically, *Peanuts* and *Calvin and Hobbes*. The sports page, however, persists in covering European soccer exhaustively.

50. Georges Goursat (1863–1934), whose *nom de la palette* was "Sem," was an illustrator and caricaturist whose work ranged from the Belle Époque through the tumultuous twenties in Paris. Besides his depictions of society from top to bottom, he drew caricatures of virtually every prominent person who occupied or passed through post-World War I Paris, including Coco Chanel, Colette, George Feydeau, Sacha Guitry, Jules

Massenet, J.P. Morgan, Giacomo Puccini and Maurice Rostand.

51. Honoré-Victorin Daumier (1808–1879) was a painter, sculptor, and printmaker whose comic depictions of the high and mighty, especially in French courtrooms, are among the great caricatures ever drawn. His comic images appeared in popular newspapers and periodicals, mocking and satirizing the monarchy, politicians, the judiciary, lawyers and the bourgeoisie.

52. My guide for English speakers curious about sumo, particularly for fans watching the bimonthly tournaments on Japanese TV, was published as *The Joy of Sumo* in 1990 by Tuttle Publishing of Tokyo and Vermont. I revised the book in 2010 for Tuttle, who republished the book, with photos, as *SUMO: A Thinking Fan's Guide to Japan's National Sport*. It remains in print after more than thirty years as the bestselling sumo book ever published.

53. Daniel-François-Esprit Auber (1782–1871) specialized in composing operas, largely of the comic variety, in collaboration with the librettist Eugène Scribe. His most notable grand opera was *La Muette de Portici (The Mute of Portici)*. He served from 1842 to 1871 as director of France's premier music academy, the Paris Conservatoire. Many images of him are available online, but none with a hat.

54. It's my habit to catch up on my Travel Diary, recording our daily experiences on the road lest we forget. Customarily, I fill in my journal at a café, where I can have a coffee or glass of wine and watch Parisians pass by. Le Relais Paris Opéra is typical, just off the beaten path at 1, rue Auber. Felicitously, this café remains in operation almost thirty years—and one pandemic—later.

CHAPTER 9

55. Henri Fantin-Latour (1836–1904) was a French painter and lithographer best known for his lush still-life paintings of flowers and fruit and for portraiture of Parisian artists and

writers in elegant Victorian dress.

56. The namesake of the boulevard Poniatowski, Prince Józef Antoni Poniatowski (1763–1813), was a Polish general and one of Napoleon I's most devoted allies, eventually named a Marshal of the French Empire. He stuck with Napoleon to the bitter end, participating in the disastrous attack on Moscow in 1812 and defending the French army's retreat after Napoleon lost the Battle of Leipzig in 1813. Poniatowski was wounded badly and ended up drowning in the Elster River.

Glossary

On behalf of linguistic cripples like myself, I've endeavored in this reminiscence to avoid the gratuitous use of foreign terms. It's inevitable, however, that a book set outside the U.S. will contain a few exotic words in the language of the country or countries frequented by the author. I've exacerbated the problem in this book by injecting terms here and there in Japanese and Yiddish. To soothe these impositions on the reader, I'm providing definitions of almost all of this volume's non-English words and phrases below:

acheteur: buyer
addition: in a restaurant, the check
agneau: lamb
ail: garlic
aile: wing
ancien: old
apache: a street criminal of the early twentieth century in Paris
arrondissement: a ward or precinct in Paris
art brut: primitive or spontaneous art—Grandma Moses was *brut.*
ascenseur: elevator
aspirateur: vacuum cleaner

assiette: plate, or plateful of food

assurance des emprunteurs: borrowers' insurance; verification that buyers of an apartment have a mortgage offer in hand

atelier: artist's studio

autre: another

avocat: lawyer

bac: ferry

balconnet: balcony

banlieue: suburb

bateaux mouche: a long, low Parisian tourist barge (literally, "fly boat"), plying the Seine daily from dawn to midnight

bâtiment: building

beau/belle: beautiful, pretty, fine

beaucoup: very much, very many

Beaux Arts: the fine arts

béton: concrete

bien sur: of course

boeuf bourguignon: beef in a rich, dark demiglace sauce, stewed in the style of the Burgundy region

bois: wood

"Bonnes gens qui par cy passez, priez Dieu pour les tréspassés.": Inscription on the church of St.-Séverin, "Good people who pass here, pray God for the dead souls."

boulangerie: bakery

boul-Mich: the boulevard St.-Michel, lifeline of the Sorbonne student body

bricolage: do-it-yourself department

broyeur: a unique Paris toilet that combines the functions of the "head" on a sailboat with the garbage disposal in an American sink. Its presence signals that the plumbing in a particular dwelling is inadequate to support a conventional Thomas Crapper flush toilet

caisse: cashier's desk

canard roti: roast duck

cave/caveau: a cellar, often used to store wine, often damp and uninhabitable. On the Left Bank of the Seine, near the river, many caves are the result of excavation that followed the great flood of January 1910, when mud poured into the ground floors of Left Bank dwellings. Since the mud couldn't be moved, most building owners abandoned the lower floors and built upward. Some mud-filled cellars were eventually dug out, mostly for storage but sometimes for more felicitous purposes. The Caveau de la Huchette on rue de la Huchette, for example, has been for many years a lively jazz club where, until his death in 1988, blues legend Memphis Slim often boogie-woogied into the wee hours for claustrophobic standing-room audiences.

cent grammes: 100 grams

centre ville: city center

c'est dommage: too bad; it's a shame

chanteur/chanteuse: singer

charcuterie: cooked pork in various forms, usually served cold; also, a pork butcher's shop or delicatessen

chateau: castle

chaud: hot

chaudier: heater

chauffage: heating

chien chaud avec la sauce des milles iles de Kraft (coinage): hot dog with Kraft Thousand Island dressing

chipmunks (coinage): two, sometimes three, young Japanese women scurrying around a foreign city draped with shopping bags from designer boutiques, constantly consulting a Japanese guidebook and a tourist map and feverishly discussing which boutique to hit next. Their mecca: Louis Vuitton.

choucroute: sauerkraut

cinquième étage: the fifth floor

circoncision des oreilles: circumcision of the ears
clair: light, bright, clear
clementine: tangerine
clochard: bum, vagabond, panhandler
cochon: pig
cochonailles: smoked pork ribs
comble: attic space
confit de canard: preserved duck, one of the most toothsome by-products of the *foie gras* industry in the Périgord and Basque regions. It is a popular bistro dish in Paris and, because it comes in a can, perhaps the best food item to bring home from France.
coq au vin: chicken stewed endlessly in a red wine sauce and served almost as black as octopus ink
coquille St.-Jacques: scallop
cotelette d'agneau: lamp chop
cour privée: private courtyard
crémerie: dairy; a shop specializing in dairy products (and fresh eggs)
croque monsieur: a French lunch and snacktime staple, a slice of ham on bread toasted beneath a thick layer of cheese, usually Gruyère
déjeuner: lunch
demain: tomorrow
dépannage: troubleshooting
déshabille: undressed, scantily clad
dix heures moins le quart: quarter to ten; 9:45
eau: water
ebi (Japanese): shrimp
église: church
en anglais: in English
en face: in front of
enfant: child

entrécote: rib steak, a cheap cut of beef that, in the hands of a good French chef, can be sublime

escalier: staircase

f: abbreviation for "franc," the french currency before the euro

flic (slang): cop

formule: a set-price meal usually composed of an appetizer (*entrée*), a main course (*plat*), dessert (*dessert*) and coffee. Wine is extra.

frais d'acte: fee for a proceeding or action

frais de dossier: fee to pay for documents or files

frais du prêt: loan fee

fraise: strawberry

fraises des bois: wild strawberries

framboise: raspberry

la France profonde: rural France, any part of France other than Paris

friterie: French fries shop

fromage: cheese

foie gras: the liver of a goose or duck, often served in a *paté* or liver paste, composed entirely of "good" cholesterol. The more you eat, the longer you live.

francs: French money (pre-euro)

gaijin (Japanese): foreigner, usually white; black foreigners are *kokujin*

gateau: cake; Marie Antoinette's *bête noire*

gauche: left hand; impolite, inappropriate

gentil: gentle, genteel, gentlemanly; classy

gratinée: cheesy (in a good sense)

haricots verts: green beans, but unlike American green beans; these are long and thin, tender as a baby's pecker

hotel de ville: city hall

ilot insalubre: unsanitary island, slum

immeuble: building

kaiseki (Japanese): a multi-course Japanese meal in a series of small, elaborately designed tidbits, ideally served by meek and deferential women in full kimono; the most expensive way to eat out in Japan

kanji (Japanese): traditional characters in Japanese writing based on Chinese ideograms

Lac Léman: Lake Geneva

lait: milk

langoustine: a Dublin Bay prawn; saltwater crayfish

lave-linge: washing machine

livraison: delivery

locataire: renter, tenant, lodger

louer: to rent

Lutetia: the Roman name for the city of Paris, which eventually reverted to the name of its original inhabitants, a tribe called the Parisii. The Lutetia is one of the most elegant hotels on the Left Bank (the café serves a splendid *chocolat chaud*).

marché: market, trading center, shopping promenade. The Left Bank's toniest department store is La Bonne Marché.

mauvais: bad

Meiji Era (Japanese): the long reign of Emperor Meiji (1867–1912), who forced Japan out of feudalism toward modern forms of government and social organization

merci: thank you

metaux: metals

métier: profession, job

mildiou: mildew

Mon Dieu!: My God!

mon petit chou: my little cabbage; sweetheart

moule: mussel

moules-frites: mussels steamed in a mariniere sauce with

thin French fries, usually served with copious amounts of beer. This is the national dish of Belgium, but it's widely available (thank God) in Paris, ideally only in months that contain an "r"

The best recipe he [the fish man on rue Rambuteau] gave me was for mussels: "Brown two chopped onions and a piece of garlic in a thread of butter, then when they're transparent, add two cups of dry white wine and a cup of water, salt and pepper and a bay leaf. Let them bubble nicely while you clean a quart of mussels for each person. With your fingers, pull off the beard (it rips off easily if you're pulling in the right direction). Throw away the mussels that are open when uncooked. Now put all the good mussels in a casserole, cover with a lid, after five minutes shake them well to change their position and in five more minutes lift them out with a slotted spoon onto a waiting dish with a cover and pour the juice through a strainer lined with cheesecloth to remove the remaining grains of sand. Serve with a baguette for a hearty first course."— Edmund White, *Our Paris: Sketches from Memory,* 1994

moulures: moulding

mur: wall

Muscadet: cheap French white wine, light, tangy and drinkable by the gallon

Nihongo (Japanese): the Japanese language

notaire: a French notary public with far more powers and responsibilities than the same professional in the United States; comparable to a paralegal

nu: nude

oban (Japanese): a post-menopausal pre-geriatric woman usually, but not always irritable and imperious, afflicted with innumerable unspoken (but readily elicited) grievances; tends to be overdressed; often moves about in groups of three or more, walking abreast so that nobody can get past them. Age does not define an *oban.* Attitude does.

Obon (Japanese): a midsummer holiday during which people honor deceased relatives and ancestors by visiting graves, holding festivals and dancing the *bon-odori,* a Japanese variation on line-dancing

offre de prêt: loan offer, mortgage approval

oie: goose

omiyage (Japanese): an obligatory gift expected by all family members, co-workers, friends and acquaintances of any Japanese person who travels away from home—especially overseas. Since the typical Japanese vacation lasts four days, and most Japanese travelers have more than twenty *omiyage*-worthy friends and relatives, shopping is necessarily the primary activity among these travelers.

O-shogatsu (Japanese): the Japanese New Year, equivalent to Christmas, Hanukkah, Kwanzaa, Saturnalia, etc.

parfait: perfect

parquet: The Boston Celtics' basketball court

(De) Particulier à Particulier: Paris' real estate publication for people selling homes without the aid of an agent

paté de campagne: hearty meat paste typical of rural France

pavé de saumon: salmon steak

paysan: peasant, philistine, redneck

Périphérique: the circular highway that marks the border between Paris and its suburbs; the Parisian Beltway

Petit Robert: the most popular French dictionary

pichet: pitcher

pied-à-terre: home away from home; literally, a foot on the ground

pierre dure: hard stone

plat du jour: blue plate special

plombier: plumber
poivre: pepper
pomme: apple
pomme de terre: potato
pommes frites: French fries
porte-jarretelle: garter belt
poubelle: garbage can
Pour qui sait aimer, les heures son roses: For those who know how to love, the hours are rosy
procuration: power of attorney
projét: project
promesse: promise, commitment, agreement
punaises en laiton: brass tacks
quai: quay, levee, artificial river bank
quatre-vingt dix: ninety
qu'est-ce que c'est: What is this?
rangement: arrangement
relais: country inn
réléve du bancaire (RIB): numbers identifying a bank account
rhumsteack: rump steak
rillettes: shredded meat (pork, duck or goose), preserved in its own fat, usually served as a spread with bread and *cornichons* (tart little pickles)
Rive Gauche: Left Bank of the Seine
roi: king
romaji (Japanese): the Western alphabet
rue: street
salle de bains: bathroom
sans: without
saucisson: sausage
sec: dry; not sweet
service de dépannage: troubleshooting service

shotengai (Japanese): a covered shopping arcade
s'il vous plait: please
So! Ne! (Japanese): Really! No kidding! You got that right!
soupçon: suspicion, hint; a small quantity
sportive: sporty, athletic, tanned, buffed, pumped and oiled
sud-est: southeast
syndic: building co-op management
tableau: picture
tarte fine aux chaude pommes: hot apple tart
tartine au buerre: a slice of buttered French bread
terrasse: terrace; sidewalk section of a café
tirage: draft
touche: push-button
Toute-Étoile: All-Star
traiteur: caterer; purveyor of delicacies
trés chaud: very hot
Trésor Public: tax agency; the French IRS
troisième étage: third floor
trop cher: too expensive
tuchis (Yiddish, Leo Rosten's spelling): derrière, bottom, tush, gluteus maximus, caboose
un petit peu: a little bit
vacanciste: vacationer
vendeur/vendeuse: seller, salesperson
venusienne: like Venus, goddess of love
verre: glass
viagère: an apartment or house purchase arrangement contingent on the death of the seller/occupant.
Ville de Paris: the city of Paris
yoot (coinage, cf. ***My Cousin Vinny***): youth

Bibliography

Adnan, Etel, *Paris, When It's Naked,* Post-Apollo Press, Sausalito, 1993

Angelou, Maya, *Singin' and Swingin' and Gettin' Merry Like Christmas*, Random House, New York, 1976

Barclay, ed., Steven, *A Place in the World Called Paris*, Chronicle Books, San Francisco, 1994

Barry, Joseph, *The People of Paris*, Doubleday, New York, 1966

Baudelaire, Charles, *The Parisian Prowler: Le Spleen de Paris,* 1862, University of Georgia Press, Athens & London, 1989

Beach, Sylvia, *Shakespeare and Company,* Harcourt, Brace & Co., California, 1959

Bernardin, Alain, *Crazy Horse: Légendaire 1951–1991,* Editions Lincoln, Paris, 1991

Bernstein, Richard, *Fragile Glory: A Portrait of France and the French,* Knopf, New York, 1990

Blume, Mary, *A French Affair: The Paris Beat, 1965–1998*, Plume Group, New York, 2000

Bremond d'Ars, Yvonne de, *In the Heart of Paris: The Fabulous Adventures of an Antique Dealer,* Victor Gollancz, London,1959

Brodrick, Alan Houghton, ed., *The People's France: Paris*, Hodder & Stoughton, London, 1950

Bryson, Bill. "Paris," in *Neither Here Nor There: Travels in Europe,* Harper Collins, New York, 1992

Callaghan, Morley, *That Summer in Paris: Memories of Tangled Friendships with Hemingway, Fitzgerald and Some Others,* Stoddart, Toronto, 1963

Calvin, Henry, *It's Different Abroad,* Perennial Library, New York, 1963

Claiborne, Craig, *The New York Times Food Encyclopedia,* New York Times Co., New York, 1985

Collins, Larry and Dominique La Pierre, *Is Paris Burning?*, Grand Central, New York, 1965

Culbertson, Judi and Tom Randall, *Permanent Parisians: An Illustrated Guide to the Cemeteries of Paris*, Chelsea Green, New York, 1986

Dark, Sidney, *Paris*, MacMillan, New York, 1936

Eliot, T.S., *Old Possum's Book of Practical Cats,* Harcourt, Brace & World, New York, 1939

Émile-Bayard, Jean, *The Latin Quarter Past and Present*, Brentano's, New York, 1921

Fitch, Noel Riley, ed., *In transition: Writing and Art from transition magazine, 1927–1930*, Anchor Books, New York, 1990

Fitch, Noel Riley, *Sylvia Beach and the Lost Generation: A History of Literary Paris in the Twenties and Thirties*, W.W. Norton, New York, 1983

Fitch, Noel Riley, *The Literary Cafés of Paris*, Starhill Press, Washington & Philadelphia, 1989

Flanner, Janet, *Paris Was Yesterday, 1925–1939*, Viking Press, New York, 1972

Gash, Jonathan, *Paid and Loving Eyes,* St. Martin's Press, New York, 1993

Gash, Jonathan, *The Great California Game,* St. Martin's Press, New York, 1991

Gentleman, David, *David Gentleman's Paris,* Hodder & Stoughton, London, 1992

Grizell, Rex, *Off the Beaten Track Southern France,* Moorland Publishing, Derbyshire, 1994

Guppy, Shusha, *A Girl in Paris*, William Heinemann Ltd, London, 1991

Gusewelle, C.W., *A Paris Notebook,* Lowell Press, Kansas City, 1985

Hazan, Eric, *A Walk Through Paris*, Editions de Seuil, Paris, 2016, Verso, London, 2018

Holmes, John Clellon, *A Wake in the Streets of Paris*, 1987

Howton, F.W., *Functionaries,* Quadrangle, Chicago, 1969

Hugo, Victor, *Notre-Dame de Paris*, 1831, Signet Classics, New York, 1964

Hussey, Andrew, *Paris: The Secret History*, Bloomsbury USA, New York, 2006

Kafka, Franz, *Metamorphosis & Other Stories*, Penguin, London, 1961

Laffont, Robert, ed., *The Illustrated History of Paris and the Parisians,* Methuen, London, 1958

Lee, Jennifer, ed., *Paris in Mind: Three Centuries of Americans Writing About Paris*, Vintage, New York, 2003

Liebling, A.J., *Between Meals: An Appetite for Paris,* Modern Library, New York, 1959

Loos, Anita, *Gentlemen Prefer Blondes: The Illuminating Diary of a Professional Lady*, Boni & Liveright, New York, 1925

Lucas, Netley, *Criminal Paris,* Hurst & Blackett, London, 1926

MacKay, Charles, *Extraordinary Popular Delusions and the Madness of Crowds,* 1841, Noonday Press, New York, 1969

Malraux, André, *Anti-Memoirs*, Harcourt Brace, New York, 1968

Matthiessen, Peter, *Partisans*, Viking Press, New York, 1955

McAlmon, Robert, *Being Geniuses Together: 1920–1930* (Revised with supplementary chapters by Kay Boyle), North Point Press, San Francisco, 1984

Nietzsche, Friedrich, *Ecce Homo*, Penguin, 1992

O'Reilly, James, Larry Habegger, and Sean O'Reilly, *Travelers' Tales Guides: Paris*, Travelers' Tale, San Francisco, 1997

Orwell, George, *Down and Out in Paris and London*, Harcourt Brace Jovanovich, New York, 1933

Paul, Elliot, *Hugger-Mugger in the Louvre*, Ballantine, New York, 1940

Paul, Elliot, *Mysterious Mickey Finn*, Avon, New York, 1939

Paul, Elliot, *Springtime in Paris*, Random House, New York, 1949

Paul, Elliot, *The Last Time I Saw Paris*, Random House, New York, 1942

Paul, Elliot, *Understanding the French*, Random House, New York, 1955

Perelman, S.J., *Eastward Ha!,* Touchstone, New York, 1977

Perelman, S.J., *The Most of S.J. Perelman,* Fireside, New York, 1942

Putnam, Samuel, *Paris Was Our Mistress*, Southern Illinois University Press, Carbondale, 1947

Root, Henry, *Root into Europe*, Methuen, London, 1992

Root, Waverley, *The Paris Edition: The Autobiography of Waverley Root 1927–1934*, North Point Press, San Francisco, 1987

Routh, Jonathan, *Jonathan Routh's Guide Porcelaine to the Loos of Paris,* Wolfe Publishing, London, 1966

Sandburg, Carl, *Smoke and Steel*, Harcourt, Brace, and Howe, New York, 1920

Santé, Luc, *The Other Paris,* Farrar Straus & Giroux, New York, 2015

Shaw, Irwin and Ronald Searle, *Paris! Paris!*, Dell, New York, 1976

Slocombe, George, *The Heart of France: Parisian, Provincial & Peasant*, Selwyn & Blount, London, 1934

Sontag, Susan, foreword to *A Place in the World Called Paris,* Steven Barclay, ed., Chronicle Books, LLC, San Francisco, 1994

Untermeyer, Louis, *A Concise Treasury of Great Poems, English and American*, Pocket Books, New York, 1942

White, Edmund, *Our Paris: Sketches from Memory*, Knopf, New York, 1994

White, Norval, *The Guide to the Architecture of Paris*, Scribner's, New York, 1991

Willams, Oscar, *Immortal Poems of the English Language*, Washington Square Press, New York, 1952

Wilson, Robert Forrest, *Paris on Parade,* Bobbs-Merrill, Indianapolis, 1925

Wiser, William, *Disappearances,* Atheneum, New York, 1980

Wodehouse, P.G., *French Leave,* Penguin, London, 1956

Wurman, Richard Saul, *Access Paris*, Harper Collins, New York, 1998

Zeldin, Theodore, *The French*, William Collins & Sons, London, 1983

About the Author

David Benjamin began his career as a storyteller in Mrs. Poss' second-grade class at St. Mary's School in Tomah, Wisconsin. His fictional memoir, *The Life and Times of the Last Kid Picked*, originally published by Random House, was reprinted by Last Kid Books in 2019. His Last Kid Books include a collection of his essays, *Almost Killed by a Train of Thought*, two short story anthologies, *The Melting Grandmother and Other Short Works* and *Christmas in a Jugular Vein* and sixteen novels, *Three's a Crowd, A Sunday Kind of Love, Summer of '68, Skulduggery in the Latin Quarter, Black Dragon, They Shot Kennedy, Fat Vinny's Forbidden Love, Witness to the Crucifixion, Choose Moose, Bistro Nights, The Voice of the Dog* and Benjamin's Jim Otis mystery series, *Jailbait, Bastard's Bluff, Woman Trouble, Dead Shot* and *Cheat*. As a journalist, Benjamin has edited newspapers, published and edited several magazines, and authored *SUMO: A Thinking Fan's Guide to Japan's National Sport*.

Since its launch in 2019, Benjamin's publishing imprint, Last Kid Books, has won more than forty independent-press awards. These include, for *They Shot Kennedy*, the Midwest Book Awards' 2021 grand prize for literary/historical/contemporary fiction, and a 2022 Silver Medal for Humor to *Fat Vinny's Forbidden Love* in the Independent Book Publishers Association's prestigious Benjamin Franklin Awards.

Benjamin and his wife, Junko Yoshida, have been married for ages. They live sometimes in Madison, Wis., and the rest of the time in Paris.